Victorian Gothic

Also by Ruth Robbins

LITERARY FEMINISMS

VICTORIAN IDENTITIES: Social and Cultural Formations in Nineteenth-Century Literature (*co-editor with Julian Wolfreys*)

APPLYING: TO DERRIDA (*co-editor with John Brannigan and Julian Wolfreys*)

THE FRENCH CONNECTIONS OF JACQUES DERRIDA (*co-editor with John Brannigan and Julian Wolfreys*)

Also by Julian Wolfreys

BEING ENGLISH: Narrative, Idioms, and Performances of National Identity from Coleridge to Trollope

THE RHETORIC OF AFFIRMATIVE RESISTANCE: Dissonant Identities from Carroll to Derrida

DECONSTRUCTION • DERRIDA

WRITING LONDON: The Trace of the Urban Text from Blake to Dickens

READINGS: Acts of Close Reading in Literary Theory

PETER ACKROYD: The Ludic and Labyrinthine Text (*with Jeremy Gibson*)

VICTORIAN IDENTITIES: Social and Cultural Formations in Nineteenth-Century Literature (*co-editor with Ruth Robbins*)

APPLYING: TO DERRIDA (*co-editor with John Brannigan and Ruth Robbins*)

LITERARY THEORIES: A Case Study in Critical Performance (*co-editor with William Baker*)

RE:JOYCE: Text • Culture • Politics (*co-editor with John Brannigan and Geoff Ward*)

THE DERRIDA READER: Writing Performances (*editor*)

LITERARY THEORIES: A Reader and Guide (*editor*)

THE FRENCH CONNECTIONS OF JACQUES DERRIDA (*co-editor with John Brannigan and Ruth Robbins*)

INTRODUCING LITERARY THEORIES: A Guide and Glossary (*editor*)

PR 468.G6
VIC

Victorian Gothic

Literary and Cultural Manifestations in the Nineteenth Century

Edited by

Ruth Robbins

and

Julian Wolfreys

First published 2000 by
PALGRAVE
Houndmills, Basingstoke, Hampshire RG21 6XS and
175 Fifth Avenue, New York, N. Y. 10010
Companies and representatives throughout the world

PALGRAVE is the new global academic imprint of
St. Martin's Press LLC Scholarly and Reference Division and
Palgrave Publishers Ltd (formerly Macmillan Press Ltd).

Outside North America
ISBN 0–333–74935–9

In North America
ISBN 0–312–23169–5

This book is printed on paper suitable for recycling and
made from fully managed and sustained forest sources.

A catalogue record for this book is available
from the British Library.

Library of Congress Cataloging-in-Publication Data
Victorian Gothic : literary and cultural manifestations in the nineteenth
century / edited by Ruth Robbins and Julian Wolfreys
    p. cm.
    Includes bibliographical references and index.
    ISBN 0–312–23169–5
    1. English literature—19th century—History and criticism. 2. Gothic revival
(Literature)—Great Britain—History—19th century. 3. Supernatural in literature. 4.
Horror tales, English—History and criticism. 5. Psychological fiction, English–
–History and criticism. 6. Psychoanalysis and literature—Great Britain—History–
–19th century. 7. Great Britain—Civilization—19th century. I. Robbins, Ruth, 1965–
II. Wolfreys, Julian, 1958–

    PR468.G68 V53 2000
    820.9'1—dc21
                                                            00–042068

10   9   8   7   6   5   4   3   2   1
09   08   07   06   05   04   03   02   01   00

Printed in Great Britain by Antony Rowe Ltd, Chippenham, Wiltshire

Contents

Notes on the Contributors

Alison Chapman teaches eighteenth-century and nineteenth-century literature at the University of Dundee. Her study of Christina Rossetti is forthcoming. She is at work on a new project on the uncanny and literary influence.

J.-A. George is a graduate of Vassar College and received her PhD from King's College, London. She teaches English and Drama at the University of Dundee. Her research interests include Old and Middle English, the Pre-Raphaelites and early drama.

James R. Kincaid is Aerol Arnold Professor of English at the University of Southern California. His many publications include *Child-Loving: the Erotic Child and Victorian Culture* (1992), *Annoying the Victorians* (1995), and *Erotic Innocence: the Culture of Child Molesting* (1998).

Roger Luckhurst lectures in nineteenth- and twentieth-century literature at Birkbeck College, University of London. He is the author of *The Angle Between Two Walls: the Fiction of J.G. Ballard* (1997) and co-editor, with Peter Marks, of *Literature and the Contemporary* (1999). The material in his chapter derives from research towards his forthcoming book, *Outside Recognised Channels*, a scientific and cultural analysis of the emergence of the concept of telepathy in the 1880s.

Peter Morey teaches English in the Department of Cultural Studies at the University of East London. He is currently completing a book on narrative and power in fictions of India.

Richard Pearson is a Lecturer in English at University College Worcester. His research interests include the work of William Makepeace Thackeray, and he is the editor of *The Thackeray Library* (1997), and assistant editor of *The Index of English Literary Manuscripts*, Vol. 4 (1993).

Ruth Robbins is a Lecturer with the Department of English at University College, Northampton. She has published numerous articles on *fin-de-siècle* fiction, and is the co-editor of *Victorian Identities: Social and Cultural Formations in Nineteenth-Century Literature* (1996), *Applying: to Derrida* (1997), and *The French Connections of Jacques Derrida* (1999). She is the author of a study of feminist criticism and its application called *Literary Feminisms* (2000).

Victor Sage is Reader in Literature with the School of English and American Studies at the University of East Anglia. He is the author of numerous articles, and, most recently, *Horror Fiction in the Protestant Tradition* (1998). He is also the co-editor, with Allan Lloyd Smith, of *Modern Gothic: a Reader* (1997).

R.J.C. Watt is a Senior Lecturer in English at the University of Dundee. He has published an introductory study of the poetry of G.M. Hopkins, *A Concordance to the Poetry of Philip Larkin*, and many articles on nineteenth- and twentieth-century poetry, textual problems in Shakespeare, and literary computing. He has also pioneered the development of electronic literary concordances on the Web.

Kenneth Womack is an Assistant Professor with the Department of English at Pennsylvania State University, Altoona. He is the author of numerous articles and is Associate Editor on *George Eliot–George Henry Lewes Studies*.

Julian Wolfreys is Associate Professor of English at the University of Florida. He is the author and editor of numerous books, including, most recently, *Writing London: the Trace of the Urban Text from Blake to Dickens*.

Marion Wynne-Davies teaches English at the University of Dundee. She is the author of *Women and Arthurian Literature: Seizing the Sword* (1996) and the editor of *The Bloomsbury Guide to English Literature* (1989) and *The Tales of the Clerk and the Wife of Bath* (1992). She has also co-edited, with S.P. Cerasano, *Gloriana's Face: Women, Public and Private, in the English Renaissance* (1992) and *Renaissance Drama by Women: Texts and Contexts* (1995).

List of Illustrations

Preface: 'I could a tale unfold' or, the Promise of Gothic

Julian Wolfreys

> I could a tale unfold whose lightest word
> Would harrow up thy soul, freeze thy young blood,
> Make thy two eyes like stars start from their spheres,
> Thy knotted and combinèd locks to part
> And each particular hair to stand on end
> Like quills upon the fretful porcupine
> > *Hamlet, Prince of Denmark* I.v.16–21

The gothic was dead, to begin with.

It is generally agreed that the gothic, understood narrowly as a narrative form given principal expression through the novel, had a life-span of approximately 56 years. It was born or, rather, given life, in 1764, with the publication of Walpole's *The Castle of Otranto*. It died, or was dismembered and interred, somewhere around 1818 or 1820, with the publication of, respectively, Mary Shelley's *Frankenstein* or Charles Maturin's *Melmoth the Wanderer*. (Recent reassessments of Thomas De Quincey's *Confessions of an English Opium Eater* [1821], such as Margaret Russett's *De Quincey's Romanticism* [1997] may allow us another provisional moment of 'conclusion' for the gothic.) Already, towards the end of its rather artificial life, gothic narrative's often galvanic animation was perceived by some of its readers as not being fully charged, a highly visible sign of which was the parody of its already monstrous form, most noticeably in Jane Austen's *Northanger Abbey*, written in 1798/9, but not published until 1817. Austen's work is a parody, aimed at the work of Anne Radcliffe in particular, as is well known. However, any parody of that which is already internally parodic (intentionally or not); that is to say, any parody of that which is marked by excess, heterogeneity, fragmentation, delirium and what Margaret Russett terms appositely a 'degraded sensibility' (1997, 17), is hard to imagine. The gothic, as a body of fiction, is always already excessive, grotesque, overspilling its own boundaries and limits. Austen's knowing comedy perhaps misses the impropriety of gothic sensibility even as it registers the decay of a genre which is best understood not so much through the perceived signs of its formulaic decline as by the corrupt condition by which gothic attains any animation whatsoever. The overly familiar relationship between the gothic as both a form and sensibility and Austen's wit at its expense is worth acknowledging once more, not because of the author's parody, but because of the tension – readable here between the distancing effect which the parodic desires, and the seduction of the writer or, for that matter, the reader – by the gothic. The gothic, though dying even from its first moments of animation, leaves its traces in its audience, only to return again and again. As Jacques Derrida has suggested in a published interview, if the reader notices, day after day, the constant announcement that someone or something is dying, or dead, and if this dying or death continues to be an event, one begins to wonder what is happening (1996, 224–5). Even at the moment when it appears to have given up the ghost, the gothic, keeps on returning, even as it dies, or appears to be decaying. It starts to be celebrated, or perhaps fed upon, by the spectre of criticism, for example, or else it feeds upon itself, adopting a knowingly self-referential manner.

The year after *Melmoth the Wanderer*, that publication chosen by many critics in the twentieth century to signal gothic's demise and the move on to more sophisticated forms of literary entertainment, Walter Scott writes and publishes his critical introduction to Walpole's *The Castle of Otranto* (which Scott attempts to dress up by insisting on its alternative identity as a historical romance; 1821, 1974). In this same year, as mentioned above, Thomas De Quincey publishes his *Confessions of an English Opium Eater*. If *Confessions* is a conclusion of sorts, it also marks the return of the gothic even at the moment of its death. This work, though not a novel, is clearly disturbed in its narrative identity by traces of the gothic, from the first instances of the house in Soho and the haunted, haunting anonymous girl, to the perpetually haunting figure of Anne, who returns to disturb De Quincey's troubled self. Even the city of London, with its dark passages and labyrinthine streets, is constructed by De Quincey in a knowingly gothic fashion; the convolutions of which, in turn, inform the often equally labyrinthine structure of the *Confessions'* narrative, with its constant deferrals and displacements of information, its promises of narrative revelations which never arrive, and its passages which, all too often, lead frustratingly nowhere.

Why then should we take notice, albeit in passing, of Scott's introduction (which is also a timely reassessment), and De Quincey's mordantly witty memoir? Both are, arguably, exemplary texts which respond to the gothic in particular ways, taking apart the gothic corpse, dismembering and re–membering it. Scott's critical appreciation subsumes the gothic in favour of historical romance as the identity given Walpole's narrative of terror. De Quincey, on the other hand, brings out the terror of the streets of the English capital, as well as the terrors of the night, giving them a resonantly *English* context, as one of the contributors to this collection suggests. If the gothic had previously been concerned, at least in part, to make manifest a fear of the foreign other, De Quincey's text brings home the fear, internalizing that in a doubly economical fashion, through the issue of narrative representation, and through the consumption of narcotics.

This double consumption is, we would argue, an emblematic figure for the location of the gothic in the Victorian period, whether that location is in the period's publications, in its images or in its cultural discourses in general. The gothic, having been dismembered, is no longer figured in the nineteenth century, from the 1820s onwards, as a single, identifiable *corpus*. (If indeed it ever was. One of the chief features of gothic in its first phase is the frequently fragmentary condition of its narrative, as many critics in recent years have acknowledged.) The twelve essays in this volume address the question of gothic remains, of what remains as the haunting spirit of the gothic throughout the nineteenth century. The essays represent current thinking on the gothic in the nineteenth century, while offering new departures on the topic and suggesting new ways in which the gothic may be understood from various theoretical, historical and cultural perspectives in relation to the Victorian epoch. *Victorian Gothic* addresses comedic aspects of gothic, questions of technology and subjectivity in the nineteenth century, the visual arts and photography, the uses of gothic imagery, issues of colonialism and gender, relationships between forms of publication and the gothic, and as (profoundly gothic) images of children and adolescents.

The range of authors and artists addressed is as broad as the Victorian period itself, and, equally, as diverse and heterogeneous. While certain writers might seem obvious choices for any revisionist discussion of the place of the gothic in the nineteenth century, others will appear somewhat unusual. Charles Dickens and Sheridan Le Fanu doubtless deserve inclusion, as do Richard Marsh, Bram Stoker, and Henry James for their contributions to *fin-de-siècle* gothic narrative. But the reader will also find Mary Elizabeth Coleridge, William Morris,

Julia Margaret Cameron, Gerard Manley Hopkins, Rudyard Kipling, and H. Rider Haggard alongside Oscar Wilde and Vernon Lee. As this brief list suggests, the Victorian gothic is no respecter of location, haunting equally the most canonical of figures, as well as those who are considered as having only the most marginal canonical status. And while writers from the 1830s onwards retain certain features in their writing – particular tropes, narrative conventions, features of form and content – recognizable as belonging to the gothic in its first literary manifestations, more often than not those features are transformed, disfigured, brought back to life, or conjured from some unspeakable place in ways which are wholly unpredictable, and all the more haunting for that. Escaping from the tomb and the castle, the gothic in the Victorian period becomes arguably even more potentially terrifying because of its ability to manifest itself anywhere. Reciprocally, The Victorians may be read as embracing the gothic, taking it to themselves in intimate and disconcerting ways. The essays in this volume respond to this, by exploring how the promise of the gothic is kept by its Victorian inheritors, repeatedly, throughout the major part of the nineteenth century, as the spirit of the gothic is unfolded in myriad strange and estranging ways.

In being so dispersed, in coming to light in numerous, unsettling, and unpredictable ways, assuming new identities, seemingly from beyond the grave, the gothic appears to mark nineteenth-century literature and culture with that haunting promise just mentioned. If the gothic in its narrow sense was, like Wilde's Bunbury or Conrad's anarchist bomb, quite exploded, its fragments spread far and wide throughout the Victorian era. The gothic became other than itself, the meaning of the term changing, metamorphosing beyond narrow definition, promising the destabilization of whatever it came to haunt, itself destabilized in itself and from itself. At the same time, the promise of the gothic was – and still is – a promise of a certain return, a cyclical revenance. It still remains as this, and its remains are readable as numerous counter signatures guaranteeing the gothic promise within the literary or photographic text. The promise of the gothic being that there is always one more sepulchral door to open, and, with that, one more uncanny tale to tell. What the tale may be is ultimately of less importance than the promise of that tale, the promise of what that tale will effect, as the words of Hamlet's father's ghost suggest. The ghost in *Hamlet* never keeps his promise, telling Hamlet instead of all too earthly acts. But the very promise of revelation is in itself seductive; it speaks to a desire, and recognizes in its articulation the move-

ment of that desire in search of the secret terror. If the gothic as a recognizable narrative form began to lose its grip over its audience, this
may have been in part because the tale all too often unfolded with the
revelation that there was no terror which could not be explained away.
Thus the promise of the gothic was itself ignored in favour of rational
explanation and the banality of closure.

However, while for some the gothic was to become unbearable, first
in the 1820s and, subsequently, in the twentieth century through
critical assessment of the gothic (this is a narrative concerned with
aesthetic proprieties which literary criticism has told compulsively
and repeatedly until recent years), for many others, it remained – and
continues to remain – *unburiable*. The promise of the gothic is comprehended in all its uncanny potentiality as both *trait* and *retrait*. The
gothic mode leaves its mark, in the nineteenth century, in the most
conventional of narratives, the most ordinary of photographs. But
even as we read that trace, we only read where the gothic has been,
we only comprehend its effect in the places from which it has already
retreated. We understand the gothic therefore as always already
spectral through and through. All that is left in the Victorian text is
the promise of the gothic, the disturbing trace, the haunting absence.
Such a narrative surrounding the gothic is, itself, a gothic narrative,
concerned with constant returns, uncanny disturbances, dismembered
remains and improper forms, deferrals and differences. The essays in
this collection recognize the condition of the gothic and, in response
to that, make their own collective promise – a promise at once shared
and multiplied – that while there are indeed yet more tales to be told,
more skeletons to bring out of closets, there are also new and
interesting manifestations of the same old stories. The promise is also
one which suggests that, in returning to the Victorians so as to understand their own gothic compulsions, their spectral and technological
manifestations of the uncanny, we begin to comprehend that the
promise of the gothic itself returns once again – to haunt our comprehension, to trouble the certainties on which we rely for our
identities, and to continue returning in ever stranger articulations of
revenant alterity.

The gothic is to be found everywhere then, but never as itself, never
in the same form twice. The gothic becomes truly haunting in that it
can never be pinned down as a single identity, while it returns
through various apparitions and manifestations, seemingly everywhere: in comic discourse, through photographic images, in the
attempted return to a pseudo-medieval sensibility, in the very form of

publication itself, in the social construction of children or sexuality, in the projection of discourses of Orientalism, via mesmerism and other 'technologies of the uncanny', as Roger Luckhurst puts it, and in countless other discourses and historical, material traces as well, as these essays suggest. To paraphrase as well as briefly cite the essays in *Victorian Gothic*, the gothic becomes restructured even as it restructures 'the new discipline of archaeology', and its discourses, when given fictive expression in a colonial context. In the same context the effect of the gothic economy is to destabilize discourses of power and knowledge, and, with that, supposedly stable subject positions. The gothic serves furthermore to formulate what is described as an 'alliance between' aestheticism and decadence, where such formulation or figuration operates through the blurring of vision, the distortion of identity once again, and the anatomization of experience. In these and other disturbing ways, the Victorian gothic 'manifests itself' as 'both a subversive supernatural force and a mechanism for social critique'.

The gothic is also bound up with the late Victorian interest in hypnosis, trance states and the construction of the modern subject, in the sense given that term by Michel Foucault. Such construction, under the influence of the gothic, is also a potential act of solicitation which invokes terror at the prospect of a 'complete loss of identity'. The gothic aspect of the construction of the subject is also manifested through photography. A technology of shadows and spectres, photography readily draws upon the 'grisly props of gothic representation' while also aiding, as a technology of the uncanny – that 'most gothic of psychic effects' – in the reconfiguration of subjectivity. Furthermore, the gothic figures not only the reconstitution of the modern subject but also a disruption of social order, as well as an implicit challenge to 'coherent structural reason'. It does so frequently through its attention to the grotesque or to its exploitation of the comic. In all such activities, the gothic may be read in all its many apparitions as being concerned with a challenge to stable identities through the 'production of a combination of conflicting sensations'.

All the manifestations and qualities of gothic effect observed by the contributors to this volume move the idea of the gothic beyond the narrow understanding of the gothic as a narrative or novel form. They address what Eve Kosofsky Sedgwick in her groundbreaking *The Coherence of Gothic Conventions*, describes as the function of the gothic. As Sedgwick argues, the function of the gothic was to 'open horizons beyond social patterns, rational decisions, and institutionally approved emotions ... [it] became a great liberator of feeling' through its acknowledgement of the 'non-rational' (1986, 3). As Sedgwick suggests, if we are to accord this definition to the gothic, we must at the very least also acknowledge the discontinuity between such a sense of the gothic and the narrow definition of gothic or what Sedgwick describes as the 'gothic novel proper' (1986, 3). It is this very discontinuity – which is also a radical transition – which serves to liberate the spirit of the gothic from its ponderous conventional body, and which comes to serve the Victorians in the numerous ways which are explored by the essays presented here. At the same time, however, the radical transformation of gothic, which is in turn a gothic transformation, makes the definition of the gothic much harder, from certain conventional critical positions, and it is with the provisional identification of the gothic in different and differing ways that criticism has concerned itself. The act of defining the gothic beyond its narrative conventions is fraught with difficulties, not least because of what Sedgwick terms the 'conflicting claims of the general and the specific' (1986, 4). Sedgwick's analysis of contingent naming focuses, appropriately enough, on the frequency of the term 'unspeakable' in gothic narrative. As she argues, the frequency of such a term may be raised critically to the level of the thematic, but, equally, the unspeakable names a certain play within narrative structure.

This problematic – which is, simultaneously, a problem of defining the gothic and a gothic problematic, that which appears as a gothic trope arriving to disturb the act of definition – is also identified by Anne Williams in her revision of the poetics of gothic. In her *Art of Darkness*, Williams, like Sedgwick, seeks to move beyond the narrow definition of the gothic as 'primarily ... a form of prose fiction, as something relative and subordinate to its early contemporary, Romanticism' (1995, 1). Williams' planned movement is articulated through the understanding that the nature of the gothic is dual, and that 'it has a "male" and a "female" genre' (1995, 1). Part of the problem in speaking adequately of the gothic has arisen, Williams argues, from conventional criticism's inscription of the gothic as an aberrant and marginal novel form, an inscription which, for the likes of Leavis, Watt and Booth, is also an erasure (1995, 1–3).[1] Williams' introduction to her study provides a useful summary of conventional, often masculine, critical attitudes to the gothic as an 'outmoded embarrassment' (1995, 4). As the keepers of the flame of realism and what she calls the 'High Prose Fiction tradition', certain critics, Williams suggests, 'have regarded the gothic as long dead, or else

(if alive) as irrational "feminine" popular romance' (1995, 6). Such definition is dependent on keeping to the narrow understanding of the gothic,
while not recognizing the radical fragmentation and dissemination of
gothic in the nineteenth century.

If, as Robert Miles suggests, the question 'What is "gothic"?' seems
easily answered, this is no doubt because of a formalist adherence to the
rote identification on the part of the critic of 'the same plots, motifs and
figures endlessly recycled' (1993, 1). Nothing could be easier, less
troubled. Yet such an approach, if we recall Sedgwick's argument, and to
follow Miles also, falters once we begin to pay attention to gothic's
affirmative resistances, or what Miles terms 'gothic's deep structure'.
gothic writing, Miles argues, following David Punter, is '"disjunctive",
fragmentary, inchoate' (1993, 1); furthermore, gothic 'worries over a
problem stirring within the foundations of the self ... Gothic ... is
not fantasy in need of psychoanalysis but a coherent code for the
representation of fragmented subjectivity' (1993, 2). There is for Miles,
after Foucault, an 'instability of discourse, its tendency, especially within
the "dialogic" space of narrative, to fragment or round on itself' (1993, 6).
Thus, for Miles, as for other recent critics of the gothic, as well as for a
number of the critics in this volume, the gothic is concerned with the
self, with the other within the self, and with what Kelly Hurley terms 'the
ruination of the human subject ... [through] the spectacle of a body
metamorphic and undifferentiated' (1996, 3).[2]

The critical move beyond the conventions of gothic narrative is
articulated then, at least in part, by the act of reading gothic's sense of
the alterity of subjectivity, and the alterity which undoes any sense of
the subject's own comprehension of coherence, presence or meaning.
Whether it is through the spectro-poetical manifestations of identity
made possible by the technology of photography, the uncanny assault
on the sense of self by the otherness of the foreign; whether it is
through either the withered or corpulent, hectic or abused figure of the
grotesque child, through the projection of spectro-sexual ambiguities
or even, as one essayist suggests, the uncanny manifestations of feet in
the poetry of Gerard Manley Hopkins as the disturbing sign of
gothic–fetish; in any of these examples, the comprehension of the
gothic is expanded through an understanding of the role gothic effects
have to play in the constitution of modern, fragmented subjectivity. At
the same time, the variety and heterogeneity of subjects addressed in
these essays point to what Jacqueline Howard terms gothic's '"multi-
voiced–ness"', its 'propensity for multiple discourse' (1994, 13, 12). If
the body and the subject are fragmented and dispersed, then so too are

the voices of the gothic subject. For the gothic subject, properly understood, is never singular; there are always other voices, other disembodied, ghostly articulations within and against the dream of full, simple, self-evident speech to be read in any apparently stable voice, such as that desired in realist narrative. Such qualities in turn speak to the 'plural dimensions of reading' (1994, 1) which, for Howard, is also a provisional definition of the gothic mode, all of which resist the imposition of a homogeneous definition of the gothic, while proving 'unsettling for the reader' (1994, 12).

However unsettling the haunting of stability, of homogeneity and the self-same may be, it directs us, in conclusion, to an act of inversion in the Victorian period, inversion as consumption *and* internalization, whereby the gothic, broken up, comes to be dispersed ✕ throughout the culture and throughout the nineteenth century. A common 'device' in the gothic narrative of the period 1760–1820 was the textual fragment, as Veejay Mishra discusses in his *The Gothic Sublime* (1994, 83–116). Not only do fragments of long-lost texts reappear, fortuitously or ironically, within novels and, to a lesser extent, plays and poems, but fragments were created in their own right, as a textual manifestation of the gothic sensibility. The fragment, of which the paradigmatic example, Mishra suggests, is the now neglected 'Sir Bertrand' by Anna Laetitia Barbauld (1994, 83), is a textual, *material* embodiment of dismemberment and of the narrative tendency in gothic to come to an impassable and unspeakable hiatus. Byron went so far as to write a fragment, self-referentially titled 'A Fragment'. As Fiona Robertson puts it in her study of Sir Walter Scott, the abrupt halt in gothic 'marks the points at which [gothic's] narratorial language breaks down and is defeated by the enormity [or, we would contend, the sheer alterity] of what it attempts to describe' (1994, 81). The fragment published as fragment is but one example of what Mishra describes as 'versions or symptoms of the extreme otherness of the gothic sublime' (1994, 83). Such fragments, and the silences which they generate speak of the unspeakable, bearing witness to an absence at the heart of meaning. The Victorian gothic takes the fragment as symptom to its heart. Whatever realist fiction cannot speak, there is the gothic fragment as other. Wherever photography in the nineteenth century seeks to re-present its subject, there in the phatic image is the disturbance of that subject. The unreal, the ghostly, the uncanny: all are maintained throughout the Victorian period as the apparitions and manifestations of fragments from some other place. Yet they return, even as they appear, not only from some other place, but from the other *within* that identity we name as Victorian. The fragment, no longer outside, unfolds itself inside those very contours which seem to define unequivocally Victorian identity.

Notes

1. On critical approaches to the gothic, see also Jacqueline Howard's excellent *Reading Gothic Fiction: a Bakhtinian Approach* (1994), which draws on both the dialogic work of Mikhail Bakhtin and the work of Todorov and others on the fantastic, to move the discussion of gothic beyond the conventional critical impasse arrived at as a result of reading the gothic, as an 'inferior genre' (5). Howard provides an overview of critical approaches (18–36), suggesting, as does Williams, that the beginnings of gothic revisionism can be located with the 1969 publication of Robert D. Hume's article 'Gothic versus Romantic: a Revaluation of the Gothic Novel' in the *PMLA*. Coral Ann Howells' *Love, Mystery and Misery: Feeling in Gothic Fiction* (1978) is one of the first book-length re-evaluations of the gothic.

    Similarly to Williams, Howard's study addresses itself to the issue of gender in relation to gothic (53–105), as does Susan Wolstenholme in her 1993 study, *Gothic (Re)Visions: Writing Women as Readers*.
2. On the subject of the gothic body and the spectacle of the body in pain, see Steven Bruhm, *Gothic Bodies: the Politics of Pain in Romantic Fiction* (1994).

1
'Designing Gourmet Children or, KIDS FOR DINNER!'

James R. Kincaid

We all know that the Victorians had dumped on them by their fore-bears a host of problems, none more vexing than 'the child'. This 'child' had been concocted very recently and hastily. It was a Rube Goldberg invention,* much ballyhooed and loaded with all sorts of national and domestic importance, given vital jobs to do before anybody had bothered to test it. The child was expected to carry the weight of a new ideology, a new figuring of the family, and a new focus on innocence and the need to protect it. 'Here you are!' the Victorians heard from the past; 'Take this and welcome to it. We call it "child". Figure out how it is supposed to work. Perfect it. Sorry we lost the instruction manual. Toodle-oo'.

The Victorians did what they could to obey these wholly unreason-able orders, obedience coming naturally to the Victorians, who had been told it was a virtue. They did, I say, what they could. What they found they could do was to figure the child as innocent and then freight that innocence with desire, take the loveable and make it also detestable, take sweetness and make it also acrid, take ...

– *It's not very clear what any of this has to do with the Gothic. This is a volume on the gothic. You should address that right off and not meander.*
You interrupted just as I was about to introduce the line that would tip me right over into the heart of gothic.

– *Sorry. What is that line?*

---

* Rube Goldberg (1883–1970), a Pulitzer Prize-winning cartoonist, sculptor and author, drew 'inventions', the purpose of which were to make easy goals much harder to obtain [eds].

The Victorians loved children so much they could, as we say, just eat them. They worshipped children with one hand on a whip and formulated a dark and powerful ambivalence that is with us still. 'Let us live for our children!' called out Froebel, the father of the modern kindergarten. The Victorians tried very hard to do just that strange thing, to invest themselves and their nation in the young, to adopt a grammar devoted to the future tense, to sacrifice themselves for the well-being of their little ones, to offer their bodies for the sustenance of babies. There is no doubt that the Victorians churned out an earnest and continuous discourse of baby- and child-loving. It seems, though, that they could manage this only if they relieved themselves and their true feelings somehow – not, however, with a direct counter-discourse or even an after-hours satiric grumbling – both too dangerous. Instead they devised a peculiarly modern double-speak that made every act of child-worship an act of desecration, every act of self-sacrifice an excuse for murder, every offering of maternal breast and paternal bread a cannibalistic assault.

– *Now we're getting gothic. Eating children is right there. Did the Victorians really do that?*

It's a metaphor for a discourse of child-hating and child-desiring that offered kids up as if they were a menu item: isolated, 'presented', sanitized and guaranteed not to cause upset, meant for our eyes and our palates only, spicy but not threatening, available for tongue and fang alike. This is an ambivalence that still structures the way we make children, the way they are for us – edible.

The Victorians took the gothic out of the castle and into the nursery.

– *Out of the castle and into the bedroom: that's a better line.*

But it's not my point. The gothic had always been fast friends with beds and what gets done in beds. The Victorians didn't sexualize the gothic; they took the sneaky erotics already there and re-located them onto kids. They made children the centre of the gothic spectacle. Why not? They couldn't decide what else to do with the child, so they figured it might as well be placed into the most familiar container they had for delicious repugnance, titillating horror. The Victorian child helped redefine the gothic; but it's probably more important to note that the gothic defined the Victorian child. The child could contain and evoke the gothic sensation, and since 'gothic' had never been a formal or aesthetic matter anyhow, it didn't matter what was used to convey it. Gothic had always meant the production of a combination of conflicting sensations; it was reader-response from the get-go. Gothic was whatever made you feel gothicky.

– *So, let's see if I have this right. This child provoked ambivalent feelings in the culture and so did the gothic, so it came natural to the Victorians to fit them together like two puzzle pieces.*

No. It's not just ambivalence that's at issue, as we shall see. But what you most have wrong is the notion that 'the child' and 'the gothic' are settled and passive cultural features. When they come together, they don't 'fit' but reconfigure; both are active and bullying. The gothic is reformed, and so is the child. Notice how quickly the Victorian child gets rid of its Wordsworthian ancestor, that frolicker in nature. The Victorian child, drenched in gothic, is urban, grim and seated. Victorian gothic becomes eerily domesticated and chillingly cute.

– *Gothca. From this point on, then – not to put words in your mouth but just to move us on a little more briskly – the discourse of the child and the discourse of the Gothic flow in one stream. The Victorians, wading in words, would find themselves up to their knees or higher in the interpenetrating currents of gothic and child. Fishing from the banks, they would …*

Not quite. It's not two currents joining but mucking one another up, strangling one another, eager to disfigure or swallow up. Look, these discourses were radically unstable, still are. Partly that's because they are discourses of the unknown and even the unknowable. Consider the gothic: it's got always to reach towards what cannot be spoken; if all can be spoken, then there is no gothic. It can gesture towards the sublime, toward the blasphemous, or towards the magical, but it must never fall into the prosaic: the gothic has to alert us to the presence of agencies we cannot explain. We cannot explain them because they lie outside the realm of the explicable, outside of language. It's not just that we don't know enough; knowledge is not the issue. If the gothic can be explained, it is no longer gothic. That's why the endings of gothic novels, the explanations, are always read by good readers as parodic. They expose the inadequacy of explanations.

– *You're saying that when we find out that there really were no ghosts we don't believe it? I do. I find those endings reassuring. They offer closure.*

The endings do; gothic doesn't. Readers who are still in the gothic mode make those endings parodic or ignore them altogether. The endings descend to speech, and the gothic is unspeakable. 'Words cannot express!' Victor Frankenstein is always howling – and me and you too, when we're inside the gothic unspeakable and unknowable. The endings offer knowingness, familiarity, discursive assurances. The endings have nothing to do with gothic or with gothic readers; they simply provide an exit to those who shouldn't have been there in the first place.

– *So why does gothic always end that way, especially Victorian gothic – with explanations and all, I mean.*

Ah, but does Victorian gothic end that way? You may be thinking of Wilkie Collins, but ...

– *No, I wasn't thinking of Wilkie Collins, as it happens. I haven't read Wilkie Collins. I was thinking of Victorian gothic generally, all Victorian Gothic.*

Minus Wilkie Collins.

– *I was thinking of things like* Jane Eyre *or* Wuthering Heights *or those sorts of things.*

Well, you're pulling me away from kids, but I think neither of the novels you cite 'explain' things necessarily. Jane is still being directed by mystic voices and the madwoman is still in that attic.

– *She's not. The madwoman is a goner.*

Try to think of that book without her there. Try to think of her not there even when we are told she's dead. Anyhow, in the other Brontë, who is to say about the horror and its source? Is it quieted at the end? Only Lockwood thinks so, and he's an idiot.

– *That's what you mean by parody, right? Lockwood goes on about how all is peaceful and serene. He says he doesn't see how anyone can imagine ghosts walking, right? That's the end of the novel. I see. Lockwood can't imagine a damned thing, lacking any imagination whatever, so when he says he can't imagine that's a signal to us that we'd better do so, if we want to be regarded as good readers. I got that right?*

Sort of. The ending of *Psycho* is clearest here, the part where the shrink yammers on and on about Norman and his mother, exposing the hopeless irrelevance of explanations of any kind, the shallowness of mere knowing and speaking. Before you interrupt, I realize, of course, that the film is not Victorian; but some features of the Victorian gothic remain with us. They all do.

Nowhere more clearly than in the unknowable nature of the unspeakable child. Like gothic sensation, the child is a species not only separate for the Victorians but endowed with the capacity for allowing and excusing feelings and attitudes one would never entertain for a knowable species. Awe, for instance, and detestation. The child is mysterious and capable of actions and responses that are both endearing and horrifying. We want to cuddle the cute little thing and slaughter it for the table. It cannot be brought into focus or spoken, because it must exist outside our realm. Like desire and like fear.

– *Maybe all this about the edible child needs more illustration. Let's introduce the Fat Boy here.*

No, we need to talk first about isolation, displaying children like
gothic monsters, objectifying – a whole lot of things. Our problem is to
order them, not to jump ahead to the Fat Boy.

– *Linton Heathcliff then, or little Miles and Flora?*

You know, I think this collaborative paper should be directed more
toward our topic and perhaps less to this give and take. I don't think
readers will be interested in us going back and forth this way. We
should probably do that off to the side, you know, and just present
here the results of our collaborative and interdependent work.

– *I thought we were doing a kind of postmodern improvisational collaboration, you know, reflecting on the very form we are resisting just as we are
  confined by it, making its very impersonality the vehicle for ...*

That may be, but it isn't very gothic, and we haven't mentioned the
child for about four pages. I'm afraid this is a shambles.

– *What about using as a transition, a segue so to speak, the way in which
  gothic has always been collaborative, in a communal groupy sense.*

That helps, since it suggests exactly what gothic isn't and what the
child isn't. The collaborative writing we're doing, highly effective as it
is, creates something of a clash with the assumptions of Gothic and
with the cultural constructions of the child, both of which assume
that, down deep, there is no community.

– *'We live as we dream, alone'. I always liked that line.*

Yes. Well, the reason gothic is so powerful and the child so frightening is that they strike at the deepest fear of all, isolation from a social
group.

– *Northrop Frye said that, said it was the essence of pathos and deeper far
  than the fear of death. You didn't make that up and you should put in a
  footnote.*

OK. I will. First, though, see if you follow me here. The key to the
gothic and to the cultural position of the child is isolation. Take the
child first: the child must be alone in order to be absolutely powerless.
The modern child has no reason for being if it isn't figured as something needing protection. The modern family comes into being around
the separateness of the child; it is the centre to be adored and detested
but always Other. The family exists as such a tight little fortress
because we are told we have something to protect, not the virtue of the
woman, whose virtue long since ceased to matter, but the innocence of
the child. The child must, then, be under siege and without any
defences of its own. Got me? We can, paradoxically, cluster round it to

gaze at it, clutch it in fondling protectiveness, beat it, or chew on it only because it is fundamentally isolated. The child has no coordinate being; it is there like a statue or a picture, isolated and with the spot-light on it. All children are, at the same time, in a perpetual beauty contest, just as they are always stepping up to the slaughter-house chopping block: all eyes fixed on them, lights up, bring the axe down, the applause up, curtain!

– *I'll have to look over your prose, but of course I follow you. Why would you think I wouldn't follow you? It's a question of whether I agree, not whether I am capable of understanding. It's not such a subtle thought as all that you're offering.*

Of course not. It's pretty obvious. Do you want to take up the gothic now and carry on the major burden, the tune – sing soprano, as it were? You probably are getting tired of being so reactive.

– *You want me to take up the gothic? In what way?*

In reference to isolation. Remember we were talking about how our seamless collaboration worked interestingly at cross-purposes with the nursery gothic of the Victorians, where nothing ever meshes with any-thing else. We were suggesting that the gothic slipped toward the nursery because one *isolato* knows another: the child and the gothic both suggest 'Thou hast been, shalt be, art, alone'.

– *You footnoting that? Matthew Arnold somewhere.*

Right. You want to carry on with gothic isolation then?

– *Gothic aloneness is proverbial. You won't find much Victorian gothic where there are parties and clubs. There are some, granted, but the parties break up early and the clubs are not much to speak of. People are by themselves a lot in all Gothic from any period, I grant you, but they are even more by themselves in Victorian gothic, where being alone reached its summit. And gothic villains are especially isolated, though of course the villains always were but not to the extent we find in Victorian gothic, where the aloneness is, so to speak, foregrounded and shoved at us.*

That has the virtue of real clarity, without which we'd be nowhere. Now, maybe relate that aloneness to late capitalist individualism or something like that.

– *No. I don't know anything about late capitalist individualism. There are Brits writing in this volume, and they can be counted on to do that sort of thing, and very well too. I think we can be absolutely sure of that. I say we do something more American, like find some humanistic and thematic line to pursue. The point, after all, is that the gothic comes to reside with and inside the child because the child becomes, at once, the centre and the stranger, the alien in our midst, the species that cannot be spoken.*

So the child is framed but never caught, right? Framed by both our visual and judicial discourse?

– *What?*

Framed as in a photo and as in a cultural plot that enmeshes the child.

– *I suppose so, but I think it's more telling to think of the gothic child on a platter: Florence Dombey about to be eaten by the witch woman, Brooke Shields served up in 'Pretty Baby', Mr. Hyde as a little boy consumed by his host, Linton Heathcliff chewed alive by his daddy, Miles and Flora sucked dry by the governess, Alice inside the belly of the Looking-Glass.*

But that sounds as if the child were nothing but gothic victim, she who gets eaten.

– *Yes, but that's only half of it. The child is formulated as a victim, certainly, always about to be snatched away. That gives the adult something to do: protect the child and watch out for the monsters. It creates the paranoid anxiety necessary for gothic and not hard to locate in our child-centred world.*

What's the other half?

– *The other half is that the child who is being threatened is also the threat. The monster and the maiden in distress are the same. The child which beckons us and invites us to eat is also a ravenous maw. Just as we are about to bite, we find ourselves inside the mouth of our own shameful desires.*

Like that's clear!

– *I know. Here, try it this way. We have in our culture modelled the child as passive and settled, an image in a photo, on a plate, in our memory. This image is also our centrefold, the definition of our desire. As we are drawn toward it, though, we are drawn toward the unspeakable, the gothic. The child is both the generator of our erotic energy, its target, and also that which exists without reference to desire in any form. The child is that which must magnetize our desire and that which can do anything but that.*

Take memory, the child in our minds.

– *Yes, the Victorians inherited the child of memory, the inner child, the child we all once were, the most alluring and demonic of all children. That child becomes our source and sustainer and the repository of all we are. It is us. It is also what we lose and must return to, our primal authenticity. But going back there is a frightening journey; it's back into the cave, where the hungry bears are. Going back to feed on our own child, we find ourselves in the lair of the ogre.*

Thus the child is both innocent and evil, explicable and empty, villain and victim, host of the party and its main course, vampire and cannibal.

– *The Fat Boy, in* Pickwick, *is a case in point. He is defined not simply by his eating but by his ability to turn flesh, any flesh, into food. His own flesh is always spilling out, offering itself, but he nurtures that bounteous feast by gnawing on anything in sight. The Fat Boy can hardly move but he is everywhere; he loves to terrify people, to make their flesh creep, but is all flesh himself. He is nothing, entirely empty, but he terrorizes the party with his invasive substance. He is innocence consumed by lust, and by the reader. He is pure gothic: without words and without fixed form. He is the child as harmless toy and raging demon.*

But not all children are as obviously demonic as The Fat Boy. I'm thinking here of Linton Heathcliff.

– *Me too. But I think we need to clarify for a second what the Fat Boy offers and demands. He draws us back into a blissful world, no doubt about that, a world that has nothing in it but ME, me and my demands. What I demand is the breast, and the whole world is a breast to me. There's nothing I don't want; but there's also nothing that won't be given to me. I just need to reach out my lips and suck, my teeth and chew. The Fat Boy exists at the heart of gothic, the undifferentiated world or self, unmarked by language and inseparable from the feeding of a desire that is never sated.*

Good. And in the more subtle case of Linton Heathcliff …

– *But the gothic is never static, of course, and the experience of the gothic is much more demanding – in fact, demands far more than it gives. As we lean toward the Fat Boy, yearn for his coherence, we find ourselves suddenly in his clothes, in his body, infantilized and thus on the table ourselves, attacked by the knives and forks of others.*

That is, the child is offered to the Victorians as a comestible, and the proper way to show your love for the child is to take it into you, allow that at your heart, at your core, is the child. That's where it belongs and you are doing the proper thing by absorbing it, possessing it utterly. And that's the lure, the basic terrifying lure of the gothic: 'just come into my house, my den, my nightmare, little one!'

OK. I know you're about to say, 'And once we're there, we suddenly find – blah, blah, blah'. But I want to stop right here a second. Just hold on.

– *You seem excited.*

I just don't want you hurrying on to the end of the chapter without making this point clear.

– *You think the chapter would be too short if we did?*

Nobody'd mind that. I am thinking rather that you'd hustle us into a paradox before the first step was secured. See what I mean? You're going to say, the Victorian gothic depends on getting us drooling over the child and that, when we try to tuck in, we find we're on the menu ourselves, the Tuesday special, stuffed reader. But I think nobody'll accept the last part, about being the meal, unless you make them see more clearly that they want to eat in the first place. Give them an example of the luscious child. Then you can move on. That's all I'm saying. It's a question of rhetoric.

– *OK.*

So, you going to do that?

– *No, I think you are.*

Right. Well, there's Linton Heathcliff, you know, who is eaten by his father. He turns the boy into a kind of Jello, a quivering semi-solid, just by sitting in the room with him. Heathcliff puts his napkin on his lap, takes a sip of water, plays a little with his knife and fork; and the boy arranges himself in a bowl. Heathcliff then slurps him up.

– *Terrific. You got that point solidified, I think. Nobody's confused now; we can be sure of that. We have our readers right where we want them.*

I doubt it. Let me offer one more example.

– *Another example of the same thing?*

Well, not the same thing. A different thing in a way – or, actually, the same thing in a different key. A different slant on the point that Victorian gothic features cannibalistic infanticide or childicide. 'The Turn of the Screw' is what I had in mind.

The Governess, our surrogate, wades into those kids as if she were in a pie-eating contest. Here's her on Flora, for instance: 'She was the most beautiful child I had ever seen ... I slept little that night – I was much too excited' (Ch. 1)' We (The Governess) soon persuade the dim-witted housekeeper to let us take her into us: 'It had been agreed between us downstairs ... that I should have her as a matter of course at night' (Ch. 1). And have her we do.

'And the little boy – does he look like her?' we ask 'Is he too so very remarkable?'

'Oh miss', says our stolid friend, '"*most* remarkable. If you think well of this one!" – and she stood there with a plate in her hand, beaming'. And he is, 'incredibly beautiful' (Ch. 2), inciting 'a passion of tenderness' that allows her (us) to 'then and there take him to my heart' (Ch. 2). He is 'indescribable', of course, but there's nothing to him except love.

Well, there's Quint, of course, and Miss Jessel and all that evil, all that sexual evil. They seem to have started lunch without us and we need to drive them away. There's only so much room at the table.

We manage it, though it isn't easy. We get the boy all cooked and ready, hitch up to the banquet, saying to the entrée, 'Now *I* have you!' (xxiii). We launch a few taunts at 'the beast' (Quint? Miles? Us?) and then we can say, 'I caught him, yes, I held him – it may be imagined with what a passion'. As we fill ourselves, we consume him, of course, he dwindles and dies. You can't have your child and eat it too, it seems, which is too bad.

– *Now?*
  All yours.

– *So the gothic child, which is to say the gothic, the Victorian gothic anyhow, certainly entices, invites, sets before us a feast. Come and get it, get the child! Catch it, recover it, and get back to it.*

   But the child never stays there, never offers itself up – or, when it does, takes on the uncanny features of us. We suddenly realize that the leg we are ready to swallow is our own. The search to cover the child with desire, to protect it, to become that child lands us in the slaughter house. Line up.

   Look at the cautionary gothic ending of Through the Looking-Glass. *Here's a gothic story which does not chicken out at the end, does not lose its nerve or abandon its cannibalistic promise. Here the sometime child, Alice, has just said her last farewell to her old pedophile lover, Lewis 'White Knight' Carroll, and has tripped over the last brook to be a Queen and mate a King. She has thoughtlessly abandoned her own childhood and, worse, her old child–lover.*

   And she moves right into the world of gothic adulthood, the great party of Queens, the feast of children. Suddenly, 'there was the leg of mutton sitting in the chair', with the White Queen floating in the soup tureen. Other guests are at once 'in the dishes, and the soup ladle was walking up the table towards Alice's chair' ready to scoop her up.

So the gothic quest comes to rest on the child; and the child which had called to us so charmingly, activated our appetite, now turns on us the face of the beast, clawing at us and rending us. The tables turned.

Victorian gothic, then, is sublimely regressive, showing us finally that we really do need to be afraid to look. Don't look now and don't look back. It's not that the monster is in the basement or the closet or the woods. It's disguised as innocence, as tenderness, as desire; and it nestles in the nursery of our own hearts.

– *Which is to say ...*
> There's no more to say.

– *We're done? You're calling this off?*
> Done.

– *I'm not done. You just want the last word. You like that line about nestling in the nursery of the great gothic day-care centre in the hell of our hearts or whatever it was. You imagine that's climactic. Unbearable!*
> I think it's time we part.

– *Fine. I don't want any part of this, then, or of you. Take my name off the title page. I just wish I could get you inside a gothic novel.*
> Bye.

2

Resurrecting the Regency: Horror and Eighteenth-Century Comedy in Le Fanu's Fiction

Victor Sage

Comedy and horror are closer than we tend to think. We know this from Elizabethan and Jacobean drama, and we can see it in later comedy too. The structure of certain kinds of comic scene, and here I mean set comic scenes, is not far from horror and one's laughter is sometimes uneasy, shading over into something which feels at first sight inappropriate but which, we discover, has been lurking there all along. These scenes are based on the total incarceration of one character in a prison of illusion, the walls of which are kept up until the last minute so that the audience can savour the confusion of the victim, even if our laughter is a recognition of an icy current welling up through the play's comic fabric at this point.

The name of Goldsmith, for example, is not usually connected with horror and yet there is a scene in the fourth act of *She Stoops to Conquer*, which I should like to start with. It is the famous coach scene, in which Tony Lumpkin has apparently sent his mother on a forty-mile journey, but in reality has simply diverted the coach in a circle through the village:

> *Hastings*:   Well, but where have you left the ladies? I die with impatience.
> *Tony*:   Left them? Why, where should I leave them, but where I found them?
> *Hastings*:   This is a riddle.
> *Tony*:   Riddle me this then. What's that goes round the house, and round the house, and never touches the house?
> *Hastings*:   I'm still astray.

Tony: Why, that's it, mon. I have led them astray. By jingo, there's not a pond or slough within five miles of the place but they can tell the taste of.

Hastings: Ha, ha, ha, I understand; you took them in a round, while they supposed themselves going forward. And you have at last brought them home again.

Tony: You shall hear. I first took them down Feather-bed-lane, where we stuck fast in the mud. I then rattled them crack over the stones of Up-and-down Hill – I then introduced them to the gibbet on Heavy-tree Heath, and from that, with a circum-bendibus, I fairly lodged them in the horsepond at the bottom of the garden.

Hastings: But no accident, I hope.

Tony: No, no. Only mother is confoundedly frightened. She thinks herself forty miles off ... (Goldsmith 1960, 281)

This cock and bull story forms the climax of this comedy in which the hypocrisy and the class pretensions of the characters are ridiculed by a hallucinatory set of literal misunderstandings about identity and location. Here, however, comic deception has reached its outer edge, so to speak, and the play's geniality is momentarily destabilized. Goldsmith, like Fielding, reminds us how unpredictable and potentially dangerous travel was in the eighteenth century – the presence of the highwayman is everywhere. The gibbet, as in the comic songs of *The Beggar's Opera*, acts here as a reminder (to audience and characters alike) of present danger and future mortality.[1]

But perhaps the most frightening thing for the victim and the funniest thing for the audience is not on an instrumental level – not just the fear for personal safety – but is rather a matter of consciousness. Deception becomes *hallucination* for the victim, not just puzzlement. It is the surrounding presence of illusion, a complete three-dimensional switch of one reality for another in which the ruling expectation that coaches are the emblem of a happily rational, goal-orientated form of human behaviour, is overturned, which dominates the structure of such practical-joke reversals; and this spectacle of a human being, entirely hidden in the capsule of expectation, and yet still able to act out a complete replica of life, with all its moral choices intact, tempts us to laugh at the victim's fear. It is an experiment in consciousness.

In Goldsmith's case, we have only a glimpse here of the intensity of Mrs Hardcastle's fear, though the next scene amplifies it. Paralysed by darkness and the expectation of imminent attack, but determined to protect her son, in a moment of great personal heroism, she kneels to her own husband, thinking he is a highwayman, and offers him her life in exchange for that of Tony, the very callous manipulator who has led her into this trap. She means it as literally as we can take, it, when she confesses at the point of revelation: 'My fears blinded me'.

This coach-diversion is re-played in a somewhat darker key some twenty years later. However, in the case of Sheridan, the scene occurs in life and it does not have quite such a strong comic shape. On 19 October 1792, Mme de Genlis tells us in her journals, there was a strange incident on the coach-road to Dover. Having entertained them at his house in London, Sheridan saw off the party, consisting of Pamela and Adelaide, the daughter of the Duc D'Orleans, on their way to Dover to embark for France. When she noticed that they were taking a different route, Mme de Genlis questioned the postilions who refused to reply. Mme de Genlis was paralysed with terror. Someone rode up and said, from outside the coach: 'Mesdames, on vous trompe, on ne vous même point à Douvres'. This French servant appears then to have stopped the equipage, turned it round, and headed the party back to London to Sheridan's residence. Mme de Genlis was convinced that he was feigning surprise when he interrogated the postillions. She says in her *Mémoires Inédits*, that everything convinced her it was a plot to abduct her daughter, Pamela, to whom Sheridan had already, bizarrely, proposed marriage.

But Mme de Genlis' French biographer, Gabriel de Broglie, working from the correspondence of the Duc D'Orleans, sees a darker and more sinister counter-revolutionary political plot in this famously bizarre and puzzling incident. De Broglie claims that the plot, cooked up by the Duc D'Orleans, was to abduct, not Pamela, but Adelaide; according to de Broglie, the King of Prussia, in league with the Duc D'Orleans, wanted to marry Adelaide to a German prince who would then have assumed the crown of France. At the same time, the Duke of Brunswick would have been placed at the head of the French army (de Broglie 1985, 228).[2] Whatever the truth of this murky affair, Sheridan prevaricated and kept the ladies with him for several weeks, before they finally returned to Paris.

Whichever way round, and I suppose it could have been both, posterity suspects Sheridan of being party to a conspiracy.

My second starting point is the ambiguous popular reputation of the Regency period among Victorians. Prince Albert died, with the same kind of mass mourning as the funeral of Princess Diana, just as the sensation novel was getting under way as a genre, in December 1861. Mary Elizabeth Braddon, in her second novel, *Aurora Floyd*, about to begin its serialization in *Temple Bar*, apparently breaks off her narrative to reflect on the differences between the Prince Consort and the Prince Regent:

> It is many years since England mourned for another royal personage who was called a 'gentleman'. A gentleman who played practical jokes, and held infamous orgies, and persecuted a wretched foreign woman, whose chief sin and misfortune it was to be his wife; a gentleman who cut out his own nether garments, and left the companion of his gayest revels, the genius whose brightness had flung a spurious lustre upon the dreary saturnalia of vice, to die destitute and despairing. Surely there is some hope that we have changed for the better within the last thirty years, inasmuch as we attach a new meaning today to this simple title of 'gentleman'. (Braddon 1996, 60)

The last sentence is both complacent and vulnerable, depending on how one reads it. Braddon's Oxford editor calls this comparison between the two figures 'hackneyed' and it no doubt is, if one takes its optimism literally: but the Victorians' desire to measure their own progress has another side, a nightmare from the past, and this nightmare is repeatedly exploited in the sensation novel. The fear of the past takes different forms in different novelists. But the fuel for the engine of these characteristically backward-looking plots – in which a secret from the past steals up to ruin the carefully built-up facade of the present – is often a negotiation between a looser moral, and perhaps a more dramatic political, age and the bourgeois stability of the present. If the dead prince is the spirit of the age, then the sensation novel swaps the corpse of one prince for the other.

Nowhere is this tension more acute than in the Irish gothic writer, Sheridan Le Fanu, who repeatedly creates plots in which this dispossessed aristocratic corpse is undead: it keeps on resurrecting itself, and ruining whatever happiness the younger generation have created for themselves and their children.

But to go back to that past for a moment. In the case of Sheridan, who is not the person whom the prince abandoned in Braddon's outburst (that is Beau Brummel), but who might have been, there is a more explicitly gothic effect than in the case of the Prince Regent and there are more explicitly political reasons for this. Sheridan died in 1816 and was given a large funeral and buried in Westminster Abbey. His elegant comedies continued to be very popular during the Victorian period, partly because they lacked obscenity.[3] On the biographical front, things are very different. The nineteenth-century biographical construction of Sheridan is a long and complex one, but sooner or later most writers who have tackled his life are forced to admit that there is something indissolubly contradictory about his character, his appearance, his language, or his actions. Often, all four.

In contemporary testimony Sheridan is persistently described, from the point at which he became a public figure, in a rhetoric that is at once adulatory and demonizing:

> His face, though very handsome, had an ambiguity which most people found fascinating. 'Even when I first knew him [early 1793] wrote [Sydney Smith], 'his forehead was very fine, and his eyes brilliant in the extreme. The lower part of the face was coarse, and not agreeable.' As he became more and more a public image, this contrast took on a mythic quality, seeming to be the outward sign of inner struggle between the divine and demonic. Lord Byron said of him that 'the upper part of Sheridan's face was that of a god – a forehead most expansive, an eye of peculiar brilliancy and fire; but below he shewed the satyr'. (O'Toole 1997, 196)

Byron, who often took Sheridan home drunk from Drury Lane, and who admired the latter's rhetorical genius and libertarian sentiments, strikes the tone of angel/demon here. Much contemporary comment was given to the eyes, their unusual, almost supernatural brilliancy:

> Sheridan's eyes seemed to those who saw him to express the divine side of his nature. As a young man, Samuel Taylor Coleridge wrote in 1795 of how his 'eye-beams dance'. Henry Brougham, who saw him in his last years in Parliament, claimed that his eye was 'singularly piercing', and that 'it had the singularity of never winking'. (O'Toole 1997, 197)

Thomas Moore and Samuel Rogers extended the demonic aspects of this picture with a set of death-bed anecdotes about his torment of his ex-lover, Harriet Duncannon, Lady Bessborough, the even more beautiful sister of the Duchess of Devonshire, who went to see him when he was dying:

> He asked what she thought of his looks. She said his eyes were brilliant still. He then made some frightful answer about their being fixed for eternity. He took her hand and gripped it hard, and then he told her that, if possible, he would come to her after he was dead. Lady Bessborough was frightened, and said that he had persecuted her all his life, and would now carry his persecution into death. Why should he do so? 'Because', said Sheridan, 'I am resolved you should remember me.' He said more frightful things and she withdrew in great terror. (Butler 1931, 300)

And then, finally, Samuel Rogers's *Table-Talk*, puts the gothic seal on this final incident:

> He sent a final *macabre* message to Lady Bessborough 'that his eyes would look up at the coffin-lid as brightly as ever'. (Butler 1931, 301)

The popular iconography, created by the newspapers, of Sheridan as the angel-devil of the Whig opposition, the Lucifer of the Regency, possessed of the devil's golden tongue and a seditious soul, with the prince in his pocket (witness his rhetorical conjuring trick in his House of Commons over the crisis of the Prince's secret marriage to Mrs Fitzherbert, a Catholic) declined towards the end of his life into 'Sherry', the red-nosed Hogarthian grotesque of the cartoons who had become a by-word for drunkenness, lechery and sedition. Byron's championing of him did Sheridan no good at all in Victorian eyes.

In fact, in the case of Sheridan, biography was mere scandalized gossip and drawing-room horror until the later Victorian period, when the Marquis of Dufferin and Ava, the great-grandson of the playwright, decided to rescue his kinsman from moral and political disgrace. He commissioned W. Fraser Rae, a liberal journalist, to produce the first full account from the Sheridan papers.[4]

The horror attaching to the image of Sheridan created in the table-talk of Thomas Moore and Samuel Rogers and inherited by the Victorians, was not only moral, but to some extent, a political horror; for some, he was the icon of sedition: he consistently opposed the King and championed the cause of catholic Emancipation on behalf of the Irish peasants; he was instrumental, in the first Whig Parliament, in repealing the 'Sixth of George the First', a manoeuvre which gave to Ireland a brief commercial, constitutional and legal independence from England; he supported the Americans in their War of Independence against the British crown; he supported the French Revolution; he was uncomfortably close to the Irish rebels of 1798, even apparently trying to help some of them escape from a courtroom; he harried Pitt's government over the suppression of civil liberties; and, a paradox for some, he became the chief spokesman for, or interpreter of, the Prince Regent outside the walls of Devonshire House. To the popular press, which he himself manipulated skillfully on occasion, he represented political radicalism, profligacy and sexual licence in equal measures. Such notoriety created a mixture of horror and popular admiration. Horace Walpole's reaction to Sheridan's speech indicting Warren Hastings playfully elides the gothic register with the language of political distrust:

> One heard everybody in the streets raving on the wonders of that speech; for my part I cannot believe it was so supernatural as they say – do you believe it was, madam? ... How should such a fellow as Sheridan, who has no diamonds to bestow, fascinate all the world? – Yet witchcraft, no doubt, there has been, for when did simple eloquence ever convince a majority? Mr Pitt and 174 other persons found Mr Hastings guilty last night. ... Well, at least there is a new crime, sorcery, to charge on the opposition. (O'Toole 1997, 218)

The devil plays all the best tunes and has all the best speeches: there is no doubt that Sheridan was feared by his contemporaries – by creditors, ex-lovers, and political opponents alike – because of his penetrating wit and extreme persuasiveness.

Even as late as 1810, when the king's illness had entered its final phase and a new Regency was in preparation, Sheridan was hoping to be appointed as Chief Secretary to Ireland in a Ministry headed by Grey and Grenville. Grenville rejected him out of hand, and Grey said that sending Sheridan to Ireland would be like 'sending a man with a lighted torch into a magazine of gunpowder' (O'Toole 1997, 428).

Joseph Sheridan Le Fanu was Sheridan's great-nephew. For him, these contradictions between the angel and the demon in the family were particularly acute. The Sheridans and the Le Fanus were close. As T.P. Le Fanu in his 1920s memoir of the Le Fanu family puts it:

All living Le Fanus are also of Sheridan blood, that is to say, they are all descendants of Doctor Thomas Sheridan, through either his son or his daughter Hester. (cited in Browne 1951, 9)

When Thomas Sheridan left his Smock Alley Theatre in Dublin, he entrusted the business to a Le Fanu. It is tempting to think of the Le Fanus as the clerkly, lawyerish side of the family; the Sheridans, the theatrical, artistic, politically radical side, but this is an overexaggeration and a simplification. What we can say is that Joseph Sheridan Le Fanu was a lifelong Tory, the son of a Dean in the Irish Church, whose impressionable youth, spent in deepest Limerick during the Tithe Wars of the 1820s, had registered the lasting image of violence offered to the family during those times (see McCormack 1991, Chs 1 and 2).

For much of his writing life, Sheridan Le Fanu was attached to the Dublin University Magazine, a staunchly Tory, Protestant Ascendancy journal, and Le Fanu wrote thunderingly anti-Catholic editorials during the repeal of the Union campaigns – an issue on which he never capitulated. The rhetoric of these editorials is sometimes close to Anne Radcliffe in tone. In 1848, just after the Young Ireland crisis, up to which he appeared to have been relaxing somewhat his astringent line, he gave vent to the following:

We leave our English readers to gather ... how far we were justified in pronouncing that the supremacy of British Law, and the practical existence of the constitution here; depend upon the conscientious loyalty of Irish protestants – a loyalty which has passed the ordeal of fearful vicissitudes – which has withstood the shocks of civil commotion – and worse – the spurning of insolence, and the coolness of neglect – a loyalty, above all, which is impervious to the secret and mortal poison of casuist tongues – which cannot be seduced by the fraudulent subtleties, or overpowered by the exorbitant tyranny of a dark and sinister theology. (DUM July, 1848)

Here the traditional anti-Catholic register shows its hand in the anti-Jesuit references to 'the secret and mortal poison of casuist tongues' and the final gothic flourish of 'a dark and sinister theology'. The implication, as in the case of the condemnation of Sheridan forty or fifty years previously, is that Protestant loyalty goes with 'candour' and 'openness'. Le Fanu's early romances were devoted to showing how that loyalty had been betrayed in the past by corrupt Whig administrations in Ireland. Yet it was his own great uncle who had a reputation for being a prime mover against all the forces of social order, religion, and the landowning class which Le Fanu's family interests stood for.

But this picture is too simple: Le Fanu himself was caught in a contradictory situation: his mother was a nationalist sympathizer who made a cult of the radical aristocrat, Lord Edward Fitzgerald, martyred in the '98 rebellion. She slept with Lord Edward's dagger, captured from him when he was betrayed and arrested, under her pillow. One of the earliest poems to come from the pen of her son was 'Shamus O'Brien', a nationalist ballad in vernacular dialect. Le Fanu himself is a complicated and divided character, in whom class and religion could combine to produce unpredictable sympathies.

The terrors of the coach incident clearly impressed themselves upon Le Fanu, because the plots of two of his novels depend upon the secret diversion of coaches and there is some direct indication in *Uncle Silas* (1863) that the source of this sinister, paranoid episode, which by the 1860s and refracted through Le Fanu's backward-looking mirror, has overtones of political violence about it, is indeed contained in the comedies of Goldsmith and Sheridan.[5] Moreover, the whole narrative crosses the barriers of genre between the comic and the gothic in a strange and interesting way.

Silas himself, born in 1771, is the living corpse of the Regency rake who has apparently hung on to life with the help of gambling, murder, fraud, Swedenborgianism and a small allowance from his brother, into the 1840s, when the action of the novel takes place (c.1843–45), reaching the ripe old age of 74. The incident in which Maud and her cousin stare at the portrait of him as a beautiful boy of eight gives the necrophiliac tone that can pin death and representation together in a single phrase: '"A very singular face", she said, softly, as a person might who was looking into a coffin' (Le Fanu 1981, 55). And when Maud looks at the other portrait of him as a more mature young man, she still falls for him, despite her cousin Monica's condemnation of him. The association with the figure of Sheridan is not improbable:

> There stood the *roué* – the duellist – and, with all his faults, the hero too! In that dark large eye lurked the profound and fiery enthusiasm of his ill-starred passion. In the thin but exquisite lip I read the courage of the paladin, who would have 'fought his way', through single-handed, against all the magnates of his county, and by ordeal of battle have purged the honour of the Ruthyns. There in that delicate half-sarcastic tracery of the nostril I detected the intellectual defiance which had politically isolated Silas Ruthyn and opposed

him to the landed oligarchy of his county, whose retaliation had been a hideous slander. There, too, and on his brows and lip, I traced the patience of a cold disdain. I could now see him as he was – the prodigal, the hero, and the martyr. (Le Fanu 1981, 59)

The hint here is that the romantic girl has fallen for an angel-devil of the Whig elite of forty years previously. In her eyes, Silas is sublime, and the storm that rages on the night that he seeks to take possession of her as his ward, seems appropriate:

And so it was like the yelling of phantom hounds and hunters, and the thunder of their coursers in the air – a furious, grand, and super-natural music, which in my fancy made a suitable accompaniment to the discussion of that enigmatical person – martyr – angel – demon – Uncle Silas – with whom my fate was now so strangely linked, and whom I had begun to fear. (1981, 145)

He is also variously described as a living corpse, a modern Bluebeard, an Erl-King, and a malign Prospero. Even rational worldly Cousin Monica thinks she can 'fancy him an old enchanter in his castle, waving his familiar spirits on the wind to fetch and carry tidings of our occupations here' (1981, 145).

When Maud finally claps eyes on him, to her obsessed perception he is like a Dutch painting: both a fiction and a figure from the past:

He rose, tall and slight, a little stooped, all in black, with an ample black velvet tunic, which was rather a gown than a coat, with loose sleeves showing his snowy shirt some way up the arm, and a pair of wrist buttons, then quite out of fashion, which glimmered aristo-cratically with diamonds. (1981, 189)

The anachronistic space in which Silas has survived is his own theatri-cal creation, and when seeking to draw Maud into it, by belittling his own daughter, he makes a number of casual-looking allusions to romance and comedy:

He said something in his clear, gentle, but cold voice, the import of which I was too much agitated to catch, and he took both my hands in his, welcomed me with a courtly grace which belonged to another age, and led me affectionately, with many enquiries which I only half comprehended, to a chair near his own.

'I need not introduce my daughter; she has saved me that mortification. You'll find her, I believe, good-natured and affectionate; *au reste*, I fear a very rustic Miranda, and fitted rather for the society of Caliban than of a sick, old Prospero. Is it not so, Millicent?'

The old man paused sarcastically for an answer, with his eyes fixed severely on my odd cousin, who blushed and looked uneasily to me for a hint.

'I don't know who they be – neither one nor t'other.'

'Very good, my dear,' he replied with a little mocking bow. 'You see, my dear Maud, what a Shakesperean [sic] you have got for a cousin. It's plain, however, she has made acquaintance with some of our dramatists: she has studied the role of *Miss Hoyden* so perfectly.' (1981, 190)

Silas's allusion to Sheridan's comedy, *A Trip To Scarborough*, here and to the character type, the comic rustic, to which the character of Milly apparently conforms, has the effect, amongst other things, of confirming the arrestation of his own cultural *points de repère* in the later eighteenth century. It also explicitly brings Sheridan back into the text on another level.

In the second half of the text, the allusions to Sheridan and Goldsmith begin to unfold. Performing the same sarcastic trick on Maud's Cousin Monica, Lady Knollys, Silas refers again to *A Trip to Scarborough*:

'This is my daughter, Milly – oh! she has been presented to you down stairs, has she? You have, no doubt, been interested by her. As I told her Cousin Maud, though I am not yet quite a Sir Tunbelly Clumsy, she is a very finished Miss Hoyden? Are not you, my poor Milly? (1981, 240)

Here he tempts her to speak her rustic dialect, to prove his witty point that she is a 'finished' primitive – a pun on education and acting, but also painting too – and a sarcastic but also self-piteous way of underscoring the jibe that he has been deprived by the family (Monica included) of the money to educate his children.

The theatrical allusion which makes Silas the author of the narrative's comic script, however, is a self-defeating paradox. Allusion to late-eighteenth-century comedy belongs, not to Silas, but to the text. So, when Dudley, his brutalized bumpkin of a son, begins to make more regular appearances, pressing Maud, at Silas's secret instigation, to marry him, he is cast by Maud, interestingly, as Tony Lumpkin:

> My uncle had his Bible and his consolations; but it cannot have been pleasant to this old *roué*, converted though he was – this refined man of fashion – to see his son grow up an outcast, and a Tony Lumpkin; for whatever he may have thought of his natural gifts, he must have known how mere a boor he was. (1981, 255)

We know that the plot is a coach-diversion, and the irony of this ambiguously prophetic remark from Maud is quite complex and illustrates this crossing over from one genre to another: this is comedy upside down. When Dudley gets cold feet, and seeks to buy his way out of his father's conspiracy to abduct and murder Maud by performing a counter-diversion of his own and driving her, not to 'Dover', but to her cousin Monica, for the sum of £20,000, Maud again has Goldsmith on her mind. But her perspective is completely perverse: indoctrinated by her own father into a set of masculine values that belong to the past, she still at this late stage misreads the situation and defends her assassin uncle. She completely misunderstands what Dudley – her own generation – is offering her. She looks down at his counterplot as the efforts of a Lumpkin without wit. The result is a use of the comic structure, which yields unexpected sparks of pathos and irony:

> I joined Mary Quince, extremely angry. As I passed under the carved oak arch of the vestibule I saw his figure in the deepening twilight. The picture remains in its murky halo fixed in memory. Standing where he last spoke in the centre of the hall, not looking after me, but downward, and, as well as I could see, with the countenance of a man who has lost a game, and a ruinous wager too – that is black and desperate. I did not utter a syllable on the way up. When I reached my room I began to reconsider the interview more at my leisure. I was, such were my ruminations, to have agreed at once to his preposterous offer, and to have been driven, while he smirked and grimaced behind my back at his acquaintances, through Feltram in his dog-cart to Elverston; and then, to the just indignation of my uncle, to have been delivered up to Lady Knollys's guardianship, and to have handed my driver, as I alighted, the handsome fare of £20,000! It required the impudence of Tony Lumpkin, without either his fun or his shrewdness, to have conceived such a prodigious practical joke. (1981, 345)

Dudley is committed from this moment on to murder her. His despair is evident to the reader, but not to Maud, the ingenue, who only sees him through the lens of 'honour'. She pompously enters arguments against what she sees as his 'practical joke' which are based on her own family loyalty and pride ('to the just indignation of my uncle' is a fine stroke of forensic irony).

There are two or three other moments like this, where Silas's coach-plot stands on the brink of discovery, almost foiled by Maud herself. For example, in the following, when Silas writes in code and Maud spots it:

> I cannot say what it was in this short advice that struck me with fear. Was it the thick line beneath the word 'Dover' that was so uncalled for, and gave me a faint but terrible sense of something preconcerted?
> I said to Madame –
> 'Why is 'Dover' underlined?'
> 'I do not know you little fool, no more than you. How can I tell what is passing in your oncle's head when he make that a mark?
> 'Has it not a meaning, Madame?'
> 'How can you talk like that?' she answered in her old way. 'You are either mocking of me, or you are becoming truly a fool?' (1981, 394)

'Dover' means Bartram-Haugh, of course; but 'Dover' is also the point of recall for the Sheridan incident with Mme de Genlis. Here the feeling that the plot is already known is irresistible, and yet curiously the almost comic effect is tilted and creates suspense and tension. The fabric of the plot is so flimsy that Maud, unlike Mrs Hardcastle, soon recognizes Bartram-Haugh and declares the 'hotel' at 'Dover' to be such (1981, 400); but again, the comic possibilities of these moments are suppressed by the fanatical and sinister violence of the narrative.

But perhaps the most strange and complex of these allusions to Sheridan is Silas's own. In trying to persuade Maud that Dudley's clumsy and disgusting attempts to propose to her are in fact tokens of a genuine love, he appeals to both Sheridan's biography and his play, *The Rivals*:

> 'You know in that pleasant play, poor Sheridan – delightful fellow! – all our fine spirits are dead – he makes Mrs Malaprop say there is

nothing like beginning with a little aversion. Now, though in matrimony, of course that is only a joke, yet in love, believe me, it is no such thing. His own marriage with Miss Ogle, I *know*, was a case in point. She expressed a positive horror of him at their first acquaintance; and yet, I believe, she would, a few months later, have died rather than not have married him.' (1981, 311)[6]

Silas appeals to the Sheridan's biography and the comedy in one frame in order to establish his own credentials as a survivor from the Regency period and a persuasive force. His emphasis suggests that he actually witnessed the change of attitude in Miss Ogle's psychology. Wittily, Mrs Malaprop is neatly converted from a comic butt, to a wise counsellor to help his sinister cause.

In *The Rose and the Key* (1871), a novel full of equally gothic elements, the coach-diversion becomes a conspiracy practiced by Lady Barbara Vernon against her daughter, Maud, to prevent her from inheriting the family estate. Maud Vernon is placed in a private lunatic asylum, while thinking that she is going for a stay at the country house of an aristocratic acquaintance, Lady Mardykes. Both Goldsmith and Sheridan are present in this plot: the coach diversion itself is terrifying and fraught with indirect violence. Maud's maid, 'honest Jones', is substituted by a trick at a Country Inn by the egregiously horrible Mercy Cresswell, an old nursery playmate of Maud's from the village, who has, unbeknownst to her, become a lunatic asylum attendant. This figure, described as 'plump, and broad, and strong, with a cunning and false gaiety in her fat face, and who laughed a great deal, not pleasantly, but rather maliciously, and at untoward times...' (Le Fanu 1994, 213) is a parody of a comic character. As Maud stares at her, she suddenly remembers the abuse she received from Mercy, as a child:

Maud had a remembrance of an occasional slap or pinch, now and then, slyly bestowed by this short, freckled, laughing young lady, who rather liked getting her into a scrape at times, and who used in playful moods, when they were running about the rooms together, and no one by, to run her into a corner, hold her to the wall, and make ugly faces, with her nose almost touching Maud's, till the child would scream with fright and anger; and then she would fall into shrieks of laughter, and hug and kiss her a little more roughly than was necessary, and after this somewhat sore and uncomfortable reconcili- ation, she would charge her – for the love she bore her own, own poor little Mercy Cresswell, who would be sent away if she did, never more to dress her doll, or trundle her cart, or roll her ball for her – not to tell nurse, or nursery-maid, or Miss Latimer, that they had had 'a falling out'. (1994, 231)

This creature appears in the coach on the journey in place of Jones, a nightmare from Maud's past, grinning and laughing inappropriately at everything that Maud says, and almost giving the game away. Mercy's grandmother, Maggie, has threatened Maud as a small child, in one of the most gothic moments of the text, for apparently taking the part of her father in her innocent prattle. The woman is dying:

The figure in the flannels beckoned, and for the first time, a little awe stole over the child; she drew near, trying to see her more dis- tinctly in the obscurity. When she did, it was not the face she knew. There was no smile there. The face was hollow and yellow, a clammy blackness was about the lips, the eyes looked at her, large and earnest; the child came to her, returning her strange gaze in silence. She was frightened that such a thing should be Maggie Cresswell.

The old woman placed her bony hand on to the child's arm and clasped it feebly. She spoke in a hard whisper, with a little quick panting at every word.

'That's Anne Holt has been saying that; it's a shame to be putting things in your head gainst your good mamma. Well it is that you are under her and not under him; no blacker villain ever lived on earth than your papa. Keep that to yourself; if you tell anyone in the nursery, I'll come to you after I'm dead and frighten you.' (1994, 72)

This is close to Sheridan's own alleged threat to Lady Bessborough as he lay dying, and it may be that Le Fanu is thinking of that macabre anecdote as a model for this scene.

The coach-diversion is initially presented as a sort of sadistic joke on dreamlike position, surrounded by three-dimensional illusion. The episode is violent in several ways. As they near 'Lady Mardykes'', Maud is faced with a mirror-image of her own abduction. Another coach is desperately trying to overtake them from which she can hear sounds:

She mistook them first for the laughter and vociferation of a rollicking party on their way home from supper. But she soon perceived, with alarm, that they indicated something very different.

They were sounds of fury and terror. She heard a voice exerting itself in short gasps and shrieks, and declaiming with frightful volubility:

'I say Vivian's my name! Murder, murder – my God! two to one – they're murdering me!' yelled this voice, which, disguised as it was with rage and terror, she nevertheless fancied she knew, and exactly as the chaise drove by, at a suddenly stimulated pace, the window was broken, and the jingling glass showered on the road close beside the wheels; and, in the flash of the lamp, Miss Vernon had a momentary glimpse of the cantering horses and the postilions lashing them, and of the hands and faces of the men struggling within, and, as the strange phantasmagoria flew by ... (241–2)

But Maud still does not realize that she is a part of this 'phantasmagoria' herself, and a comparable violence is being done to her own personal liberty. In fact, this is the insane son of Lady Mardykes whom the postilions are desperate to restrain and get to the asylum.

Inside the house, the illusion that it is Lady Mardykes' Carsbrook is kept up, and the sequence is like a sinister, hallucinated reversal of the 'mistakes' in Goldsmith's comedy. Le Fanu projects a similar pattern of prolonged misunderstanding, not that a house is an inn, but that an institution is a private house. The result is a comic defamiliarization, shot through with discomfort and fear, as the reader supplies Maud's puzzlement:

'This is Miss Maud Vernon, daughter of Lady Vernon, of Roydon Hall', said Darkdale, performing this odd office of introduction in a dry, rapid way.

'Half an hour later than we expected,' said Mr Drummond, pulling out a large old-fashioned silver watch by the chain, from which dangled a bunch of seals and keys on his comfortable paunch; and then, glancing back, it was to be presumed at a clock, in the interior, 'no, twenty-five, precisely five-and-twenty minutes late', and he turned from the corners of his eyes upon Miss Vernon a shrewed [*sic*] glance, and quickly made her a respectful bow.

'I'll tell you about that by-and-by', said Darkdale.

'I hope the young lady will find everything to her liking, I'm sure.'
'Miss Vernon's come for a short visit to *Lady Mardykes* here, a few weeks or so', interrupted Darkdale. (1994, 251)

All of naive, protected Maud's purely aristocratic expectations are transposed into 'oddity', striking false notes. They are speaking in code all around her and the reader frantically reads the signs – the punctilio, the jailer's bunch of keys, and the way Darkdale (his gothic name gives the game away), the madhouse-keeper, who, Maud thinks, puzzled, is 'dressed like a poor schoolmaster', talks across her as if she isn't there, like a child, instead of one of his betters – these things the character is entirely unable to read, and perhaps doesn't even perceive.

The climax of this adapted form of comic misunderstanding comes in the garden, which is a complete mock-up of Lady Mardykes' croquet-lawn, where she finally meets the inmates. The tone of these chapters is extravagant and almost surrealist, anticipatory of *Alice in Wonderland*, which was published soon after this novel. There Maud meets the Spanish Ambassador:

He is a tall man and well-formed, with a short black cloak thrown, Spanish fashion, in spite of the heat of the weather, across his breast and over his shoulder. He has a broad-leaved black felt hat looped at the front with something that looks like a little buckle of brilliants. His face is dark and handsome, with an expression of the most ineffable pride and self-complacency. His chin is high in the air, his movements are slow and graceful, he wears white kid gloves, and carries in his hand an ebony walking cane, with a gold head, formed something like a crown, in which glimmers a brilliant. He is evidently dressed in 'shorts', for the more advanta-geous exhibition of his handsome legs; he wears black silk stock-ings, and he turns out his toes as he walks like Sir Christopher Hatton. (269)

This last detail is another allusion to Sheridan, this time to *The Critic* (1779):

Sneer: ... But tell us, who are these coming? –
Puff: These are they – Sir Walter Raleigh, and Sir Christoper Hatton. – You'll know Sir Christopher, by his turning out his toes – famous you know for his dancing. I like to preserve all the traits of character. (157)

The allusion tends to suggest an analogy between the madhouse which masquerades as a grotesque country house party, and Puff's anachronistic play within a play: but Le Fanu has hybridized Sir Christopher Hatton, crossing him with Sheridan's Don Whiskerandos, and Mercy Cresswell reports that 'in the servants' hall' (i.e. amongst the madhouse attendants), they call him 'Don Ferdnando Tights'. In reality, he is a mad Welsh slate-quarry owner from Carnaervon called Ap-Jenkins.

Sheridan's latest biographer, Fintan O'Toole, suggests that *The Critic* is a more politically sensitive play than the mere self-conscious *jeu d'esprit* it is often taken to be. He takes it that, after 'the devastating mockery of English heroic history' which is the inset *Spanish Armada*, the finale invites the audience 'to see through the kind of appeals to warmongering euphoria that were, and would continue to be, so central to conservative politics' (O'Toole 1997, 152). Le Fanu's allusions to Sheridan's play within the play, tend to twist the latter's hall of mirrors into a grotesque carnival, which, like a lighted comic bubble, exists inside, and parodies, the gothic madhouse run by Dr Antomarchi whose interview room, to a now enlightened and suspicious Maud, 'might be the first audience-chamber, in a series, in the Inquisition'(283). The Italian, Antomarchi, is apparently named after Napoleon's physician on St Helena (it is weakly implied that he is a relation [1994, 174]). Maud thinks of him as a Jesuit whose eyes, when roused, became 'wild and burning'. Antomarchi is a mesmerist, it seems, and a gothic villain, whose sinister methods revive a number of past, but also more recent, fears about French imperialism.[7] In his 'slightly but studiously averted gaze, there is a hinting of treason', thinks Maud (1994, 216), and for a Victorian reader the word has perhaps slightly more political significance than simply a term for personal betrayal.

To be sure, Le Fanu is a special case. He clearly 'recognizes' his fellow-Irishmen and they form a personal tradition for him, particularly his kinsman Sheridan. The series of allusions to a genial but sophisticated form of comedy shows how concerned Le Fanu is to draw his reader's attention to the (theatrical) level of representation, of staged illusion, within his own narrative texts, and the sharp turn into the macabre, the grotesque, the sinister, and the violent, which he characteristically initiates is never far from comic structure, despite appearances. This re-appropriation, however, has an external reflex: it is also a form of cultural memory, in which the nightmares of the past are explicitly, but subtly, revived, often revealing the bankrupt heritage of an aristocracy that has lost its capacity to resist its own history and is willing to prey upon its own young in order to retain power.

Notes

1. Cf. Katherine Worth's point here about this scene: 'Stage illusion is still more important in Tony's third practical joke, when he takes his mother on the "dangerous" journey which goes round in a circle and lands her in her own garden. The audience know she is being gulled, but if they are to feel the force of her panic (as one should, in farce) they too must share a little of the impression of an unknown, threatening world of quagmires and highway-men which Tony conjures up out of the most ordinary materials – the essence of stage illusion. In the National Theatre's 1984 production a large overhanging tree, atmospherically lit, conveyed an effect appropriate both to the real place and the characters are in, the garden, and Crack–skull common where they think they are' (Worth 1992, 91).

2. Incidentally, Sheridan may have also got the idea from his mother, who also suffered from this anxiety:

   > 'Even Sheridan's highly intelligent and sensible mother went into hysterics on arriving safely with her children at the Hotel Picardie in Paris where her husband was waiting for her; for on hearing the word Picardie, she had imagined that the coachman was abducting them' (Butler 1931, 48).

3. But it is interesting that Wilkie Collins in the 1860s, in his sensation novel, *No Name*, slyly uses her amateur performance as Sheridan's Julia in *The Rivals* to start Magdalen Vanstone on the road to conventional ruin as an actress.

4. Le Fanu was in correspondence about his antecedents, including Sheridan, with the Marquis in the 1860s. See W.J. McCormack, *Sheridan Le Fanu and Victorian Ireland* (1991, 205).

5. The connection between the plot of Le Fanu's *Uncle Silas*, Sheridan, and Mme de Genlis, was noted by W.J. McCormack, in *Dissolute Characters* (1993, 61).

6. See McCormack (1991, 205) for some biographical comment on this passage.

7. Some of Le Fanu's unpublished correspondence from the 1850s in the Brotherton library, Leeds, refers to invasion by the French, in an anxiously playful manner. For example, in 1851 he wrote to his sister-in-law:

   > As to politics they have got into such a monstrous and menacing jumble that I have given over conjecturing what may emerge from them – I hope at all events we may not have 150,000 Frenchmen in London, as Captain Maurice seems to expect, with "*materiel*" etc.

3
'I wants to make your flesh creep': Notes toward a Reading of the Comic-Gothic in Dickens

Julian Wolfreys

It is the fear one *needs*: the price one pays for coming content-edly to terms with a social body based on irrationality and menace.

Franco Moretti

Gothic novels are technologies that produce the monster as a remarkably mobile, permeable, and infinitely interpretable body.

Judith Halberstam

A baby savage, a young monster, a child who had never been a child, a creature who might live to take the outward form of a man, but who, within, would live and perish a mere beast.

Charles Dickens, *The Haunted Man*

Love your other

The gothic is always with us. Certainly, it was always with the Victorians. All that black, all that crêpe. All that jet. All that swirling fog. If there is a transition in the nature of the gothic from the end of the eighteenth century to the middle years of the nineteenth century, it is marked by an inward turn perhaps. There is an internalization to be considered not so much as a denial of the gothic as it is a form of intimacy. In writing of the nineteenth century which manifests a gothic turn, there is an embrace of the uncanny within ourselves rather than a displacement or projection on to some foreign or distant other. In part, the turn inward and the interest in the otherness within is signalled in part during what is termed the high Victorian period by

31

the intense fascination, obsession even, with English manners, with Englishness and all that is the most alien to the definition of Englishness, not in some foreign field, but in England, the heart of darkness itself. It is through what James Twitchell describes as the sober English concern with darkness, mesmerism and Satanism (1981, 33), that the gothic aspect of Englishness is revealed. Far from disappearing, it may be argued, the gothic, ingested and consumed, becomes appropriate, 'a legitimate subject of literature', to employ Twitchell's phrase (1981, 33). It is not so much that the vampire is sought out. Rather, vampiric feeding on otherness constitutes a significant aspect of English letters. In particular, that which is fed on are images of children and the idea(l) of the feminine.

The mid-nineteenth century interest in children, adolescents and women represents a transitional moment in the gothic, for, as is well known, the gothic of the latter years of the eighteenth century focused its terror of the other on foreigners, on Catholics, on distant lands and long-ago days, on creepy castles and even creepier foreigners, most of whom were explicitly Mediterranean 'of a certain sort', if not out-and-out 'Oriental', in the well-known sense given that word by Edward Said. After the moment to which I refer – a moment admittedly forty years or so in length – the Victorian gothic turned once again to the foreigner, to the outsider, to the otherness of colonized lands and imperial subjectivities, as essays at the close of this volume discuss.[1] But for that double moment traced, as it were, parabolically, from the moment at which Victoria came to the throne to that other moment when many of the Victorian writers thought of specifically as Victorian were either dead, dying, or consigned to writing mostly poor poetry on the Isle of Wight, the gothic mode of representation was turned on the British by the British. If there is, as James Kincaid says in Chapter 1 of this volume, a turn from the castle to the nursery, there is also a turn from some foreign field that is most decidedly not forever England, to the playing fields and private gardens of the English, to domestic interiors and to the streets of England's capital.

The gothic is thus found among the hedgerows, in the rosebushes, along country lanes. It is to be found on the Yorkshire moors and throughout the exotic Babylon of the Empire's capital, London, particularly in the back passages of the metropolis. It is to be found equally in boarding houses and amongst the houses of quiet squares. This is true at least of the literary, between the years 1840 and 1870. Most especially and insistently, the gothic is always to be found in the texts of Charles Dickens, from *The Pickwick Papers* in 1836–37, to *The Mystery of Edwin*

Drood, in 1870. That escape from the uncanny is impossible, we acknowledge, at least since Freud. That the return of the repressed is inescapable and inevitable, we acknowledge equally. These qualities are our own, they inhabit our being in its most intimate recesses, even, and especially, when we project them as though they were being projected from elsewhere, from some *other* place, other than the other within. But what if we seek to embrace this alterity? What if we revel in its haunting quality, as, I argue, did the Victorians? What if we play Oprah Winfrey, Sally Jesse Raphael, Montel Williams or even – nightmare of nightmares – Jerry Springer, to that gothic aspect of ourselves, always already lurking in the moments of anxiety and the fearful perception of imminent terror which our daytime selves simultaneously deny, yet secretly anticipate? As all good, or even mediocre therapists will tell you, you'll never get rid of the uncanny, the other. So give it a good hug, love your other as you loathe yourself. Perhaps even tickle it, solicit a little laughter. Like a visitor who has overstayed their welcome, the uncanny may not take the hint when you begin to clear the coffee table, but at least you can amuse yourself at its expense.

The Fat Boy

The title of this essay is well known. It comes from that most famous of narcoleptics (literary or otherwise), the 'Fat Boy', AKA 'young opium eater' (1988, 345) – no doubt in deference to Thomas De Quincey – from *The Pickwick Papers*. The scene is equally well-known, but no less comical and worth repeating for all that.

> It was the old lady's habit on the fine summer mornings to repair to the arbour in which Mr. Tupman had already signalised himself, in form and manner following: – first, the fat boy fetched from a peg behind the old lady's bed-room door, a close black satin bonnet, a warm cotton shawl, and a thick stick with a capacious handle; and the old lady having put on the bonnet and shawl at her leisure, would lean one hand on the stick and the other on the fat boy's shoulder, and walk leisurely to the arbour, where the fat boy would leave her to enjoy the fresh air for the space of half an hour; at the expiration of which time he would return and reconduct her back to the house.
> The old lady was very precise and very particular; and as this ceremony had been observed for three successive summers without the slightest deviation from the accustomed form, she was not a little

surprised on this particular morning, to see the fat boy, instead of leaving the arbour, walk a few paces out of it, look carefully around him in every direction, and return towards her with great stealth and an air of the most profound mystery.

The old lady was timorous – most old ladies are – and her first impression was that the bloated lad was about to do her some grievous bodily harm with the view of possessing himself of her loose coin. She would have cried for assistance, but age and infirmity had long ago deprived her of the power of screaming; she, therefore, watched his motions with feelings of intense terror, which were in no degree diminished by his coming up close to her, and shouting in her ear in an agitated, and as it seemed to her, a threatening tone, –

'Missus!'

Now it so happened that Mr. Jingle was walking in the garden close to the arbour at this moment. He too heard the shout of 'Missus,' and stopped to hear more. There were three reasons for his doing so. In the first place, he was idle and curious; secondly, he was by no means scrupulous, thirdly, and lastly, he was concealed from view by some flowering shrubs. So there he stood, and there he listened.

'Missus', shouted the fat boy.

'Well Joe', said the trembling old lady. 'I'm sure I have been a very good mistress to you Joe. You have invariably been treated very kindly. You have never had too much to do; and you have always had enough to eat.'

This last was an appeal to the fat boy's most sensitive feelings. He seemed touched as he replied, emphatically, –

'I knows I has.'

'Then what do you want now?' said the old lady, gaining courage.

'I wants to make your flesh creep', replied the boy.

This sounded like a very blood-thirsty mode of showing one's gratitude; and as the old lady did not precisely understand the process by which such a result was to be attained, all her former horrors returned.

(Dickens 1988, 92–3)

The scene is stage–comic, and, in its stage management, provides the would-be gothic writer – or scourge of timid old ladies everywhere – with a textbook example of how to bring a scene off that is at once both gothic, potentially terrifying in its eventual outcome, as all good scenes of gothic tension should be, and, simultaneously, unremittingly comic. Although all is soon revealed after the last moment described above, as is usually the case in the novels of, for example, Anne Radcliffe, when the rational explanation arrives to calm down the unbearable agitation of being (for both the reader and the principal subject), nonetheless, Dickens works the scene in at least two different directions at once. The scene relies for both its gothic tension and its knowing comic solicitation of that tension on producing the simultaneity of feeling, while, also, providing the reader with a Hitchcock-like view from above down onto the terror-stricken old lady, rather similar to the elevation permitted the reader over Catherine Morland by Jane Austen, in *Northanger Abbey*. We know, because we have been told repeatedly, that the old lady is deaf. This is why the Fat Boy bellows. Nonetheless, this does nothing to allay the old lady's fears. If anything, they are increased. Furthermore, his bellowing in anticipation of the revelation of a secret goes directly contrary to the laws of gothic. He shouts when he should be whispering, and it is a summer's day at a country cottage, and not the dead of night or dead of winter in some far-off chateau, castle or monastery. We might even suggest that the scene is knowingly anti-gothic, that Dickens is just having a laugh at the expense of tired form, a form he loved as a child and continues to embrace throughout his career, were it not for the fact that the deaf old lady is genuinely terrified. She is made even more an abject figure by her being unable to scream. The comedy of the scene only works because there is such a departure from routine, as Dickens makes quite clear, and because the force of the old lady's emotions is not to be denied. It is in part the cruelty of this scene which makes us laugh, whether or not we choose to admit it.

The moment in the garden is, then, exemplary of the comic-gothic. The reader works – and is expected to work – in a number of ways at once here, not least in accommodating the ludic oscillation between comedy and cruelty, the latter as the necessity for the former, the former the outcome of what happens when you get close enough to the gothic to see how the special effects work (which is precisely what Dickens does). At the same time, the scene sets for us all sorts of normal patterns of behaviour, which we are asked to take for granted, solely for the purpose of departing from them so excessively. Yet something remains unsettling in this scene, two things to be precise, moments when the gothic never quite resolves itself away. The first is the Fat Boy's own agitation, that nervousness of demeanour as he prepares himself for his greatest performance (walking in and out of the arbour is merely for the purposes of warming up). The second is the Fat

Boy's outburst, which serves as the title for this essay: 'I wants to make your flesh creep'. Why the Fat Boy should wish to do this is a mystery, unless he is merely relishing the effect, like all good stage villains. Also, the news he has to impart is hardly the sort to make the flesh creep. The gothic is quite exploded, though the uncanny remains, thereby intimating the return, if not of the repressed, then, at least, of that which cannot be described. Quite.

To make someone's flesh creep is, we might say, Young Opium Eater's desire. Anyone less like Thomas De Quincey, the man who made even Wordsworth gothic, is hard to imagine. But the desire of the Fat Boy's finds its target in the terrified old lady. The Fat Boy understands that creeping flesh is a necessity if the narrative he wishes to unfold is to be deemed successful. He relishes his role, his performative status in the whole event. It is participation that is important. The Fat Boy is thus exemplary of the domestic gothic. He no longer is content, like so many good British subjects, with sitting back and enjoying being scared. He wants to take part. The English, no longer afraid – temporarily – of Catholics and foreigners (the Irish of course are always an exception, but that has to with proximity to home, as all good cultural historians will acknowledge) need to scare themselves, to cut a caper at home, put on a sheet and run around going 'hoo, hoo', for their own delight and terror. There are no bogeymen abroad, so why not pretend to be a little spooky in one's own back yard? As Sam Weller's knowing sobriquet for the Fat Boy attests, the other is within us, in this case in the form of the drug possible addict. And of course, it doesn't really matter if the Fat Boy is addicted, what matters is that he might be. The perceived drug addict as the most gothic of figures, then, haunted from within, tremulous without. Right in our own gardens. This is what we are witness to, and the Fat Boy plays it up unmercifully. As James Kincaid notes in his essay in this volume, the Fat Boy is double, both 'harmless toy and raging demon'. Doubleness is, of course, a feature of the uncanny, as Freud acknowledged (1953–1974 v.17, 233). It is this doubleness which Dickens remarks through the ambivalence of the comic-gothic.

Kincaid also raises the issue of the boy's appetite, his constant desire to consume flesh, and to turn whatever he consumes into flesh. It is interesting to speculate, in the light of Kincaid's remarks, on a possible connection between the Fat Boy and the contemporary concern with cannibalism, in relation to the distrust of medical science's advocacy of anatomy, as H.L. Malchow discusses (1996, 110ff).[2] As Malchow suggests, there were growing worries about 'domestic, if metaphoric, cannibalism' as a manifestation of the gothic in the form of anatomical dissections in the 1830s, given voice in places both high and low, in *The Lancet* and in popular songs of the day (Malchow 1996, 110). Perhaps from a fear of the anatomist's knife and its implied relation to 'barbaric' practices, a grim humour, a '[d]issection-room humor' arose during the period, and 'Dickens made much use of this kind of humor' from *Pickwick* to *Our Mutual Friend*, as Malchow acknowledges (114–15). Malchow cites the dinner scene between the medical students Bob Sawyer and Ben Allen, who joke about the 'source' of their meat (a child's leg), terrifying Mr Pickwick. He also recalls the meal consumed by Wegg and Mr Venus in *Our Mutual Friend*, in the taxidermist's shop, where the two men are surrounded by jars containing the pickled remains of 'Indian and African infants', along with scenes from *Bleak House* (1996, 115). Harry Stone also notes the frequency of the 'comic mode' in relation to the theme of cannibalism, citing the example of the Fat Boy (1994, 77–9). As Stone makes clear, Young Opium Eater makes little if any distinction between animal and human flesh (78). Such comedic business succeeds, argues Stone, in banishing the gothic quality of such moments. However, I would argue that the gothic element remains potent precisely because it is never banished absolutely. Instead, it operates as gothic because of its immanence and its promise, laying below the surface and getting under our skins, waiting suggestively to make our flesh creep. As with many instances of alterity, the comic-gothic operates through proximity and intimacy.

The scenes with the Fat Boy and other scenes in Dickens' writing clearly revel in the comic–gothic as it pertains particularly to children, where the young become the source of sustenance and comedy. There is the grimly comic moment in *Great Expectations* when Magwitch begins to eye hungrily Pip's fat cheeks, saying 'Darn Me if I couldn't eat 'em ... and if I han't half a mind to't!' (1994, 5). Eating young boys is much on Magwitch's mind, for he conjures the spectral young man who, Pip is promised, will find a way to Pip's heart and liver, in order that they may be torn out and roasted (1994, 6). As fascinating as such moments of potential cannibalism are, and departing from Malchow's study, Dickens is, we would suggest, not so much interested in bringing the foreign, gothic other home, as finding it already at home, at the dinner table, locating the gothic *within* English humour. The grotesque is a necessary component of such comedy. In turn, comedy devours, it feeds off the other, often to hilariously ghoulish effect. The Fat Boy is, in a figurative, if not literal sense, the embodiment of comic cannibalism (again, see Stone's argument). Consuming flesh and fowl, he also has digested the gothic sensibility, to regurgitate it in a particularly stagey and English manner.

Written on the Body

The Fat Boy impresses us, of course, because, not to put it too coyly, he is *fat*.[3] His excessive, grotesque, quivering corporeality names him. This mountain of flesh, who consumes more flesh and sleeps, is known by his body, by the excessiveness he embodies. Were he not fat, could we laugh at him, could he provide us with comic and gothic moments? Probably not. The flesh is everything, it makes the act believable, and it is his size, as well as his creepy proximity, which terrifies the old lady. Dickens knows this, no doubt, and relishes the blubbery monstrousness of the boy, seeing in it not only a good turn but also a sure-fire commercial winner, guaranteed to keep us coming back for more. It is almost as if one can imagine Dickens advertising the Fat Boy in the words reserved for Mr Whackford Squeers, speaking of his son: '"Here's flesh!" cried Squeers, turning the boy about, and indenting the plumpest parts of his figure with divers pokes and punches. ... "Here's firmness, here's solidness"' (1986, 517). There is a slight difference between the boys however, it should be noted. While the Fat Boy provides comedy by inflicting (metaphorical and psychological) pain, here it is the almost equally rotund Master Squeers who feels the pain while being part of the comedy. Fatness is not the bodily articulation of comic pain and gothic, grotesque excess so much as it is the medium through which such discourses may be expressed, and onto which they may be inscribed. What we as readers comprehend from one fat boy to another is the use to which the child's corpulence may be put, the abuse which it endures for the sake of the joke, at a moment where pain and pleasure are inextricably linked. The experience of both and their simultaneity is, for the reader, of the flesh made word and the word fleshed out, embodied. It is, as with so many gothic narratives, an 'experience rooted in the body', as Steven Bruhm puts it (1994, xv). And for all the comedy, both the Fat Boy and young Whackford perform for us as gothic bodies, in Bruhm's definition of this corporeal and textual phenomenon, for it is principally their bodies which are 'put on display' in all their 'violent, vulnerable immediacy' (1994, xvii).

It is through the figure of the figure that Dickens, by such examples, draws upon the discourse of the gothic, a form of writing which 'needs to be regarded', as Robert Miles argues, 'as a series of contemporaneously understood forms, devices, codes, figurations, for the expression of the "fragmented subject"' (1993, 3). Young Opium Eater and Young Whackford overflow their limits, their identities breaking down to become excessive and grotesque articulations. They are exploited and made to work. Dickens understands therefore, in the words of José Gil, that the body 'carries the symbolic exchanges and correspondences between the different codes that are in play'. He continues: '[t]he body is the exchanger of codes ... on its own the body signifies nothing, says nothing. It always speaks only the language of the other (codes) that comes and inscribe themselves on it' (1998, 99). This seems particularly true of the Fat Boy, who, despite his corpulence, his idleness and glut-tony, is, as James Kincaid puts it, hollow, this hollowness in all its gothic splendour being 'the mysterious hollowness of fascinating caverns' (1992, 95). Dickens writes the boy as hollow in order to fill him from other places; he writes him as fat in order to write large the conjunction of the comic and gothic discourses which find their meeting place in the particular scene already considered. It is not that the Fat Boy is always in gothic mode, although, arguably, his constant state of being-narcoleptic is suggestive of zombies or the undead, albeit of a carnivalesque order. We might even suggest, given his often death-like state – extending the performative aspect further – that the Fat Boy's performance is analogous to an act of mesmerism on Dickens' part,[4] as well as an act of ventrilo-quism through the mesmerized boy by the author. Dickens puts on a theatrical turn by having the Fat Boy adopt a gothic mode of discourse, arriving with the promise of a tale to harrow the old woman, in a low, comic parody of Hamlet's father (both, after all, involve gardens in one way or another).

But is it possible to find the conjunction of the comic and the gothic in bodies which are decidedly not obese? One possible example of this is worked through in the scene leading up to Oliver asking for more food, as Harry Stone discusses (1994, 81; for more concerning Stone's discussion, see below). Another example comes from *The Uncommercial Traveller*. In the article entitled 'Wapping Workhouse', the narrator, on his way to that institution, encounters a rather strange boy who is referred to four times in two pages as an *apparition* (1987, 19–20). The ghastly and grotesquely comic come together in the bodily form and voice, whose most noticeable features are 'a ghastly grin and a [voice] like gurgling water' (1987, 19). The unnerved narrator remarks of the locks by which they are standing '"A common place for suicide"', to which the uncanny figure, returns in a possible jest (which may just be a misheard response), '"Sue?" returned the ghost with a stare' (19). With music-hall timing, not missing a beat, the proper name of one of the dead comes back, with that gallows humour to be found everywhere in Dickens' writing. Yet it is not merely the pun which is important, the joke at the expense of self-slaughter. Importantly, the scene is set up through the body of this ghostly creature, especially in that humorous *rictus* and in the voice of the drowned. The body of the apparition is, once more, expressly written as an empty figure on which are traced the comic and the uncanny. Everything about the young man is uncanny, uncomfortable, especially his wit, which insists on disrupting the meaning of words.

Thus Dickens, again, abusing identity in order to entertain, raising a laugh as well as raising the dead. We may turn for our next example of the empty body across whom the language of the other is inscribed to that favourite turn from *Martin Chuzzlewit*, Bailey Jr.

Bailey Jr.

Bailey Jr., who like the Fat Boy and Whackford is in the food line of business, is first encountered in the kitchen area of Todgers', illuminated by 'a frequent gleaming *of mysterious lights* in the area' (1986, 199; emphasis added).[5] This is a small detail, so small in fact that the reader might ignore it altogether, yet it is significant in preparing the stage for the boy's entrance. The boy, who is a 'conspicuous feature among the peculiar incidents of the last day of the week at Todgers's' (1986, 200), bursts in on the Miss Pecksniffs, who are working by the fire, suitably lit only by a single candle, as gothic moments should be. Bailey's purpose is to carry news of tomorrow's dinner to the sisters, which he does by adjuring them not to eat the fish. This, we are told, is delivered as a 'spectral warning', after which, he 'vanished again' (1986, 200). Later in the evening, Bailey returns briefly, 'squinting hideously behind the back of the unconscious Mrs Todgers' (1986, 201). The comic scene is punctuated by the merest hints of the gothic, as we can read in Dickens' choice of words, while it is also equally staged, rather than simply described. First made visible by mysterious lights, this strange apparition intrudes unexpectedly in dimly lit places, in best gothic fashion, to make portentous utterances, only to disappear, then to return figured synecdochally by the disturbing squint.

Bailey's appearance is thus written according to a range of discursive effects, already discussed above, his identity traced in this manner, his subjectivity constituted by the comic, the gothic and the theatrical. The fragmented gothic body, even as it signifies nothing, to recall Gil, nonetheless is the material place in Dickens' text where contemporaneous codes are exchanged and overwritten. The scene itself is also coherent and consistent in terms of the gothic: mystery is suggested, events are startling and remain unexplained fully, atmosphere is established, and the harbinger of calamity vanishes. Dickens is careful to determine the comic moment according to gothic convention, so that the overwriting of Bailey Jr.'s body overflows the limits of that body onto the form and the representation of the scene itself. Saturday night supper is expressed through the gothic mode, while the ludicrous nature of Todgers' boarding house reciprocally impresses itself onto the gothic, not exactly domesticating it but transforming it into a peculiarly English moment.[6] This process is, arguably, itself gothic, inasmuch as there is the intimation of an excess that overspreads particular identities, spreading from form to scene to character and back again, 'extending by contiguity, a particular chain of attributes', to borrow Eve Kosofsky Sedgwick's definition of a particular gothic convention (1986, 149).

The overwriting effect extends to naming, which also operates in the example of Bailey Jr. as a 'particular chain of attributes' and which the temporary renaming of the Fat Boy may well be one more sign. Bailey Jr. is known by several names, all of which are given by the lodgers at Todgers', and all of which reveal a melodramatic and gothic pedigree. Dickens tells us that the boy's name may have been Benjamin, although this is merely gossip rather than fact (1986, 201). This is changed to Uncle Ben, or just Uncle. In turn, the boy's name is transformed into Barnwell. He is also named Young Brownrigg, or otherwise given the names of 'any notorious malefactor or minister' (1986, 201). Even the name 'Bailey Jr.' appears to be a name provided with reference to the law court, rather than the boy's real name. This is not certain, however. For, the reader is informed that the name of Bailey invokes a somewhat gothic tale, involving 'the recollection of an unfortunate lady of the same name, who perished by her own hand early in life, and [who] has been immortalised in a ballad' (202). The ballad of the female suicide notwithstanding – who unwittingly provided posterity with the comic, though grim, spectacle of hanging herself with her garters – Bailey is established by his various names as having an impeccably scurrilous literary and cultural pedigree. The names inscribed on the boy mark him with a history of violent spectacle and morbidity belonging to the City of London. Dickens uses the boy to recall various eighteenth-century grotesqueries and *grand guignol* events, fictional and real, which the various names countersign against the propriety of nineteenth-century society. George Barnwell is an apprentice in Lillo's play *The History of George Barnwell, or the London*

Merchant, who murders his uncle and robs his employer. Mother Brownrigg whipped three apprentices to death, subsequently hiding the bodies in the coal-hole, before being caught and hanged. Moreover, while not particularly gothic in itself, at least two acts of renaming mark Bailey with a certain female otherness, as though the grotesque and femininity were somehow aligned (of which more in the discussion of Jenny Wren, below).

As with the Fat Boy, then, the propriety and property of the proper name hardly appears to matter with regard to Bailey. As far as these two characters are concerned, the proper name is decidedly improper. It is erased, as if to make the figure either hollow or blank, fresh for further inscription. Identity becomes the function of a series of performative *personae* read from some other place, rather than being intrinsic to the self. In the case of Bailey Jr., his identity is all too often deemed villainous and mysterious, good for nothing except hanging (201), even though, simultaneously, this situation appears to the source of comedy rather than horror.

Indeed, it appears that Bailey enjoys a joke as much as the next person, for he consciously performs in a comic-gothic register for the members of the lodging house, and most especially for Merry and Cherry Pecksniff, as the scene described above attests. At another moment almost immediately after the spectral warning concerning the inedibility of fish, Bailey frightens *and* amuses the young ladies in an act of gothic pantomime:

> He entertained them on this occasion by thrusting a lighted candle into his mouth, and exhibiting his face in a state of transparency; after the performance of which feat, he went on with his professional duties. (1986, 200)

It is all but impossible to imagine the performance of this act without imagining the pain which Bailey inflicts upon himself for the amusement of the sisters, but the moment is striking in its effectively rendering the boy nothing but an illuminated head, as though he were a spectre or Jack-o'-Lantern.[7] While this term today suggests more immediately a pumpkin carved to resemble a face (and Bailey inverts the conceit, making his head resemble the Hallowe'en pumpkin), the phrase has more fantastic origins, being a term dating back to the latter part of the seventeenth century, and being synonymous with *ignus fatuus* or will-o'-the-wisp. Thus Bailey's act is, like his various names, indebted to a tradition of popular narrative. Furthermore, the very pain involved in 'thrusting a lighted candle' into his mouth, suggests an unnerving irrationality about the boy, which disturbs precisely because the infliction of pain on the self cannot be explained.[8] What we can suggest is that the act is theatrical and spectacular. Dickens side-steps the internal coherence of the scene to present the reader with the moment of comic yet, at some level, terrifying melodrama, of what John David Moore describes in his work on early nineteenth-century theatre as 'vulgar popular art' (1982, 444). Such low instances of intrusive alterity are frequent in Dickens, and it is particularly important to recognize in Bailey Jr. the coming together of various, heterogeneous forms of otherness, through naming, speech and performance. Moreover, in making himself suffer for the amusement of others, Bailey brings together the supernatural with the murderous criminality that his various names authorize. This is, itself, another gothic narrative convention, as E.J. Clery points out.[9] However, it is clearly an internalized gothic – and in this Dickens unwittingly (unconsciously?) pre-empts Freud, who took, in the words of Mark Edmundson, the 'props and passions of terror Gothic ... to [relocate] them inside the self' (1997, 32). For it is as if, in miming the consumption of the candle, Bailey Jr. promises to illuminate the darkness inside us all.

For such a revelation and a willingness to play the part, Bailey Jr. must of course be punished, if only so that he can figure as a pantomimic version of the return of the repressed – or, in Bailey's case, the return of the irrepressible. In one of *Martin Chuzzlewit's* several notable violent scenes, the carriage in which Bailey travels, with Montague and the gothic Jonas, is overturned (1986, 723–7). To all intents and purposes it appears that Bailey is mortally injured. Indeed, we told this on more than one occasion: 'the boy was past holding up, or being held up, or giving any other sign of life than a faint and fitful beating of the heart' (726); then, 'but [the surgeon] gave it as his opinion that the boy was labouring under a severe concussion of the brain, and that Mr Bailey's mortal course was run' (727); finally, the news of the alleged death is relayed by Poll Sweedlepipe: '"It ain't anybody's wife", exclaimed the little barber. "Bailey, young Bailey!" ... "He hasn't been adoing anything! ... He'll never do anything again. He's done for. He's killed ... and if you was to crowd all the steam-engines and electric fluids that ever was, into this shop, and set 'em every one to work their hardest, they couldn't square the account, though it's only a ha–penny"' (1986, 827). It is not too fanciful, perhaps, to read that reference on Sweedlepipe's part to 'electric fluids' as an acknowledgement of the much vaunted powers of galvanism in the nineteenth century, and through that, indirectly, to *Frankenstein*, to acknowledge once again how Dickens recalls the gothic through the slightest of touches. However, despite the reassurances of mortality, as with all good gothic tales, the hero–villain, in the shape of Bailey, does return. Shortly after Pecksniff is both reviled and revealed by Old Martin, Sweedlepipe, a *'monstrously-excited* little man', comes 'bursting up the stairs, and straight into the chambers of Mr Chuzzlewit, as if he were *deranged'* (1986, 892; emphases added). Such comedic grotesquerie is counterposed by Dickens against the ironically labelled 'sublime address' of the departing Pecksniff. In what amounts to an hysterical state, Sweedlepipe rushes in and out, repeating himself, until 'a *something* in top-boots, with its head bandaged up, staggered into the room, and began going round and round, apparently under the impression that he was walking straight forward' (893; emphasis added). Bailey appears finally, providing both those in the room and the reader with a comic rendition of bodily monstrosity and spectacular pain, so common to the gothic. Reduced to a 'something', an 'it', no longer human yet raised from the dead – we're not told how – Bailey Jr. manifests himself once more, his body abused for the sake of the comic entrance.

Scaring children is fun

If children are, from certain perspectives, constructed socially and through various cultural narratives as different from adult, rational human beings, this is no doubt a self-sustaining process which, in fearing the otherness of the child, the adolescent, the teenager, rewrites the narrative of childhood being in order to maintain its alterity, precisely for the purpose of punishment. The child's world is, as James Kincaid says, 'unnecessary, useless'; strictly speaking, it is a made-up world, creative rather than mimetic (Kincaid 1992, 221). In recognizing this, the adult may recognize a certain lost world, and seek to punish its other for the loss of that which we failed to keep within our grasp. So, we might say, what we want is facts, not fantasy. And what better way at getting back at the childlike delight in the gothic – that which scares us because we have grown ever so sensible, rational – than to punish it with that mode of representation by which the child can create laughter? Even while children may triumph occasionally in the text of Dickens, it remains a fact nonetheless that, at some point, they are punished in some fashion for their difference. All too frequently, the writing of punishment in Dickens' novels takes a gothic turn (which is never comical), as in the process of 'education' at Dotheboys Hall, in the death of Paul Dombey, or in the manifestation of a school master named Bradley Headstone.

There are, however, other ways of punishing the child whereby the gothic mode may be maintained and in which Dickens indulges, while comedy is reintroduced for the amusement of the (no doubt) adult reader, who may, like any number of Dickens' adult characters, tend to understand children as 'naturally wicious'. Because at some level the child, adolescent or teenager is perceived in all his or her (frequently gothic) otherness, so fun may be made through the gothic mode. Not all children get to have the last laugh, as does Bailey Jr.[10]

Oliver Twist provides one example of comedy – albeit of a very dark variety – at the expense of the child, as Oliver progresses from the workhouse, to the undertaker's, to Fagin's den (all gothic structures), where other children enjoy themselves but not Oliver. (No doubt there is something of the morality tale here; all children, being naturally wicious, have criminal propensities, Oliver's plight is a warning to us all, my dears, concerning the inevitable recidivism of childhood.) Harry Stone offers a fascinating discussion of the well-known moment when Oliver asks for more (Stone 1994, 79–81). This moment, argues Stone, is equally laughable and fearful:

> the scene in which Oliver asks for more ... is generated by a bizarre and laughable fear. Everyone is familiar with the scene itself, but how many remember the fear that generates the scene? That fear flows directly from a terrifying cannibalistic threat, but this threat – a threat made by one workhouse boy that he will devour another – is cauterized by its outlandishness and its humour: we chuckle rather than shudder, and we dismiss the threat as a bit of humorous Dickensian grotesquerie; the threat, we feel, has no abiding importance. But Dickens does not dismiss the threat, nor does he discount it or forget it. (1994, 81)

This is an admirable reading of the comic-gothic event, though I would argue that it is not a question of dismissing the threat so much as seeking to domesticate it, making it manageable through emphasizing the comic register. This is a precarious moment for, in the potential effect of making manageable, the economy of the workhouse – that which seeks to make children manageable – may become reproduced in and by the textual satire. Dickens will not let us do this, however, for his text maintains the fearful and the comic, the gothic and the humorous, in a precarious balance where the seemingly opposing discursive and psychic poles in question here open between them an uncanny *aporia* into which either mode threatens constantly to overflow and commingle.

The other well-known Dickensian scared child is Pip who, like Oliver, spends much of his early life in gothic surroundings – whether the marshes, his parents' gravestones, or Miss Havisham's – or in proximity to gothic moments, such as that of the soldiers' arrival at Joe's door, in search of Magwitch, described as an 'apparition' (1994, 30). Of such moments, the most comical for the reader, though not for Pip, is the following:

> It was a rimy morning, and very damp. I had seen the damp lying on the outside of my little window, as if some goblin had been crying there all night, and using the window for a pocket–handkerchief. Now, I saw the damp lying on the bare hedges and spare grass, like a coarser sort of spiders' webs. ... The marsh-mist was so thick, that the wooden finger on the post ... was invisible to me until I was quite close under it. Then, as I looked up at it, while it dripped, it seemed to my oppressed conscience like a phantom devoting me to the Hulks.
>
> The mist was heavier yet when I got out upon the marshes, so that instead of my running at everything, everything seemed to run at me. This was very disagreeable to a guilty mind. The gates and dykes and banks came bursting at me through the mist, as if they cried as plainly as could be, 'A boy with Somebody-else's pork pie! Stop him!' The cattle came upon me with a suddenness, staring out of their eyes, and steaming out of their nostrils, 'Holloa, young thief!' One black ox, with a white cravat on – who had to my awakened conscience something of a clerical air – fixed me so obstinately with his eyes, and moved his blunt head round in such an accusatory manner that I blubbered out to him, 'I couldn't help it sir! It wasn't for myself I took it!' Upon which he put down his head, blew a cloud of smoke out of his nose, and vanished with a kick–up of his hind legs and a flourish of his tail. (1994, 16–17)

Between the pie and the cattle, there is more of gravy than of grave about this scene,[11] even if, despite its clerical air, the black ox bears more than a passing resemblance to the devil rather than any clergyman, while Pip's behaviour recalls in parodic fashion Hamlet's words concerning the reaction of guilty creatures, given certain stimuli. There is a subtle distance between Pip's older, narrating self, and his younger, other identity. While the elder Pip may well be able to construct the narrative comically at his other's expense, his younger self clearly is not in on the joke, and is terrified by the spectral cattle and the animated features of the landscape. The goblins, spiders' webs and the dripping phantom finger-post operate within a gothic mode, as the supernatural scene displaces the real world in leading to the comedy of frightened childhood.

That there is a discernible gap between the older and the younger Pip suggests to what extent the child as other has to be punished by its older manifestation. There is a double movement here, in imagination and memory, for while the elder Pip remembers the scene, he is also shaping its narration in a particular gothic fashion. His younger self's terror is transformed into a medium for entertainment. And this is not the only example of Pip's comic-gothic abilities at the expense of the young. His manipulation of gothic discourse is presented when, in London, he hires a 'boy in boots' (1994, 216). Invoking *Frankenstein*, Pip remarks that he makes a '*monster*' of the boy, who has 'little to do and a great deal to eat' (notice once more the obsession with children eating), these being the '*horrible* requirements' with which 'he *haunted* my existence' (1994, 216; emphases added). Furthermore, Pip refers to the boy as an 'avenging phantom'. Whether or not Pip intends to be humorous, his description of the boy in boots is comical even while it is indebted to gothic discourse; more to the point, we can read that the gothic child is inescapable. It is always present, and always hungry – for something.

Jenny Wren

Bodily monstrosity and excessiveness when figured or disfigured in writing may be said to be a performance of catachresis, reworked as and, importantly, *through* an image of the subject. Such embodied catachresis is familiarly recognized as the grotesque, and the grotesque is never far from gothic modes of representation. Thus far, the comic-gothic examples given have been boys – Joe, the Fat Boy and Bailey Jr. In both cases, their physical transformation is not natural to them, effected through various abusive processes, whether overeating or violent occurrence. Their bodies may be said, therefore, to have been written, not only by Dickens, but also through the impression on the individual body by social activity. The Fat Boy need not eat so much (although, chances are this is idle fantasy), and Bailey, it seems, will recover. At some level then, the grotesque identity of male children is constructed, not essential. (Arguably, even Smike's condition is exacerbated by neglect and abuse to the point of gothic excessiveness; systematic punishment by Squeers has written the boy's body as the reader encounters it, there is no Smike other than the creature whom we read.)

In distinction to the boys, and turning to our final example of the comic-gothic, Jenny Wren, we might consider that her misshapen body is a *natural* body. The strangeness of her behaviour, attitudes and identity appear to spring from her physical deformity. As a figure of female, rather than male gothic, she shares certain aspects of her identity with the boys, but is also somewhat different. In this final example, we wish to explore how Jenny's body only *appears* natural from certain perspectives, and that her writing is an altogether more complex affair.

Unlike the Fat Boy and Bailey, Jenny Wren is not the passive recipient of uncanny or grotesque names meant to approximate her identity or otherwise provide a fictive identity for her. She names herself, twice: as Jenny Wren and also as the person of the house. Jenny takes it upon herself to reinvent her identity and thus pre-empt, at least in part, the act of gothic determination imposed on the child by the adult. We should also recall at this juncture that Jenny's real name is Fanny Cleaver, which is itself suggestive enough of gothic narratives and potential acts of dismembering.

Also, unlike the Fat Boy and Bailey, who create gothic scenarios out of the every day for the entertainment of others, the dolls' dressmaker engages with the gothic mode, as much for herself as for those with whom she comes into contact. Her gothic performance is an act of self-identification, of psychic reflection and re-enforcement. Her sense of humour is not farcical, it is darkly disturbing, frequently satirical, unsettling in its ability to find as a corollary to her own physical deformity the deformity of identity or spirit in others. In this manner, Jenny is able to laugh at the gothic alterity, the psychological monstrosity within all others, hers being an act of reading rather than projection. By comparison, the laughter evoked by our two previous examples is all surface play even if it does bespeak a condition of otherness.

Jenny is the most uncanny of gothic characters in *Our Mutual Friend* where, as Adrian Poole puts it in his introduction to the novel, '[m]ost of the life ... tends to a state of suspended animation. Nothing seems certainly dead nor entirely alive' (1997, ix). Jenny's ethereal condition seems part of this certainly, and she invests her dolls with imaginative animation that manages to make the flesh creep with the ease of a seasoned music-hall performer. Even the house in which Jenny lives, exists amongst a row of houses in a square, which is described as having a 'deadly kind of repose on it, more as though it had taken laudanum than fallen into a natural rest' (221–2). This is perhaps Dickens' first clue that appearance should not be taken for granted, but should be read as an induced or constructed, rather than a 'natural' state. Jenny first appears in the second book, when Charlie Hexam and Bradley Headstone come to her house to visit Lizzie Hexam:

> The boy knocked at a door, and the door promptly opened with a spring and a click. A parlour door within a small entry stood open, and disclosed a child – a dwarf – a girl – a something – sitting on a little low old-fashioned arm-chair, which had a kind of working bench before it. ...
>
> The queer little figure, and the queer but not ugly little face, with its bright grey eyes, were so sharp, that the sharpness of the manner seemed unavoidable. (1997, 222)

These initial descriptions are supplemented by others during the puzzling conversation maintained by the dolls' dressmaker, as if to make fun of and so disconcert both Charlie and Headstone:

> The person of the house gave a weird little laugh ... and gave them another look out of the corners of her eyes. She had an elfin chin that was capable of great expression; and whenever she gave this look, she hitched this chin up. As if her eyes and her chin worked together on the same wires. ...
>
> It was difficult to guess the age of this strange creature, for her poor figure furnished no clue to it, and her face was at once so young and so old. Twelve, or at the most thirteen, might be near the mark. (1997, 224)

Everything about Jenny is sharp, from her pointed comments, to her fingers, her chin and the looks she gives the master and his pupil. Dickens makes no distinction as to a limit or border between physiological sharpness and its counterpart in the girl's personality and manner. As if to erase the divisions between one aspect and another, Dickens intimates the fantastic possibility of Jenny's being an automaton of sorts, connected by wires, whether those of a marionette – thereby aligning her uncannily with her dolls – or some *thing* given artificial life by galvanic current. Her uncanniness, amounting to a daemonic spriteliness, is inscribed by a number of undecidables and ambiguities.

This daemonic condition is hinted at by the later description of her as 'of the earth, earthy' (1997, 243). Her age is indeterminate, she appears 'queer' though not ugly, and it is impossible to tell exactly what she is, so that the final definition must, of necessity be indefinite – she is a *something*. Like Bailey Jr, although in an altogether different register, Jenny is not human, not quite. Yet while Bailey is a comic monstrosity, Jenny's is an abject figure. Jenny is configured by Dickens as a figure for the uncanny, for that which is unknowable. Defying definition or identification, she is the figure in gothic narrative which Joseph Andriano terms the 'daemonic feminine' (1993, 139) which troubles the masculine self through an address to the blind-spots within masculinity, while resisting recuperation.

And even while she haunts the story, she provides mischievous laughter, often at the expense of men, and especially at the expense of her father. As Rosemary Jackson, Joseph Andriano and Barbara Warren all suggest in different ways, the 'haunting Other may be a projection of the haunted Self ... [the]inner daemon, [is] a psychic entity unrecognized as such by the male ego' (Andriano 1993, 2).[12] As such, Jenny Wren can be read as the externalized, gothic other of the self, who deploys her pointed comedy to hold up the distorted mirror of the psyche to her male victims. One example of this is Jenny's relationship to her drunken father. Her humour is to reinvent her father as her child, as is well known. Her transformation of him is both gothic and caustically comical, as he becomes a 'wretched spectacle', a '"naughty, wicked creature"', while her scolding turns him into a 'shaking figure, unnerved and disjointed from head to foot' (1997, 239). Though deformed, Jenny has the narrative and symbolic ability to re-form, if not reform, others, to create the male subject and thereby exert control through the verbal punishment of her humour.

Of all Dickens' comic-gothic characters, Jenny is then, arguably, the most complex of figures. 'Compounded of opposites', as Malcolm Andrews suggests, she is apparently marked by both physical and psychic inconsistencies (1994, 89). Yet the inconsistencies of which Andrews speaks are only such if Jenny Wren is read within normative or realist parameters. She only appears as natural. Her inconsistencies are wholly consistent within a certain representation of the grotesque, and she is written by Dickens with a wholly symbolic function in mind. Mary Russo's eloquent introduction to the female grotesque serves usefully in helping to come to terms with Jenny Wren. Drawing on the work of Geoffrey Galt Harpham, Russo discusses the figuration of the grotesque in Renaissance art, with its 'combination of the fantastic with ... [the] rendering [of] realistic detail' (Russo 1994, 5), an ability which 'so astounded and even infuriated critics like John Ruskin' (5). Such combination is clearly at work in Dickens' articulation of Jenny, with her queer, though not ugly, face, her weird laugh, and her beautiful hair. Also, as Russo points out, the grotesque is in itself 'suggestive of a certain construction of the feminine' (1994, 5). Jenny's deformity and her marginal relationship to the narrative of *Our Mutual Friend* bespeak this construction and also its cultural necessity, for 'subjectivity', as Russo argues, 'requires the image of the grotesque body' (1994, 9), even as masculine identity requires the marginalized feminine for the purposes of self-fashioning. Dickens may be read as inscribing physical deformity onto Jenny, making her a comic grotesque in order to foreground from the margins, wherein such identity is written, and to which it is con- signed, the cultural projection of the female in general. Marginalized and yet necessary to what Russo terms the psychic register, woman is always deformed within and by patriarchal discourse. The ambiguity, the undecidability, the 'inconsistencies' of Jenny are merely the traces of the 'uncanny grotesque body as ... monstrous, deformed, excessive' con- structed through the 'discursive fictions' of nineteenth-century bourgeois culture (Russo 1994, 9). What appears 'natural' in Jenny is revealed by Dickens through the deployment of undecidability and irresolution as the tireless work of construction, and Jenny's revenge is that she is able, through her satirical reformulations, to bring out the gothic monstrosity of men, which had been hidden all along inside them, and not in the foreign or female, or indeed the child.

Jenny's gothic mode is not merely an effect of the grotesque. She com- bines those elements of grotesquerie with the uncanny, which manifests itself not only in the unresolvable ambiguities which write Jenny but also in Jenny's own sense of an 'individualized, interiorized space of fantasy and introspection' (Russo 1994, 8). As much as Jenny jokingly toys, often viciously, with the men with whom she comes into contact, she also performs for their troubled perplexity her own psychic life. She refers to herself in the third person, calling herself the 'person of the house', as already noted, or else the 'child'; she projects imagined lives for her dolls, and speaks in conundrums (Dickens 1997, 222–3). She imagines various fantasy scenarios worthy of the Brothers Grimm or as a strange parody of gothic narrative, such as locking children in the vault of a church and blowing pepper at them through the keyhole (1997, 224). She has visions of fantastic and cruel empowerment with regard to her father (mentioned above), imagining, as Harry Stone puts it, punishing and tormenting him, even ... torturing him' (Stone 1994, 501). Her flights of fantasy take a particularly gothic turn when, as Stone reminds us, 'she envisions ravenous creatures battening upon' her father (1994, 501). Such narratives are not only strange; they *estrange* both the subject and the reader and render the person of the house distinctly unhomely. It is important at this juncture that we do not forget that Jenny Wren, is herself a child (despite the fact that she rails against children), and one who was, as she herself seems to imply, at one time 'chilled, anxious, ragged [and] beaten' (1997, 238). Like the idea of the female (of which we have spoken above), the child in Victorian culture was constructed in a position of passive centrality *and* simultaneously marginalized, rendered monstrous. Jenny's gothic narrative concerning her father transformed into a child serves to remind us of the abject fate of the child, while pointing to the ways in which marginalization and punishment originate as a form of psychic projection manifested in material conditions.

Her uncanniness is given its strangest and most eloquent expression in Chapter Five of Book Two (1997, 266–80). Sitting on the roof with Lizzie, the person of the house, now no longer in the house but above it, she imagines disturbing yet transcendent possibilities which she expresses thus, to Riah and Fledgeby: 'But it's so high. And you see the clouds rushing on above the narrow streets, not minding them, and you see the golden arrows pointing at the mountains in the sky from which the wind comes, and you feel as if you were dead' (279). As the two men leave, Jenny calls out repeatedly, in a sing-song voice 'Come back and be dead, Come back and be dead!' (279). At one level, this may be read as yet one more example of Jenny's sense of humour, an uncanny humour no doubt, but imbued with a playfulness all the same. However, in another manner, Jenny's gothic lyricism imagines or desires a space beyond abjection. The fantasy of shared death is a response to the unspeakable freedom of death imagined beyond the house. Jenny's discourse operates vertically, away from the streets, away from the internal and confined space of the house, and towards the immanence of her identity freed from its body, doubled and projected onto what Mary Russo describes as the 'aerial sublime' (1994, 29). Sublimity is of course a correlative to the grotesque and gothic. Not so much a binary or polar opposite, the sublime is the imagined configuration of the 'high', to the grotesque's 'low other'. Jenny's discourse figures the movement towards the sublime, from low to high, from materiality and mortality to spirituality and immor-tality, from excessive and deformed details of the material conditions of existence to the ethereal and inexpressible possibilities of a place 'beyond' or 'to-come'. Thus Jenny Wren articulates the possibility of movement which leads nowhere in true gothic form, as Fiona Robertson makes plain (1994, 72).[13] From the all-too-material terror of

existence, there is envisioned the immaterial terror of the absolutely
other, the unspeakable, which produces anxiety in the face of mystery
and, ultimately, suspense.

The performative in-joke or, raising a laugh and raising the dead

To return to an earlier moment. Sam Weller gives away more than
perhaps even he knows when he describes the Fat Boy as 'young opium
eater'. He writes onto the Fat Boy's body a gothic identity *par excellence*,
and yet one which is also knowingly constructed, given as a textual
performance by its author, Thomas De Quincey. Weller provides Joe
with a narrative that self-consciously has already involved itself in a
knowing act of fictional performance. This gothic identity is not a
simply comprehended subject, but a complex textual performance. The
name which Sam appropriates requires a recognition to make it work;
like a literary in-joke, if you don't know the reference you won't find
the moment tellingly comical, and the gothic is misunderstood. In a
different manner, the various names imposed on Bailey Jr. operate
according to the same logic. The humour of intertextual reference
relies upon a knowledgeable audience, a community of readers within
a common cultural frame. Sam Weller brings it home to us then that
the gothic is not out there, not far afield, not in a foreign and exotic
place but right here, with us and in us, ingested and inscribed, and
actively regenerated. The melodramatic seriousness of De Quincey's
gothic self-haunting becomes transformed from one of unending desire
to a figure of local, recognisable plenitude and excess.

And let us not forget that the full title of De Quincey's most famous
text provides a national identity for the opium eater. There is the very
question of Englishness at work, as if to unsettle several identities at
once, as if to make plain that the uncanny is already here, that the
repressed didn't have to return from very far at all. This is a point made
by De Quincey himself, early on in the *Confessions* when he slyly suggests that more public figures in English political life are addicts than
either they, or we, would care to acknowledge. Joe is one such barely
disguished affront to bourgeois guilt and secrecy, exposing himself in
all his adipose and somnambulant glory.

However, to come back to the question of textual acknowledgement.
What Dickens' young comic-gothic characters share is a certain knowledge regarding their textuality. This is not to say that they knowingly
imitate or impersonate other characters, so much as they are written

according to particular textual models, albeit given an ironic reflexivity by Dickens, so as to speak beyond themselves, beyond their own individual cognizance about the ways in which children and adolescents are constructed in nineteenth-century culture. Parents did not necessarily see their children in a gothic light, at least not at any conscious level which they would willingly have acknowledged. But what we may read from Dickens' text, glancing at it from a rather odd angle of parallax, is a recognition on Dickens' part of the gothic aspects of childhood's construction, and his willingness to engage this construction against the grain, so as to shed light on the very practices of cultural configuration.

To turn back to De Quincey, following Margaret Russett's argument from the first chapter of her *De Quincey's Romanticism* (1997 14–52), Thomas De Quincey knowingly constructs his other self in his memoir within a recognizable gothic paradigm, while locating this addicted subjectivity as distinct from the narrating subject. Particularly, he produces his childhood other as a gothic child, an interpreted figure, somewhat like Bailey Jr., founded, as Russett puts it 'on strictly textual antecedents' (1997, 16). Dickens, we suggest, pursues a similar act of identity formation for certain of his children and adolescents, exploiting the conventions of the gothic by making them figures from a gothic tale, yet nudging the reader into a position of recognition through the comic self-consciousness of such a ploy.

If, as Russett argues, De Quincey knowingly 'adumbrates reader-response ... more explicitly than ... the novels of Ann Radcliffe do' (17), then Dickens, arguably, brings his ensemble of effects to an even greater pitch. It is as if Dickens, recognizing the unintentionally humorous aspect of gothic narrative, turns to the comedic mode in order to fashion a strength from an aesthetic weakness. Comedy knows what the gothic does not, it knows itself and understands that it returns from within rather than being merely the monstrous without. Comedy has the ability to sneak up on its audience, and to take them hostage through an uncanny moment of comparison and identification – of similarity – in the very same moment when the audience believes itself to be set apart from the subject of comedic discourse. Comedy is predicated on reader-response and Dickens connects the comic – whether the belly-laugh and excessiveness or the pointed dark satire at the expense of masculinity – to the gothic in order to manipulate the reader beyond even De Quincey's imagination.

However, it is not a question of manipulation for its own sake, whether it is a question of the manipulation of the character, the

scene, or the reader. In each example considered, the work of manipulation involves a ceaseless movement between form and content,
between character or subject and scene. Furthermore, this is not a
simple question of appropriating the various nervous tics of the
gothic mode. The very act of knowing intertextual contamination is,
itself, gothic. To show how this works, let's remain with De Quincey
a moment more, this time through J. Hillis Miller's reading of the
older Opium Eater. In *The Disappearance of God: Five Nineteenth-
Century Writers*, Miller describes De Quincey's acts of opium-induced
memory in the following manner: 'The dreamer who is endowed
with the power of resurrecting the past is a *vampire* who drinks the
fountains of his own vitality' (1965, 65; emphasis added). The image
of De Quincey as a self-consuming member of the undead is one of
the earliest recognitions in criticism of the extent to which the
Confessions are, in part, gothic. Miller's delineation of the gothicness
of his subject, and the ways in which writing manifests the act of
vampirism by feeding on an other self for the purposes of production, suggests a practice of inscription as consumption through
memory.

Dickens performs similar acts in his creation of comic-gothic adolescents. Dickens turns vampire on his own memory of narratives heard
or read in childhood, infusing the bodies of his literary children with
the life-force of others' texts. His act is, moreover, a vampiric manifestation in that it feeds off the literary and dramatic corpses which haunt
the Victorian psyche in general, but, perhaps, the lower-middle and
working classes in particular. If proof were necessary, one final example
might be the double occurrence, the return, of *Timour the Tartar*, in
both *Great Expectations* and *Nicholas Nickleby*. In the former, the play –
written, by the way, by Matthew 'Monk' Lewis – is chosen as entertainment by Mr Wopsle, while in the latter, Vincent Crummles recalls its
performance with great fondness. Dickens' use of intertextual reference
has the power to transcend time and space (as De Quincey's opium
dreams do, to recall Miller's argument once more). Returning from the
past, such spectral moments step outside their own identities while
transforming also the present moment and, with that, the present
identity. Dickens thus recognizes the ability of the gothic mode to
exceed formal limits, to transgress the limits of identity across time,
and thereby to suggest, through such play, the transgressive continu-
ation of transgression. In overwriting his comic-gothic children with
the traces of prior discursive and textual formations, the author
acknowledges an already fragmented body, which is nothing less than

an alternative and dissident tradition within English culture and literature. For the Fat Boy, Bailey Jr., and Jenny Wren each speak to us of
other identities, of the otherness within English identity, without the
constant melodramatic and, occasionally, anarchic eruption of which
there can be no sense of Englishness at all.

[Gothic narrative at the end of the eighteenth and, again, at the end of
the nineteenth century sought to assert a sense of national identity in
response to fears of the foreign. Such irrational fears sought to identify
and marginalize the other and all that was not-English, as is well known.
Perhaps closest to home in the nineteenth century is the equally well-
known representation of the Irish as monstrous.[14] What we may come to
understand from Dickens, however, is that the gothic, the monstrous, the
other, is a lot closer than we are comfortable in acknowledging.] Taking
the gothic and exploring it comically is one method of assuming
proximity, if not intimacy, with the subject. Comic discourse and
performance brings down the defences of the psyche. It allows the connection to be made between high and low, self and other. In so doing, it
seeks to make us face the 'monstrous' within ourselves, so to make our
flesh creep, making us tremble, simultaneously with laughter *and* fear,
just enough so as to allow us a view of ourselves we had always striven to
deny and to project onto others.

Notes

1. On gothic images of race, see H.L. Malchow (1996), who discusses the literary representation of the foreign as gothic other from the Napoleonic
   period to the fin-de-siècle, addressing usefully questions of monstrosity,
   cannibalism, vampirism and homoeroticism to the figure of 'half-breed' as a
   gothic form.
2. See also Chris Baldick (1987, 106–20), on the monstrous and Dickens'
   gallows humour. Baldick discusses the comic references to galvanism, from
   Sawyer and Allen forward, and to the 'animation of the apparently in-
   animate' (107). He also considers how the comedic effect is achieved
   through a dark exuberance on the author's part, discussing as well the question of dismemberment and dissection. Baldick argues that there is 'more to
   all this ghoulishness than a gratuitous *frisson*; it is of a piece with Dickens'
   synecdochal, Carlylean representation of character and of the fragmented
   body' (110). Furthermore, for Baldick, Dickens maps monstrosity onto the
   body as a product of 'crushing social pressures' (112). This may be true in
   part, but there is a certain distortion in Baldick's argument inasmuch as he
   takes the issue of fragmentation as directly Carlylean – Dickens' produc-
   tions being a manifestation akin to the anxiety of influence perhaps –

rather than seeing Carlyle's writing as similarly produced, and not the original source as Baldick seems to assume implicitly. Arguably, the 'contamination' of fictive discourse with traces of scientific, anatomical and gothic
textuality, speaks of the general historicity and materiality of Dickens' text,
in which materiality Carlyle is also enfolded. The gothic as genre provides
Dickens with a recognizable form of bourgeois entertainment which mis-
shapes and in turn is distorted by contemporaneous discourses of the
period.

3. On flesh, fatness, and their carnivalesque relation to the erotic in
   Pickwick, with particular attention to the Fat Boy, see James R. Kincaid's
   essay 'Fattening up on Pickwick' (1995, 21–35). Elsewhere, Kincaid argues
   that the stories we tell today concerning child abuse are, in their
   structures and circuitry, essentially gothic narratives, filled with so much
   terror that we become paralysed by them, unable to act (1998, 10–13).
   From this perspective, what is perhaps particularly terrifying in Dickens'
   gothic reinventions is that he is able to invest the gothic with humour. Of
   course, there are many children in Dickens who are neither fat nor funny,
   who inhabit the realm of the gothic and who are systematically abused, as
   is the case of the children of the workhouse in *Oliver Twist* or the boys of
   that other gothic pile, Dotheboys Hall, in *Nicholas Nickleby* as mentioned
   in the essay. Dickens' sense of the gothic in his depiction of such insti-
   tutions works on the reader to appal at the recurring institutional abuse
   which occurs through the lack of nourishment, whether literal or metaphorical. Where children are comical in Dickens, and not merely the
   subjects of humour (and this is the distinction between the Fat Boy and
   Whackford, between Bailey Jr. and Oliver Twist; see the section 'Scaring
   children is fun', above) the gothic mode can be read as being put to use as
   a revenge, rather than a return of the repressed. Precariously enough, the
   comic-gothic, coming from some other place within, promises to effect
   destabilization of normative social relations and the circuitry of power
   which such relations maintain.

4. On questions of mesmeric agency, see Chapter 6 by Alison Chapman and
   Chapter 8 by Roger Luckhurst. For a full-length study of mesmerism and its
   popularity as a form of entertainment, see Alison Winter's excellent study,
   Mesmerized: Powers of Mind in Victorian Britain (1998).

5. Bailey is not the sole proponent of the comic-gothic in *Martin Chuzzlewit*,
   though he is its most knowing practitioner. As an instance of the way in
   which the comic-gothic overflows the limits of the individual to make
   itself manifest in the discourse of others, in a particular setting or in the
   atmosphere of a scene, we might recall the moment when Merry, in conversation with old Martin Chuzzlewit in the churchyard, sees Jonas
   Chuzzlewit, crying out, 'What a perfectly *hideous monster* to be wandering
   about church-yards in the broad daylight, *frightening people* out of their
   wits! Don't come here, Griffin, or I'll go away directly' (1986, 466;
   emphases added). Arguably, Merry is not conscious of her comic abilities
   as is Bailey (or, at least, she is not as conscious). However, her comment
   partakes of the gothic mode even while it is comic. It nicely conflates the
   conventions of gothic narrative – while chastising Jonas for appearing in
   daylight; Merry appears to be aware that in gothic tales monsters in

graveyards only appear at night – with a particular feature of gothic architecture, the griffin. If Merry were more conscious, and less indebted to the gothic for the expression of her repulsion, she might recognize Jonas for the monster that he is, rather than the one she imagines him to be. Dickens appears to be offering us a warning, not so much against the gothic as against the gullibility of the gothic reader.

6. As I have argued elsewhere, Todgers' boarding house serves as a synecdochic figure for the condition of London (Wolfreys 1998, Ch. 4) This symbolic and structural relationship, in its play between domestic architecture and urban topography, provides a suitably gothic space. This is intimated in the passage above with regard to Todgers', while Kelly Hurley has argued that Dickensian narrative 'figures the urban space ... as a gothic one' (1996, 165). Certainly this is true in Dickens' city narratives, where boys can be kidnapped, women frightened, and men stalked.

7. It is interesting to speculate, given the author's interest in theatricality and stage performance, that Dickens is describing the fire-eating trick practiced by fakirs and others, where they make sure that their actions are so rapid that the heat of the flame is never in fact in contact with the skin long enough to cause burning.

8. On the body in pain as gothic trope, see Steven Bruhm, *Gothic Bodies: the Politics of Pain in Romantic Fiction* (1994), on which I have drawn in this section of the essay.

9. Clery writes: 'In Gothic Fictions, smugglers and bandits opportunistically inhabit spaces ...[such as] the deserted wing of the castle, the ancestral crypt. Like spectres they are of necessity creatures of the night and they exploit this kinship by using popular superstition as a cover for their illegitimate activities' (1995, 133–4). I am not suggesting that Bailey is either supernatural or criminal, merely that Dickens brings together in the boy's performance, in his names and acts, the discursive kinship discussed by Clery and frequently exploited in gothic narrative.

10. If the difference between the child who causes laughter and who is laughed at in Dickens can be described briefly, perhaps the question is one of class, and of the child's class position. Both Bailey and the Fat Boy are working class, their 'low' position indicated through their speech, through non-standard spelling and the emphasis by Dickens on idiomatic expression. Neither boy speaks the standard English of the middle-classes or of the narrator. Oliver Twist and Pip on the other hand, always speak standard English, without the trace of idiom or accent peculiar to the working class. They are thus implicitly given 'universal' voices. Within the narrative logic of *Great Expectations* Pip's 'voice' may of course be explained away: he is the adult narrator, recalling his own boyhood, and he has undergone education which has erased any signs of local accent which he may have had as a child. Oliver, on the other hand, always speaks English 'correctly', thereby signalling that, even as a child, in the workhouse or in Fagin's hideout, he has always already transcended both class and locale. It would seem then, as a provisional thesis by which to explain the difference between those who generate humour and those who are its objects, that the comic-gothic is, for Dickens, a working class mode of articulation, which shares certain proletarian affinities with the grotesque,

the carnivalesque, the melodramatic, and the music hall; in short, with all forms of popular entertainment.

11. The words are of course those of Ebenezer Scrooge in response to Marley's ghost (1988, 19). Although not a child, Dickens has Scrooge respond in a manner which is instructive with regard to the comic-gothic. Following the well-known retort, Dickens remarks, 'Scrooge was not much in the habit of cracking jokes, nor did he feel, in his heart, by any means waggish then. The truth is, that he tried to be smart, as a means of distracting his own attention, and keeping down his terror; for the spectre's voice disturbed the very marrow in his bones' (19). Despite Dickens' protestations, the line is, of course, funny, whether it was intended or not. However, the inadvertent recourse to humour in opposition to terror provides the reader with one more comic-gothic moment, which is, again, connected to consumption, to what is inside us. This is expressed both in Scrooge's remark, and those preceding the gravy pun, but also, importantly in Dickens' own expression of spectral disturbance in 'the very marrow in [Scrooge's] bones'. The ghost makes Scrooge's flesh creep, while the text moves spectrally across the boundary of the character's remarks to those of the narrator.

12. Andriano cites both Jackson and Warren on this point. Jackson suggests that 'the history of the survival of Gothic horror is one of progressive internalization and recognition of fears generated by the self', while Warren states that 'the phantom lady is essentially the man's most vital spirit' (Jackson and Warren, cited in Andriano 1997, 2 n.3). The works to which Andriano refers are Rosemary Jackson, *Fantasy: the Literature of Subversion* (1988) and Barbara Warren, *The Feminine Image in Literature* (1973).

13. In establishing the conventions of the gothic for a reading of Walter Scott, Robertson highlights the ways in which there is narrative and architectural correspondence in gothic novels, where passages, in both senses of the word, lead nowhere. Jenny's fantastic transport also promises to lead nowhere, strictly speaking.

14. See, for example, the well-known cartoon by John Tenniel, 'The Irish Frankenstein', published in *Punch* (20 May 1882), where in a typical conflation between the name of the creator and his creature, the Irish are represented as a monstrous, bloodthirsty, masked creature. H.L. Malchow's *Gothic Images of Race in Nineteenth-Century Britain* (1996), provides what is to date the most sustained consideration of the relation between the aesthetics and politics of representation, from *Frankenstein* to the *fin-de-siècle*. On related matters of race and the connections made between 'foreigners' and women, see Meyer (1996); also on the issue of race and degeneration, see Greenslade (1994).

4
Hopkins and the Gothic Body

R.J.C. Watt

The gothic element in Gerard Hopkins's writing has not often been explored. My intention here is to trace some general gothic affiliations in his poetry, prose and aesthetics, as well as among his circle of contemporaries, and then to focus more particularly on the representation of the body, ultimately on one particular part of the body as it appears repeatedly in his work.

Some of Hopkins's best-known poems are illuminated when seen in relation to late nineteenth-century gothic writing. The terrors of a complete loss of identity, an implosion of the self, are recorded in Hopkins's 'Sonnets of Desolation,' sometimes called the 'Terrible Sonnets'. Those poems are usually seen simply as records of a dark night of the soul, a harrowing personal struggle, to be interpreted biographically and religiously. One way to counter this prevalent and sometimes weak interpretation – something I shall only sketch here – is to show that they also have a political dimension. Written in exile in Ireland, they inscribe Hopkins's overwhelming unease and ambivalence as an English patriot who now found himself surrounded by Irish Jesuit colleagues dedicated to the cause of Home Rule, a movement he was inclined to condemn out of hand. Consequently, for the first time, the two great internalized authorities in his life, his English patriotism and his membership of the Catholic church, were completely at odds with each other. The result was a 'war within', as he called it in one of his last poems ('St. Alphonsus Rodriguez'), a personal manifestation of that political irreconcilability. Such a reading is one way to liberate these poems from the realm of the purely biographical, and once that is done it should be easier to recognize yet another dimension in them. For they are also gothic psychodramas which chart the terrifying collapses of the self, its recoveries and relapses, in ways very similar, for example, to R.L. Stevenson's novel *Dr. Jekyll and Mr. Hyde*, with which the poems are exactly contemporary (1885).

> Not, I'll not, carrion comfort, Despair, not feast on thee;
> Not untwist – slack they may be – these last strands of man
> In me.
>
> 'Carrion Comfort' (1990)

The feelings, if not the diction, would hardly be out of place if they came from Jekyll. Caught in the grip-like vice of despair, Hopkins discovers the taste of damnation:

> I see
> The lost are like this, and their scourge to be
> As I am mine, their sweating selves; but worse.
>
> 'I wake and feel the fell of dark' (1990)

The sense of an identity fractured in two, but with the two halves still bound to each other, locked in struggle, is strong:

> let
> Me live to my sad self hereafter kind,
> Charitable; not live this tormented mind
> With this tormented mind tormenting yet.
>
> 'My own heart let me have more pity on' (1990)

Such doubleness brings the kind of alienation where he speaks to his own self as to a friend/adversary beside him (outside him, beside himself):

> Soul, self; come, poor Jackself, I do advise
> You, jaded, let be; call off thoughts awhile
> Elsewhere; leave comfort root-room ...

The clear analogues of these split identities are to be found not only in Stevenson's novel but in its generic kin, those novels of uncanny doubleness and alienation which are one of the most characteristic forms of nineteenth-century gothic, such as James Hogg's *Confessions of a Justified Sinner*, Mary Shelley's *Frankenstein*, Emily Brontë's

Wuthering Heights, or Oscar Wilde's *The Picture of Dorian Gray*. Both Wilde's novel and Stevenson's may usefully be seen as fundamentally concerned with what David Punter calls 'the problem of the liberation of repressed desires' (Punter 1980, 255). If we read Hopkins's late poems from this perspective, it helps to explain the intensity of the *impasse* they record, since for him, subject as he was to a strict Christian conscience, the liberation of desire was out of the question, except through obliquity, symbolism, and displacement, as we shall see as this chapter unfolds.

Wilde's novel illustrates another familiar nineteenth-century gothic trope which is also found in Hopkins: the association of sordidness and sin with places urban or metropolitan. The city, above all, becomes the nineteenth-century equivalent of the gothic labyrinth, and representations of its concealed horrors and complexities shade into attitudes to urbanisation and industrialism. In Chapter 4, for example, Dorian talks of 'this grey, monstrous London of ours, with its myriads of people, its sordid sinners, and its splendid sins'. Hopkins, though not normally thought of as a poet of urban decadence, uses unexpectedly similar language, writing in 'The Sea and the Skylark' of 'this shallow and frail town', 'our sordid turbid time', and a populace who 'drain fast towards man's first slime' – a phrasing which points up post-Darwinian fears about reversion to origins that can be found elsewhere in the decadents. The town in question in 'The Sea and the Skylark' was actually Rhyl in North Wales, and the almost comic disparity between that town's scale of sin and London's shows that this is a common idiom, the discourse not so much of individuals as of a particular historical moment. Not that Hopkins was sheltered from the great urban labyrinths: periods of exhausting parish work among the worst slums of Liverpool and Glasgow were his personal experience of the city as living hell. Although it is usual to think of Hopkins the priest as the diametric opposite of a figure such as Wilde the man of scandal, at least in terms of their moral allegiances, as writers they have things in common. One of the few critics to do justice to this was Donald Davie in his outstandingly perceptive essay 'Hopkins as a Decadent Critic'. Davie quickly identifies him as a decadent poet too, sharing with the other decadents qualities such as a self-regarding and frantic ingenuity and a constant tendency to 'the refinement and manipulation of sensuous appetite'. To Davie, Hopkins is the greatest poet of a decadent age 'because he cultivates his hysteria and pushes his sickness to the limit' (Davie 1969, 171).

One mode of opposition to the decadence of urban civilisation was ecological, a cult of the wildness of nature, which is strong in Hopkins in poems such as 'Inversnaid' –

> O let them be left, wildness and wet;
> Long live the weeds and the wilderness yet

– and 'God's Grandeur', where the human world is 'seared with trade, bleared, smeared with toil', but by contrast:

> nature is never spent;
> There lives the dearest freshness deep down things.

The terms of this contrast are familiar from much Romantic and pre-Romantic writing, though given a new inflection by the huge growth of the nineteenth-century cities. Things veer closer to gothic, however, when nature is repeatedly associated with storm and violence. Hopkins found delight and horror in wrecking and storm. 'Wreck' was a key word in his thinking which he applied to all kinds of life situations, not merely to shipwrecks, his subjects in 'The Wreck of the Deutschland' and 'The Loss of the Eurydice'. His casual use of the word 'wuthering' to describe the great storm-bird in 'Henry Purcell' is another sign of the same fascination. In her novel Emily Brontë had coolly glossed 'Wuthering', that 'significant provincial adjective', as 'descriptive of the atmospheric tumult to which its station [i.e. the situation of the Heights] is exposed in stormy weather', but for readers of the novel, Hopkins included, the word points beyond the merely atmospheric to a human turmoil. What we see in Hopkins, then, is that turmoil or violence projected onto nature where it can appear safely removed from the human realm of passion and immorality which was so dangerous for a strictly self-denying priest.

The diverse elements of gothic have often been noted. It is, says Fred Botting, 'a mode that exceeds genre and categories' (Botting 1996, 14). Botting has described the process of diffusion, even domestication, which gothic undergoes in the nineteenth century: as the gothic novel ceased to be a genre in itself, many of its elements came to pervade other genres. To identify gothic elements in Hopkins is not, therefore, simply to categorize him as a gothic writer. In fact the surprise would be if he did not reveal, along with the abundant signs of the post-Romantic inheritance in his work, gothic traits too. Yet they have seldom been pursued by Hopkins critics. One of the few to have done so is Tom Paulin, who in his study of Thomas Hardy's poetry observed that:

> Hopkins, Hardy and Browning (whom Hopkins disliked but must have learnt from) all value the uniqueness of speech-tones – their instress – and with this valuation goes a total respect for the absolute uniqueness and integrity of people and things: 'All things counter, original, spare, strange.' Each in his own way is a Gothic artist, an enemy of veneer and 'constructed ornament'. (Paulin 1975, 86)

'Constructed ornament' and 'veneer' are Hardy's own terms from a passage in his *Life* (that strangely disavowed self-revelation, published under his second wife's name but mainly written by himself) where he writes of:

> the Gothic art-principle in which he had been trained – the principle of spontaneity, found in mouldings, tracery, and such like – resulting in the 'unforeseen' (as it has been called) character of his metres and stanzas, that of stress rather than of syllable, poetic texture rather than poetic veneer; the latter kind of thing, under the name of 'constructed ornament', being what he, in common with every Gothic student, had been taught to avoid as the plague. (Hardy 1975, 301)

Though Hardy's love of gothic began with his training as an architect, here he extends a concept of gothic well beyond the sphere of architecture, enabling its application to the aesthetics of language, the values of poetry, and moral values in general. It comes to denote a rugged authenticity, an originary purity of language, and a native tradition which its supporters hoped might stand as an alternative to both classicism and an emergent modernism; and in embodying these values in his writing Hardy helped father the myth of a 'true', 'native' strain of '*English* English poetry' which has persisted in the twentieth century at least until Larkin.

Two key figures, for both Hardy and Hopkins, in showing how a concept of gothic could be extended from the visual to the verbal arts were Ruskin and William Barnes.[1] Ruskin's influence on Hopkins was deep: from him Hopkins and many another Victorian learned that their prime duty was to *see*. Yet that seeing, which might appear as the neutral act of an objective observer laying himself humbly open to fact and reality, actually took highly specific modes. As Paulin says, 'Like Hardy in his justification of the Gothic art-principle behind his poetry, Ruskin sees irregularity and imperfection as essential constituents of gothic art, and when he describes the Gothic builders' "love of fact" he distinguishes a feature that is central to Hardy's art and to the way his imagination works' (Paulin 1975, 107). It was also a seeing imbued with assumptions about value. One such assumption was that the act of seeing was itself of the highest value, whether moral or aesthetic. (Pater was one of Hopkins's tutors.) A great deal of Hopkins's poetry rests on that view, dedicating itself to the pleasure and the excitement of the gaze, as in 'The Starlight Night':

> Look at the stars! look, look up at the skies!
> O look at all the fire-folk sitting in the air!

There, the slightly coy nonce-compound 'fire-folk' is a piece of Barnesian gothic diction. For both Hopkins and Hardy saw Rev. William Barnes as a touchstone. His Dorset-dialect poetry and his campaign to reform modern English along Anglo-Saxon lines seemed to offer a glimpse of a fantasy made actual, the fantasy of recovering an authentic speech in which meaning would be made whole and pure again and the lost age of innocence would live once more. Barnes wanted to root out the Latinate, compound, polysyllabic strain in English and replace it with something supposedly more native. He advocated, for example, that a perambulator should be called a push-wainling; if he had his way, grammarians would talk not of 'degrees of comparison' but of 'pitches of suchness'.

Of Barnes's book of English grammar (1878) Hopkins said that it was 'written in an unknown tongue, a sort of modern Anglosaxon, beyond all that Furnival in his wildest Forewords ever dreamed' (Hopkins 1935a, 162). 'It makes one weep to think what English might have been ... no beauty in a language can make up for its want of purity. In fact I am learning Anglosaxon and it is a vastly superior thing to what we have now.' Though Hopkins was realist enough to see that Barnes's re-invention of English on gothic principles was a splendidly lost cause, one of 'utter hopelessness', he did not seem to see how analogous it was to his own linguistic practice, which so often creates its best effects by antiquarian forcing of diction and syntax done in the name of authenticity. For every apparent liberty he took with language in his poetry, Hopkins could quote a precedent, showing that the apparently outlandish was in fact of good native origin.

It is in the light of Barnes's gothicized English that we should see some of Hopkins's best-known terms: 'inscape' and 'instress', 'keepings', 'fetch', and 'sake', for example, all have the fake-authentic ring of newly-invented native quaintness, though the charm and good taste imparted by Hopkins's exceptional sensitivity to language have tended to obscure their *ersatz* element – which, to be fair, Hopkins would have called originality. Writing of Barnes's language he said

> He comes, like Homer and all poets of native epic, provided with epithets, images, and so on which seem to have been tested and digested for a long time in their native air and circumstances and to have a *keeping* which nothing else could give; but in fact they are all rather of his own finding and first throwing off. (Hopkins 1938, 222)[2]

In Hopkins not only these words but their meanings too are often part of the quest for a sure and original foundation for things. As Michael Sprinker has noted, both *inscape* and *sake* 'offer a hypothetical origin for the coherence that Hopkins seeks but cannot locate in nature and in language' (Sprinker 1980, 62n.). The same critic reminds us that the fascination with human origins, indeed, is something Hopkins shared with writer after writer in the period, Darwin, Nietzsche, Freud, and Sir James Frazer among others. In his undergraduate notebooks it took the form of daring speculation about the etymologies of words; in middle life it burst out again in a long correspondence with his friend Baillie pursuing to exceptional lengths the idea that Greek mythology originated in Egypt. Like these efforts, and like Pre-Raphaelitism in art, Hopkins's Barnesian–gothic diction was an attempt to get back in time far enough to cross a barrier into a pre-lapsarian state.

Hopkins's religious beliefs were deep and sincere and the struggles he underwent during his conversion to Roman Catholicism were painful. Nevertheless, part of the appeal of High Anglicanism and Catholicism lay in something much more superficial, their trappings or 'keepings'. To some of his circle this appeal was overwhelming. Probably the most important emotional encounter of Hopkins's life, his biographers agree, was with a young man called Digby Mackworth Dolben, a distant cousin of his friend Robert Bridges. Dolben's father had spent 25 years adding gothic encrustations to his ancestral home, and the son grew up attempting to live out his life as a fantasy appropriate to his surroundings (Martin 1992, 81). He developed an excessive and ostentatious religiosity, quasi-Catholic and ritualist, and cultivated it in poems and in his daily life. By the age of 16, while still an Eton school-boy, he had joined a pseudo-monastic order and acquired a monk's habit. 'He particularly liked the reactions of rural people on seeing a barefoot sixteen-year-old monk in full monastic garb. In the country he would put on his habit at night, slip out of a window, and prowl the countryside on chilly feet in the hope of meeting passers-by' (Martin 1992, 81). In summer 1866, Dolben created a sensation by appearing thus in Birmingham, not only in church but in the streets, where he was hooted at and pelted with mud (Martin 1992, 142–3). Hopkins wrote 'He went in his habit without sandals, barefoot. I do not know whether it is more funny or affecting to think of' (1935a, 7). Sandals and bare feet will recur shortly, as we shall see. Soon afterwards Dolben was dead by drowning, completing the gothic *vignette* of his life. This was the boy to whom Hopkins had a strong emotional attach-ment. The homoerotic element is very clear, but also easily misunder-stood by the late-twentieth-century mind. In the earnest young men of the 1860s, spirituality was suffused with emotion, and emotion was charged with desire, but the distance between the religious and the erotic was in different ways both greater than and less than we might assume. In those circles, young men were disturbed by passionate attachments to each other 'not out of fear that they were abnormal but because they made [the other] into a spiritual and physical rival of Christ' (Martin 1992, 89).

The whole flirtation with Catholicism among Hopkins's circle had the crucial gothic quality of transgression, for it was regarded with horror by Anglicans such as Hopkins's own family. 'Pervert' was the word for convert. It was one of the few modes of rebellion open to ultra-conservative temperaments: to find a mode of religion, or for that matter of poetic diction, which was shocking and outlandish to con-ventional minds, but which could also be defended as more authentic, more true to origins, and hence more respectable than contemporary bourgeois respectability itself. Dolben's religious exhibitionism was transgressive enough to get him thrown out of Eton, though he was later re-admitted. He had a melodramatic burning of his own poems and Hopkins followed him in that two years later, though both took care that other copies existed first. They also toyed with religious flagel-lation. One of Dolben's poems is about it, and so is one of Hopkins's, 'Easter Communion':

> You striped in secret with breath-taking whips,
> Those crooked rough-scored chequers may be pieced
> To crosses meant for Jesu's;

That is, the criss-cross marks left by the whip can be seen as resembling Christ's cross. This is a characteristic application of the imagination to bodily damage, for as we shall see, flagellation is only one area where religion, bodily violence and sexuality meet.

Hopkins's sexuality has been much discussed by recent writers.[3] Most attention has naturally focused on his obvious attraction to male beauty. Nobody discusses the fact that one of the most striking drawings in his early notebooks is of a young woman wearing a long loose garment like a night-dress and holding a whip.[4] This is quite characteristic – one might say normal – in the period, which, as Steven Marcus noted, produced an immense literature of flagellation (Marcus 1964, xvi). Its power over the imagination stemmed from its being a transgressive fantasy of class relations as well as sexual ones, for the literature of flagellation always involves 'women of rank and fashion' (Marcus 1964, 254). As we shall see, Hopkins's writings about male bodies often involve a different but analogous fantasy of class transgression, being about rougher trade, men of the labouring class. A further element which helps to account for the widespread flourishing of flagellation fantasy in the period is as a reaction to ideas of masculinity. The female doing the whipping is almost always a surrogate mother (Marcus 1964, 258). The man whipped is the obverse of the ideal of manliness, the Victorian standard for grown-up male behaviour: whipping reduces man to child, the solid citizen to the cringer, the honest person to the role-player. As such it can sometimes be seen as 'a compromise with and a defense against homosexuality' (Marcus 1964, 264), a perspective which makes it possible to relate one characteristic of Hopkins's sexuality to another: the minor mode of flagellation, which seems to have held his attention only briefly, to the dominant homoeroticism of his adult life. Much gothic writing of the late century adumbrates similar uncertainties about sexuality.

Significant affiliations with contemporary gothic tropes, then, are clear in Hopkins. Of course, I am not trying to suggest that Hopkins's work is in every respect gothically influenced. His refreshingly open-minded attitude to science, for example, is quite free of the usual gothic terrors and clichés. His poetry, though often preoccupied with the problem of evil, is, so far as he possibly can achieve, purged of the overtly immoral or corrupt. He does from time to time relish melodramatic narrative, but his ghost stories are respectable Holy Ghost stories. It is the territory we have already embarked on, though, which deserves fuller exploration: the representation of the body and bodily horror in his writing, both poetry and prose.

Gothic, as David Punter has argued, is 'intimately to do with the notion of the barbaric' (Punter 1980, 404–5). As a Catholic convert and Jesuit priest, Hopkins could scarcely have avoided gruesome tales of martyrdom, yet it is notable that some of his favourites involved the *disjecta membra* of women's bodies. His poems about them tend to be unfinished as he wrestles with an unmanageably volatile mixture of mutilation, religious fervour, and sexuality. One such poem is on the martyrdom of Margaret Clitheroe, who suffered death by *peine forte et dure*. His draft falters the moment the horror itself is mentioned: 'Word went she should be crushed out flat'. (The 'word' here is what leads to her crushing.) Another female martyr with an enduring hold on his imagination was St. Winefred. In the legend her head was severed by Caradoc in anger and frustration after she escaped from his attempt to rape her. Hopkins returned to Winefred in various poems and planned a tragic drama, of which only a few fragments got written:

What have we seen? Her head, I sheared from her shoulders, fall,
And lapped in shining hair, I roll to the bank's edge; then
Down the beetling banks, I like water in waterfalls,
It stooped and flashed and fell I and ran like water away.

'St. Winefred's Well', Act II

The fragments of this drama share with 'Epithalamion', which we shall come to shortly, a loose, over-extended form in which fantasy is given too much room to expand. It seems these pieces proved impossible to finish because they are drawn to, and then silenced by, the horror of their subjects: the physical mutilations are both a compulsion and a revulsion; the intense emotion the martyrs arouse compels him to try to speak, but also destroys the attempt. Hopkins proved much less able to deal with the conjunction of dismemberment, religion and sex than others who have tackled similar topics, such as John Ford in *'Tis Pity She's a Whore,* or the smiling, bleeding martyrdoms depicted in mannerist painting.

The archetype of all such martyrdom and bodily violation is, of course, Christ. A remarkable sermon by Hopkins on the Sacred Heart – a topic which had its religious vogue in the later nineteenth century, and which reminds us that Catholicism is less squeamish than Protestantism about such isolated body parts – confronts directly the paradox of venerating what is gruesome and violent, and in doing so it raises questions about the nature of metonymy and fetish.[5] In this prolonged meditation – the whole sermon occupies itself with Christ's heart – it is precisely the metonymic incongruity which Hopkins confronts. Even as he insists that worship of the Sacred Heart is really worship of the whole Christ, that the bodily part stands for the soul, he cannot stop reverting to the oddness which he clearly feels acutely. The mere mention of the Sacred Heart will have, he acknowledges, 'an unpleasing and repulsive sound' to some (Hopkins 1959, 101). Yet he gets in deeper: Christ's 'body is two things, flesh and blood … the body consists of solid parts which are permanent … and of liquid parts which move to and fro. … The heart is one of these solid parts, of these pieces of flesh'. Some people, he admits, will object that it is repulsive 'to have one piece of Christ's flesh thus nakedly thrust upon their mind's eye'; they will prefer to worship the whole man, not 'every separate and dissected detail'. In seeking to argue away this objection he only brings it more vividly before his hearers: 'There would no doubt be something revolting in seeing the heart alone, all naked and bleeding, torn from the breast'. By now his large Liverpool audience had heard the word 'repulsive' twice and 'revolting' once applied to the object they were being urged to venerate.

Anthropology makes a useful distinction between a fetish and an idol. An idol is worshipped as the image, symbol, or occasional residence of a deity; a fetish is worshipped in its own character. Like any Christian, Hopkins well knew that idolization, worship, can become idolatry, and repeatedly warned himself about the 'dangerous' nature of physical attraction, as in his poem 'To what serves Mortal Beauty', where he disciplines himself to turn away from the 'lovely lads' towards 'God's better beauty, grace'. Avoiding crossing the line into idolatry, it was proper for Hopkins to idolize the body as the residence of God's presence within man, dwelling-place of the soul, and a reflection of Christ's beauty. But to regard God as present in a *part* of the body, especially an extremity or a detached part, risks the incongruous, and grows hard to reconcile with the notion of the immateriality of the spiritual. Hence any repeated stress on a part of the body may tend towards worship for itself, not as the image or residence of a deity: towards fetish not idol. It is this which Hopkins's language registers acutely as he struggles with the topic of the Sacred Heart.

The connection between fetishism and metonymy, substituting part for whole, has often been noted. In this sermon, then, Hopkins attempts to cope with the horrors of the physical by reducing fetish to metonymy, noting how sailors and labourers are called 'hands', great thinkers 'minds', and so on. Hence, talk of Christ's great heart really just denotes spiritual qualities. So, he says, the heart is 'not the piece of flesh so called, not the great bloodvessel only' but the index of Christ's greatness of soul. But even as he does so he reverts again and again to the literal, physical, bleeding heart which he keeps claiming is not the point: Christ's heart is that 'which in his Agony with frightful and unnatural straining forced its blood out on him in the shape of teeming sweat, and after it had ceased to beat was pierced and spent its contents by the opening in his side'. By constant reversion to the claim which it repudiates, Hopkins's sermon turns the Sacred Heart of Christ into a stage-prop of Jacobean horror.

Severed heads and bleeding hearts are, however, only the *hors d'oeuvre* in Hopkins. The main work which his imagination did upon the body was focused, as it happens, on feet; feet both shod and bare. Although I shall show that Hopkins's preoccupation with feet took highly distinctive form, it is true that bare feet are one of the commonest symbols in Victorian writing and painting, and we may begin with a look at their function in some of his contemporaries. In a number of Pre-Raphaelite pictures bare feet suggest freedom but also transgression and fall. Women with bare feet are common in William Morris's romances; they are a striking feature of Burne Jones's angels. As in the Bible, bare feet can be signs of humility and grace, but throughout nineteenth-century writing they are also associated with one of their most obvious causes, poverty. For Hopkins that meant the poverty of people like the parishioners whose condition and behaviour caused him so much anguish during his parish work in Liverpool. Catholics were at the bottom of the urban proletariat and poverty was accompanied by drunkenness, fecklessness and violence. He wrote of the sinners in his parish, 'Feet may go bare and hearth be cold but the fire in the throat must be quenched with liquor or rather with liquor fanned to flame' (Hopkins 1959, 42). If the real thing was distressing and even repulsive, the same ragged and barefoot poverty could, when counterfeited or an artistic image, be an object of studied interest among the middle classes, as when Charles Dodgson (Lewis Carroll) pointed his camera at an archly-posed Alice Liddell, barefoot and dressed as a beggar.

For the Victorians in particular, the partly-clothed body was more erotic than the wholly naked one; the act of undressing, even if only very partial, more erotic than the state of undress. If this is a universal verity, it is one which even Jean Baudrillard, endorses (1981): in his analysis of fetishism he asserts that 'the symbolic and sexual truth' of the body 'is not in the naive conspicuousness of nudity, but in the *uncovering* of itself' (Baudrillard 1981, 97). Lewis Carroll was an expert in this territory so far as children were concerned. As his hobby was photographing naked little girls, he had to be exceptionally sensitive to the limits and nuances of propriety, and his letters cajoling mothers to allow their children to undress for him are revealing as to how far the limits could be pushed. Carroll repeatedly asserted that complete nudity was more innocent than a partly-undressed state or any suggestion of transparency in clothing, both of which were unacceptably suggestive. He assured one anxious mother 'I hope my mention of my admiration of children's feet did not make you think I meant to propose taking *Annie* with bare feet. I shall propose no such thing, as I don't think she knows me well enough' (Carroll 1979, I: 345–6). When instructing Harry Furniss, his illustrator for *Sylvie and Bruno*, he was more frank: 'When children have, what is not always the case, well-shaped calves to their legs, stockings seem a pity' (Carroll 1979, II: 653). And again: 'I *wish* I dared dispense with all costume; naked children are so perfectly pure and lovely, but Mrs Grundy would be furious – it would never do. Then the question is, how little dress will content her? Bare legs and feet we *must* have, at any rate' (Carroll cited in Pearsall 1971, 431).

Hopkins's thoughts ran on similar lines, though it was men's, not children's feet which he came back to repeatedly. Even in his sermons and devotional writings, where his imagination was strictly on the leash, working to a professional end, feet can be unruly. The proper function of feet in the religious life, as he noted in a scrap of a sermon, is to show 'readiness to march and obey or proclaim the Gospel' (Hopkins 1959, 234).[6] But they get up to other things. In the Gospels John the Baptist talked of the coming Christ as 'one mightier than I ... the latchet of whose shoes I am not worthy to unloose' (Luke 3:16; cf. Matthew 3:11). In his private retreat notes of 1888 Hopkins's imagination seized on this image and produced a fantasia. He imagines John addressing the crowd in these words:

> I take your garments and your footgear from you when you go down into the water; all sorts of men come to me and I know the difference between a light sandal and the soldier's heavy *caliga*: I tell you my fingers have not the force to wring open this man's laces, though I stoop and bend my body to the task; if he washed himself, my arms have not the strength to lift his boots. (Hopkins 1959, 268)

This elaborate conceit is pure invention triggered by a single biblical phrase. First Hopkins appoints John the Baptist an expert on 'footgear', an expertise acquired as a side-effect of his baptismal trade helping bathers to undress. Then he exaggerates John's metaphor of unworthiness to unlace Christ's shoes into a physical incapacity to do so. The shoes themselves take on colossal proportions, becoming 'boots' which John's robust arms 'have not the strength to lift'. It is a fantasy of gigantism and of male physical power.

Most notable of all in the language of this passage is the anguished verb 'wring' which John employs in his imaginary attempt to get Christ's boots off. It is the very word which Hopkins repeated in two crucial passages in his poems. One of them again stresses Christ's foot's superhuman power:

But ah, but O thou terrible, why wouldst thou rude on me
Thy wring-world right foot rock? lay a lionlimb against me? scan
With darksome devouring eyes my bruisèd bones? and fan,
O in turns of tempest, me heaped there; me frantic to avoïd thee and flee?

'Carrion Comfort'

This mighty foot is strong enough to 'wring' the world but now, it seems, is terrifyingly directed against him alone. We shall see what 'wring' really means when we have looked at the other passage where it is used: the striptease in 'Epithalamion'. That poem was meant by Hopkins to be a present for his brother Everard's marriage in 1888, a celebration of spousal love. But contemplating that prospect led him within a short time to his usual transference, and what the poem gives us is not a tribute to man and wife at the altar but glimpses of boys and an older voyeur getting undressed for bathing. The figure whom we see undressing has himself just watched the crowd of boys swimming, – 'unseen / Sees the bevy of them' – the sight of which turns him in a moment from 'a listless stranger' into one seized with 'a sudden zest' to strip and swim. This doubleness of the voyeur's role – we, with the poem's narrator, watch the stranger undress just as he has spied on the boys – shows that the voyeur is really a displaced image of the narrator or the self: [7]

> ... off with – down he dings
> His bleachèd both and woolwoven wear:
> Careless these in coloured wisp
> All lie tumbled-to; then with loop-locks
> Forward falling, forehead frowning, lips crisp
> Over fingerteasing task, his twiny boots

>Fast he opens, last he off wrings
>Till walk the world he can with bare his feet ...

The immediate point of undressing turns out to be not so much to swim but rather to bare the feet and feel the earth, a point we shall see again later. Some critics have mocked this episode as a laughable careless oversight on Hopkins's part in that he makes the bather take off his trousers *before* wringing off his boots. But Hopkins was always the careful observer. After all, children, and even adults in a hurry, sometimes do try to take off trousers before shoes in the excitement of getting ready to swim. More to the point, for a foot-admirer the leaving of the boots till last is the proper culmination of the striptease. It must have become obvious to Hopkins that this poem skidding out of control would hardly make a suitable wedding present, and the draft was abandoned a few lines later.

Why the triple recurrence of that anguished verb 'wring', improbably connecting the retreat notes and the poem on Christ's power with the voyeurist fantasy? The word is a token of sin. In 'Carrion Comfort' Christ's right foot wrings the world as chastisement for human weakness. Christ is able to use the power of the foot directly, but in the case of the two humans it is different. John the Baptist's fingers try to wring open Christ's laces; the bather in 'Epithalamion' finally wrings off his twiny boots. Their wringing is the action of fingers or hands: it is *a wringing of hands over feet*. In short, the body-language of shame or despair accompanies the unveiling of the erotic, and the one tense verb inscribes both delight and guilt at delight. Or as Freud, that near-contemporary of Hopkins, put it, 'The force which opposes scopophilia, but which may be overridden by it ... is *shame*' (Freud 1991, 70).

The practices of fetishism take a variety of forms, but the term fetishism has an even wider range of meanings, many of them highly abstract and theoretical. Indeed, in his complex analysis of some of its extended meanings, Jean Baudrillard wittily warns of the way in which the concept of fetishism is over-used, exploited, in fact itself fetishized in social analysis: the term fetishism 'turns against those who use it, and surreptitiously exposes their own magical thinking' (Baudrillard 1981, 90). Although cultural theories of the fetish will be useful a little later, for now it is sexual fetishism, the territory of abnormal psychology, which is at issue. Sexual fetishism also takes various forms. It can be a defence against fear of sexual rejection which works by substituting an object that cannot reject, but there seems to be nowhere in

Hopkins's writing that this is present. Binet's explanation of fetishism in terms of what is seen during an early sexual experience is also, I think, unhelpful or irrelevant in Hopkins's case. Fetishism can also be a kind of bodily metonymy, substituting one part of the loved one for the whole. This is the mode of fetishism relevant to Hopkins's treatment of the Sacred Heart, and as I've suggested he is highly ambivalent about it and about other horrors of mutilation. Krafft-Ebing and Sacher-Masoch both wrote of the fetishism of objects, materials, and articles of clothing. But the shoes and boots which figure so notably in Hopkins are not the objects of desire but are usually begging to be wrung off and cast aside. They are often clumsy or even comic impediments to the real object, the feet.

The mode of fetishism which fits Hopkins's writing closely, then, is that of transference. It is said to arise through the repression of sexual desire – which is after all a systematically necessary practice for a highly scrupulous priest – and takes the form of substituting a part of the body which is not prohibited for the sexual parts. Feet, then, are not guilty because they are remote from the guilty. Hopkins's focus on feet is unusual because of its imaginative intensity, but in other respects it is not uncommon. A widespread emphasis on the erotic potential of foot and shoe, not necessarily amounting to fetishism, seems to have been characteristically Victorian. According to Ronald Pearsall 'the chief fetish of the age became the shoes'.

Commenting on women's fashion and the raising of hemlines by three inches to reveal foot and ankle, he writes

> The foot became a new and attractive erogenous area, and particularly useful in that it could be written about and sung about. The number of times foot, ankle and boot appeared in music hall songs is incredible. The boot and shoe had a double appeal – as an indication of this novel sexual territory and as sexual symbols in their own right. (Pearsall 1971, 426)

Hence the constant emphasis on shoe and foot can be seen as one of the milder, if odder, consequences of Victorian respectability's repression of direct reference to sexual matters. The indirection – the coded language – which Victorian writers could adeptly employ to deal with sex is here re-inscribed upon the body in a physical obliquity, a pedalian circumlocution. Repression, which Freud called 'the oldest word in our psychoanalytic terminology' (Freud 1991, 352), is a concept which has not always been thought to carry over well into social analysis. But the doubts which Michel Foucault has raised about the 'repressive hypothesis' are perfectly consistent with (in fact, they entail) the re-emergence of sexuality as discourse. Foucault's remark about modern societies applies very well to this endless discourse of feet: 'not that they consigned sex to a shadow existence, but that they dedicated themselves to speaking of it *ad infinitum*' (Foucault 1984, 316). It was, of course, not just the emphasis on a single part of the body but even the Victorian concept of the mind itself which shows the traces of the forces which drove sexuality into the dark. Psychoanalysis, as Pearsall noted, is 'a form of psychology framed for the Victorian mentality' (Pearsall 1971, 515). As sexuality was pushed underground in respectable society, so it was in Freud's account of the mind, where the unconscious was a gothic realm of mysterious repressed forces, shadowy, energetic, threatening, pervasive, and easily seen as evil. Freud in this sense may be said to have gothicized sexuality; he located the gothic within, and ascribed a large element of human behaviour to its influence.

A number of Hopkins's critics have felt that, like other writers who adopted a Ruskinian scopic intensity in viewing the world, Hopkins is very wise about sea and sky and trees but not so wise about people; that his people poems are few in number and not as successful as his nature poems. It should have been easy enough, for the people he does give us are all full of grace and beyond reproach. As Michael Sprinker notes, they are lesser avatars of Christ (Sprinker 1980, 17): Harry Ploughman, Tom in 'Tom's Garland', Felix Randal, the boy in 'The Bugler's First Communion', the Soldier. The problem, of course, is that they have human bodies. The dangers of too direct an encounter with erotic attraction sometimes made such poems awkward, sometimes impossible to complete. But I want to suggest that in two of his most highly finished poems about people, 'Tom's Garland' and 'Harry Ploughman', he overcomes the difficulty of encountering the working-class male body by a double strategy: an employment of stereotype, and a focus on feet. Feet, by becoming the object of the gaze, actually make these poems writable, enabling their completion by the transference of disturbing emotion onto a supposedly permissible part of the admired male body. Occasionally in the presence of male beauty the roles are reversed, so that it is his own feet which Hopkins sees as engaged. In 'The Bugler's First Communion', a young soldier-boy comes to take communion from him. As the boy, 'breathing bloom of a chastity in mansex fine', kneels at the priest's feet, he responds professionally, fetching him the Eucharist, but with an alacrity which soon gets into his pedal extremities: 'how fain I of feet / To his youngster take his treat!' The joy of it lets him 'tread tufts of consolation / Days after'. But more usually, the focus is clearly on the feet of the other.

The major poems in which Hopkins represents the labouring male body have something in common with the modes of vision found in Pre-Raphaelite art, aestheticism, and even decadence. They are verbal equivalents of close portraiture. The poem becomes an instantiation of, or substitute for, the gaze. In none is the close-up carried further than in 'Harry Ploughman', which opens with a focus on the downy golden hairs on the ploughman's arms, as if the viewer has placed his eye only inches away, before crawling over the other parts of the body:

> Hard as hurdle arms, with a broth of goldish flue
> Breathed round; the rack of ribs; the scooped flank; lank
> Rope-over thigh; knee-nave; and barrelled shank –
> > Head and foot, shoulder and shank –
> By a grey eye's heed steered well, one crew, fall to;
> Stand at stress.

This is not unlike Lord Henry's first sight of Dorian Gray 'with his finely-curved scarlet lips, his frank blue eyes, his crisp gold hair' (Ch. 2). There, as in Hopkins, the gaze moves from feature to feature, evaluating and praising. Yet in the poem the eye/I effaces itself as if in shame, never appearing in the text, so that the subject-positions of the gazer and his object are made problematic: how *did* he get that close? And did the ploughman stare back? 'It is only the gaze which can... reduce me to shame at my very existence', as Elizabeth Grosz, commenting on Sartre, puts it (1990, 80).

The body is treated in 'Harry Ploughman' as if it were the grammar of a complex sentence: it is parsed into its constituent parts, each with its function; the articulation of the parts working together is the body's syntax:

> > Each limb's barrowy brawn, his thew
> That onewhere curded, onewhere sucked or sank –
> > Soared or sank – ,
> Though as a beechbole firm, finds his, as at a rollcall, rank
> And features, in flesh, what deed he each must do –
> > His sinew-service where do.

Body parts here have become autonomous agents, acting like powerful machines. That is a characteristic which the poem shares with one kind of pornographic writing, which may account for the unease some readers have felt about it. At the same time it is in these poems above all his others – 'Harry Ploughman', 'Tom's Garland' – that Hopkins's language is at its most difficult. The syntactic involutions, the relationships between clauses and parts of speech, become as obscure and disjointed as those between parts of the subject's body. The gaze fragments its subject. The grammatical wrenching is the sign of unacknowledged shame and discomfort, the price paid for that over-close gaze, a syntactical equivalent for the wringing of hands over feet.

> He leans to it, Harry bends, look. Back, elbow, and liquid waist
> In him, all quail to the wallowing o' the plough. 'S cheek crimsons; curls
> Wag or crossbridle, in a wind lifted, windlaced –
>   See his wind-lilylocks-laced –;
> Churlsgrace, too, child of Amansstrength, how it hangs or hurls
> Them ...

This 'builds up the beauty of the object, transforming it into something satisfying in itself'. The words are Laura Mulvey's in her classic analysis of the operation of the gaze (Mulvey 1975). 'Harry Ploughman' is a perfect example of that gaze which is both inquisitive and controlling, turning the person observed into an object, a magnificent physical specimen. These are the processes which Freud associated with scopophilia, ideas which have proved so fertile in subsequent cultural analysis, in cinema theory, feminism, and post-colonial studies, but which critics have apparently been reluctant to apply to Hopkins.

'Harry Ploughman' builds to its climax at the end, where, after standing still and tense through most of the poem (a point lost on many a reader because of the clotted energy of the language), the ploughman suddenly swings into action and surges along the next furrow. By now it should be no surprise that that climactic moment is imaged in terms of his feet:

> – broad in bluff hide his frowning feet lashed! raced
> With, along them, cragiron under and cold furls –
>   With-a-fountain's shining-shot furls.

'Frowning' there was probably meant to evoke the wrinkles in the leather of his boots, but its obvious transference as an adjective of the forehead – from the furrows on a brow to the punning furrows (in leather and in earth) surrounding his feet, from one bodily extremity to the other, each as remote as possible from the genitals – only underlines the process of substitution by which feet gain their significance. Truly these are feet being asked to carry rather more weight (so to speak) than they can bear. These are compulsive channels for Hopkins's imagination: the voyeur in 'Epithalamion' is likewise 'frowning' as he fumbles with his boots, wringing his brow as he wrings his hands over his feet. The frown of anxious concentration or shame is the cost of making these poems, and the male body, writable. The guilt of sexuality is conducted away towards the earth through the feet, in Harry's case actually to be concealed half-buried in the furrow of the field.

It would, however, be inappropriately empirical to see a poem like this as simply the recording of the activities of an observing eye/I. With its lavish over-elaboration of detail, its loving over-valuing of language, its staged and impossibly close perspective, its fixation on fully rendering a fixated gaze, it is the poem itself and its discourse, not merely the object of that discourse, which has become fetishized. As it happens, in 1887, the very same year as Hopkins wrote 'Harry Ploughman', Alfred Binet's essay on fetishism described the sublimation of writing as a form of textual perversion. As Emily Apter puts it, 'Binet unearthed the fetishism submerged within writing itself' (Apter 1991, 19; see 19–24).

This brings us to Hopkins's most overtly political poem, 'Tom's Garland', subtitled 'Upon the Unemployed'. Hopkins presents a pair of (employed) day-labourers, navvies, the shock troops of the century who in digging the canals and then the railways had changed the face of Britain with the sheer power of their muscles. He tries to render all this dangerously attractive strength harmless by turning them into stereotypes: they are Tom and Dick, any old working men. (Harry, who completes the cliché trio, we have already met in his field.)

> Tom – garlanded with squat and surly steel
> Tom; then Tom's fallowbootfellow piles pick
> By him and rips out rockfire homeforth – sturdy Dick;

Hopkins begins by crowning this useful member of the community, but he has to turn him upside down to do it, for the 'garland' of 'squat and surly steel' is the nails on the soles of his boots. Since they have ceased work for the day, Hopkins can call Tom and Dick 'fallowbootfellows', though fallow also means light brown or reddish yellow, so that the two labourers, feet of the commonwealth, are 'humorously treated as a pair of pale hide boots' (MacKenzie in Hopkins 1990, 487).

Hopkins piles on the foot images like a remorselessly sustained joke: Dick 'rips out rockfire homeforth' with his hobnails. 'Rockfire', for spark, is pure Barnes–gothic again.

He contrasts those at the top of society with those at the bottom, the sovereign with the labourer:

> lordly head,
> With heaven's lights high hung round, or, mother-ground
> That mammocks, mighty foot.

The navvy is that 'mighty foot' of the commonwealth who 'mammocks' the mother-ground – a playful though violent tearing, since the word unmistakably alludes to Shakespeare's *Coriolanus* whose little boy amuses himself by mammocking a butterfly (I.iii.65). Tom is equally childish and innocent in his simple acceptance of his lowly station. The tense class conflicts of *Coriolanus* are highly relevant to the poem. In fact, Hopkins seems to have drawn, consciously or not, on this exchange in Shakespeare between patrician and labourer:

> Menenius: What do you think,
>   You, the great toe of this assembly?
> First Citizen: I the great toe? Why the great toe?
> Menenius: For that being one o' th' lowest, basest, poorest
>   Of this most wise rebellion, thou goest foremost:
>   Thou rascal, that art worst in blood to run,
>   Lead'st first to win some vantage.
>   But make you ready your stiff bats and clubs;
>   Rome and her rats are at the point of battle;
>   The one side must have bale.

> I.i.153–62

For once, it appears, the feet in 'Tom's Garland' symbolize the body politic more than the body sexual. But in reality the two kinds of threat – the revolutionary potential of the lower orders and the dangerous sexuality of the male body – have been merged. And in the case of Tom and Dick, humbly but usefully employed and content with their lot, those threats have been neutralized. The way the poem conveys that absence of threat is by making them *well shod*.

> Tom Heart-at-ease, Tom Navvy: he is all for his meal
> Sure, 's bed now. Low be it: lustily he his low lot (feel

That ne'er need hunger, Tom; Tom seldom sick,
Seldomer heartsore; that treads through, prickproof, thick
Thousands of thorns, thoughts) swings though.

In his sturdy footwear Tom is kept safe himself, so that he 'treads through, prickproof, thick / Thousands of thorns', and in addition he poses no risk to others, for he also treads invulnerably through 'thoughts', accepting the hierarchy of class difference without question. The real risk, to the body politic and the body masculine, would come if he exposed himself by taking his boots off. And that is precisely what Hopkins unleashes when, later in the poem, he turns from the safely employed navvies to consider the unemployed, the dispossessed who have no stake, however humble, in the commonweal:

> But no way sped,
> Nor mind nor mainstrength; gold go garlanded
> With, perilous, O no; nor yet plod safe shod sound;
> Undenizened, beyond bound
> Of earth's glory, earth's ease, all; noone, nowhere,
> In wide the world's weal; rare gold, bold steel, bare
> In both; care, but share care –
> This, by Despair, bred Hangdog dull; by Rage,
> Manwolf, worse; and their packs infest the age.

No reader can get through this thicket of syntax for the first time without resorting to Hopkins's prose crib which he had to write to explain the poem. This state of things – class inequality – is, he says,

> all very well for those who are in, however low in, the Common-
> wealth and share in any way the Common weal; but … the curse of
> our times is that many do not share it, that they are outcasts from it
> and have neither security nor splendour; that they share care with
> the high and obscurity with the low, but wealth or comfort with
> neither. And this state of things, I say, is the origin of Loafers,
> Tramps, Cornerboys, Roughs, Socialists and other pests of society.
> (1935a, 273–4)

The disaffected revolutionary unemployed ('Loafers, Tramps', etc. in the paraphrase) are seen as a nameless, de-humanized gothic night-mare – 'Hangdog', 'Manwolf' – in the poem, in terms typical of many nineteenth-century representations of working-class upheaval. The poem draws upon the conventional Victorian distinction between the deserving and undeserving poor, updating it to apply to the new issue of the 1880s, unemployment. Fear of revolution, which had been so strong among the middle classes for much of the first half of the century but which had receded somewhat with the prosperity of the sixties, was now back again, with riots, strikes and mass rallies, one of which turned into Bloody Sunday. But only Hopkins would inscribe the social and political order upon the body in quite these terms. He represents the dangerousness of the dispossessed as an inability to 'plod safe shod sound'. That is, they are shoeless and therefore flighty, their feet as 'bare' (line 17) of steel nails as their heads are of coronets. By contrast, Tom's mighty boots stay on, guaranteeing his masculine harmlessness and political docility. Images of the working class were always potentially contradictory, liable to oscillate between the benign and the fearful. Hopkins projects that uneasy doubleness onto the part of the body which was already invested via sexual transference with both fascination and fear, so giving us a curious symbolic politics which distinguishes the power and danger of bare feet from the plodding safeness of booted feet.

In these poems about Tom, Dick and Harry, stereotype and fetish go together. This would come as no surprise to analysts of the gaze in post-colonial theory, which applies well to Hopkins here. Homi K. Bhabha in *The Location of Culture* has argued for an intimate connection between stereotype and fetish. He points out that 'the stereotype is not a simplification because it is a false representation of a given reality. It is a simplification because it is an arrested, fixated form of representation' (Bhabha 1994, 75). I would add that in Hopkins the related strategies of stereotype and fetish both seem to serve the purpose of making the working-class male body writable by going some way to neutralize its dangerous attractiveness. Stereotype does so by generalizing or de-person-alizing the encounter, and fetish by displacing the focus from an unspeakable to a speakable part of the body.

Hopkins's focus on feet shows how displaced or repressed energy could burst out in the most prosaic – and prosodic – of places. For Hopkins's great attempt to remake prosody, Sprung Rhythm, is nothing more or less than an attempt to liberate feet in verse. In conventional English scansion, which Hopkins called 'alternating rhythm' and saw as tyrannous and restrictive, each foot is con-demned to have the same number of syllables as every other, as well as having the same number of stresses. By removing the first require-ment and keeping the second, Hopkins created a new freedom of movement for poetry:

This then is the essence of sprung rhythm: *one stress makes one foot, no matter how many or few the syllables.* (1935b, 22–3)

This is what Hardy, in the passage which I quoted near the beginning, identified as part of 'the Gothic art-principle', the principle 'of stress rather than of syllable'. Defining feet by their stresses not their syllables grants them freedom to be what Hopkins believed they really are: their vital quality is stress, that vocalic, physical attribute. In this way he re-connects verse with the body, since for him the essence of verse is speech and the essence of speech is stress. 'Stress' is a word he often uses of bodily or muscular tension, as when Harry Ploughman's limbs 'stand at stress', or when in 'The Wreck of the Deutschland' he describes a night of terrifying spiritual wrestling with God: 'the midriff astrain with leaning of, laced with fire of stress'. Stress, then, embodied in the foot, is for Hopkins the link between the technic of poetry and the physicality of the body, between the prosodic and corporeal senses of 'feet' which might otherwise seem connected only by the punning logic of dream.

Above all what Hopkins wanted for feet was freedom. In 'God's Grandeur' he laments the mess humans have made of the world:

Generations have trod, have trod, have trod;
And all is seared with trade; bleared, smeared, with toil;
And wears man's smudge and shares man's smell: the soil
Is bare now, nor can foot feel, being shod.

That poem as a whole is a visionary indictment of nothing less than man's relations with his fellows and with all of the natural and man-made world, from which vast perspective the evils of industrialization are just the latest twist. It is bizarre that the image which he uses to sum up such a huge failure is a modern disinclination to go barefoot: 'nor can foot feel, being shod'. Bathos is close. But for Hopkins bare feet and freedom were an obvious conjunction. On holiday in the west of Ireland in 1884 he wrote 'Great part of the population are very pleasantly shod in their bare heels and stockinged in their bare shins. How gladly I would go so! The struggle I keep up with shoemakers, murderers by inches, I may say ever embitters my life' (Hopkins cited in White 1992, 370). Here facetious exaggeration comes to his rescue, while the images tell of himself and his shoemakers locked in a mortal struggle for possession of his feet an inch at a time. Then again, death and feet were not always a jesting matter. During Hopkins's time at

Stonyhurst 'one of the cleverest boys' committed suicide by hanging. 'His body was naked except that his shoes were on' (Martin 1992, 213). This is death's grim parody of the erotic state, body clothed but feet bare. In another case, Hopkins's college friend Poutiatine was found dead in a pool of water beside a French railway line: 'His name they could find nowhere but in his boots and for some time they thought it was the maker's' (Hopkins ed. House and Storey 1959, 229). As sex and death are so closely associated in Romantic and post-Romantic poetry, it is perhaps no surprise that Hopkins occasionally associated feet with both.

He himself took freedom from shoes and murdering shoemakers as far as he could, and it gained him a reputation for effeminacy. Everyone recollected Hopkins's 'oddly feminine walk' (Martin 1992, 176), but one of Hopkins's colleagues at University College Dublin, a bluff, no-nonsense Jesuit called Father Joseph Darlington, went further. He recalled Hopkins's eccentricities of manner, speech and appearance, giving as an example 'the very slippers he wore; the kind little girls of 10 or 12 used then to wear: with ancle [*sic*] straps!!' (Martin 1992, 420). Darlington, like Hopkins, was an English Catholic convert with an Oxford education, but they were clearly poles apart, divided by Darlington's suspicion of Hopkins's effeminacy. Darlington, incidentally, remained at his post to become one of the tutors of the young James Joyce and the man who probably first told Joyce the meaning of the word 'epiphany'.[8]

These sandals played a prominent part in Hopkins's symbology of the foot. Wearing sandals could be referred to as going barefoot. Sandals were a sign of cultivated, artistic, progressive middle-class values such as those of the Hampstead family from which Hopkins came and with whom he remained in touch all his life. H.G. Wells's novel about education, *Joan and Peter*, describes a school for infants run by admirers of William Morris where the children have 'bare legs and brown smocks and Heidelberg sandals' (Wells n.d., 103). In the words of a detractor, it was the kind of place 'where socialism and play-acting are school subjects, and everybody runs about with nothing on' (Wells n.d., 128).[9] To the conventionally-minded, then, sandals were suspiciously bohemian, probably foreign, tantamount to naked feet, and suggestive of revolutionary sympathies.

Consequently, it is not surprising that 'sandal' in the poetry is a word which Hopkins uses to startle, just as his little girl's 'slippers with ancle straps' startled Dublin. 'Poor Felix Randal', the subject of one of his best-known poems, is even renamed for the sake of them. The real name of Hopkins's dying farrier parishioner had been Felix Spencer, but the poet altered the surname in order to work the poem up to a triumphant closing rhyme:

This seeing the sick endears them to us, us too it endears.
My tongue had taught thee comfort, touch had quenched thy tears,
Thy tears that touched my heart, child, Felix, poor Felix Randal;
How far from then forethought of, all thy more boisterous years,
When thou at the random grim forge, powerful amidst peers,
Didst fettle for the great grey drayhorse his bright and battering sandal!

Felix Spencer/Randal's trade was to use his admired physique, 'big-boned and hardy-handsome', for the heavy labour of taking shoes off and putting shoes on horses' feet. The brilliant effectiveness of the poem's close lies in the sheer inappropriateness of 'sandal', with its connotations of delicacy and interlacedness, when applied to the bright steel shoe and the 'battering' power of the heavy horse. Sandal was a complex word for Hopkins, and it reveals its cheeky strain here in this splendid misapplication. Another of his finest poems, 'Binsey Poplars', about his grief at the felling of trees, deploys the word very similarly:

My aspens dear, whose airy cages quelled,
Quelled or quenched in leaves the leaping sun,
All felled, felled, are all felled;
     Of a fresh and following folded rank
        Not spared, not one
        That dandled a sandalled
    Shadow that swam or sank
On meadow and river and wind-wandering weed-winding bank.

Again, 'sandalled' here is wonderfully unlikely as applied to the trees' shadows. Far-fetched though visually accurate, it is an image of interlaced patterns of sunlight and shade coming through the moving branches, dancing light-footed over the ground. But it carries another charge besides. Hopkins was so distressed by the felling of those Oxford trees that he probably enquired as to who had done it and why. He would have been told that the wood was going to make brake *shoes* for the Great Western Railway (Martin 1992, 302). The delicacy of the poem's language, and the airy insubstantiality of the play of the light and shade through the trees, as they 'dandled a sandalled /

Shadow', is not only Hopkins's recuperation of the trees' lost beauty; it is also, it seems, his defiance for what became of them, those clamping, squealing, heavy wooden shoes fitted to truculent wagons. 'Sandalled', then, is an act of linguistic industrial sabotage where the *sabot* is on the other foot, with sandal standing for everything that *sabot* does not, except for the rebelliousness the two terms share.

The effeminacy of the sandalled male was all the clearer in a period which set store by the outward signs of the masculine virtues and the pursuits which embodied them. Football was one such game, evocative of hearty masculinity, rough and tumble, the ethos of the playing-field: the very opposite of the effeminate. A liking for football was a guarantee of freedom from any hint of homosexuality. As it happened Hopkins quite liked the game himself, and not surprisingly gave the conventional masculine connotations a wry twist. More than once he sees *himself* as the football, the object of the kick: contemplating the fact that as a Jesuit he was liable to be moved around the country at a moment's notice, he wrote 'I have long been Fortune's football and am blowing up the bladder of resolution big and buxom for another kick of her foot' (Hopkins 1935a, 183). More literally, when he played the game while teaching boys at Newman's Oratory, the 'fattest and biggest' boy lamed Hopkins with a kick on the ankle (Hopkins 1938, 32). The unwelcome attentions of the ugly child make for a comic reversal of the potentially erotic.

The nature of masculinity in poetry became the topic of a keen debate between Hopkins and Coventry Patmore. In a review, Patmore had classed Keats with 'the feminine geniuses among men' (Hopkins 1938, 233); Hopkins responded by quoting Matthew Arnold on 'the true masculine fibre in Keats's mind' (Hopkins 1938, 234); but as the debate went on Hopkins made concessions to Patmore's view: 'Since I last wrote I have reread Keats a little and the force of your criticism on him has struck me more than it did. It is impossible not to feel with weariness how his verse is at every turn abandoning itself to an enervating and unmanly luxury' (1938, 237). At the same time, though, 'his mind had ... the distinctively masculine powers in abundance, his character the manly virtues, but while he gave himself up to dreaming and self indulgence of course they were in abeyance'. Unmanly but manly, then: the concept is clearly under some pressure. 'An enervating and unmanly luxury' is a particularly ironic charge for him to bring against Keats in view of the Keatsian sensuality of Hopkins's own early poetry. And then there is his own middle name. It was his father who was Manley Hopkins; he himself preferred to write Gerard M. Hopkins and to most people, in speech, he was simply Gerard Hopkins. It is highly ironic that the masculinist patronymic has stuck to the priest and poet whom people remembered as 'gentle and feminine' (White 1992, 382). In short, although there is a conventional, even tedious element in the concept of masculinity here, it is also a concept which can be shown to be unstable and the focus of contention.

By the end of his life Hopkins was becoming a one-man campaign for freedom for feet. In the November 1888 issue of the *Stonyhurst Magazine* there appeared a letter to the editor written by Hopkins but signed only with the name 'Gymnosophist'. It is headed 'Football Barefoot':

> Sir, Football is sometimes played barefoot in Ireland. A friend tells me that the club he belongs to challenged some village clubs in his neighbourhood; when the game came to be played their opponents stripped their feet and took the field barefoot. He and his company were surprised, and thought the bare feet would need to be tenderly dealt with ... but the countrymen told them they could not play with any ease, unless unshod. And the event proved they had no need for apprehension. The bare-footed men played as boldly as they did.

Bare feet, physical energy and prowess, and class difference are once again in conjunction, for the 'countrymen' are the peasantry, encountered by educated city men. They played 'boldly', having 'stripped' their feet. 'Football barefoot' involves a doubling both of word and of physical sensation. Hopkins continues:

> The ball did not seem to be kicked with the end of the toe, but it was kicked strongly. In point of strength no loss could be seen, and in point of activity the lightness of the foot may have made a good deal of difference.
> It is likely that those who are accustomed often to go barefoot feel this difference in nimbleness and fleetness keenly ...

The mock-solemnity of this, adopting the familiar tones of the Victorian amateur scientific observer, provides a way of seeming to repudiate too close an interest in the topic. After relating several further instances of barefoot feats and games, Hopkins switches to open jocularity as another way of doing so:

> If at Stonyhurst you would try playing football and other games barefoot you would find it an advantage on many grounds.

> Gravel however is not one of those grounds: you must play on grass.[10]

And on that happy note we may leave it. The emphasis with these bare feet is on accessibility, the recovery of an originary intimacy with mother earth, and the (almost) guilt-free naturalness of healthy outdoor pursuits. When they came as part of a hearty masculine game, the cover-story was nearly perfect. As Freud said about the transference of desire, 'In later life, the fetishist feels that he enjoys yet another advantage ... the fetish is not withheld from him: it is easily accessible ... What other men have to woo and make exertions for can be had by the fetishist with no trouble at all' (Freud 1991, 354). The only qualification necessary to make this apply to Hopkins is that it seems certain he was not fully aware of the extent to which he had become focused on feet: he would have been aghast.

Most of the feet, shoes, sandals and boots we have been considering come from the late period of Hopkins's life, the Jekyll and Hyde years, when he was also writing of the fracturing of the self which I began by discussing. In 1885 he confided to a friend:

> The melancholy I have all my life been subject to has become of late years not indeed more intense in its fits but rather more distributed, constant, and crippling. ... When I am at the worst, though my judgment is never affected, my state is much like madness. (1938, 109)

This time it really could be Jekyll speaking, diction and all. The horrors of those years were personal and real for Hopkins, but as they reach us in his writing they must also be seen to be both political and highly literary, given form and voice by the moment in which he lived and by the language he shared with others. In that writing the gothic terrors of the over-strained mind, with its 'cliffs of fall / Frightful, sheer, no-man-fathomed', are accompanied by a bodily analogue, a displacement of sexual and political fears and energies onto feet, a displacement which is sometimes joking but sometimes tense, anguished and hand-wringing. The diffusion of the gothic mode in the nineteenth century meant that it turned up again, lightly disguised, in some unexpected places. Gerard Hopkins's feet are one of them.

Notes

1. The influence of both Ruskin and Barnes on Hopkins and Hardy is discussed by Paulin.
2. 'Inscape' and 'instress' are terms which every student of Hopkins comes to grips with. On the special meaning of 'sake', see Hopkins's letter to Bridges of 26 May 1879: 'It is the *sake* of "for the sake of", *forsake, namesake, keepsake*. I mean by it the being a thing has outside itself ... something distinctive, marked'. For 'keepings', see his letter to Dixon of December 1881 (1935b, 98–9). As for 'fetch', see 'The Wreck of the Deutschland' stanza 19, and compare *The Sermons and Devotional Writings of Gerard Manley Hopkins* (1959, 200).
3. A detailed account of some aspects of Hopkins's sexuality is in Norman MacKenzie's introduction to his book *The Early Poetic Manuscripts and Notebooks of Gerard Manley Hopkins in Facsimile* (1989).
4. The drawing may be found in the *Facsimile* (1989) but in reproduction it has lost a good deal of its impact, being much more arresting in the actual notebook, which is in Campion Hall, Oxford, and not generally accessible because of its deteriorating condition.
5. As the editor of Hopkins's sermons notes, devotion to the Sacred Heart had its roots in the seventeenth century but became much more prominent in the nineteenth, being 'first extended to the whole Church by Pius IX in 1856' (1959, 281)
6. Hopkins is writing about Ephesians 6:15.
7. Compare Jacques Lacan: 'What the voyeur is looking for and finds is merely a shadow, a shadow behind the curtain. There he will phantasize any magic presence, the most graceful of girls, for example, even if on the other side there is only a hairy athlete' (Lacan cited in Grosz 1990, 78).
8. See Oliver St. J. Gogarty, *As I was Going down Sackville Street* (1937, 285). By way of revenge Joyce put Darlington into *Stephen Hero* as Father Butt, dean of the college and Professor of English (White 1992, 382). The dean of studies who humiliates Stephen in *Portrait of the Artist* is Joyce's later version of Butt/Darlington.
9. My attention was drawn to Wells's novel by Ellen Jordan in a contribution to the Victoria electronic discussion list, 20 May 1997; and I am also indebted to members of the list generally for several other references to Victorian bare feet.
10. This letter is not in the published volumes of Hopkins's letters. It appears to have been undiscovered till 1953 when it was reprinted in the *Stonyhurst Magazine*. It can also be read in full in *The Dublin Review* (1965, 289–92).

5
From King Arthur to Sidonia the Sorceress: the Dual Nature of Pre-Raphaelite Mediaevalism

J.-A. George

> The medieval revival was a complex and yet coherent move-
> ment. ... Although medievalism involved varying and some-
> times contradictory ideas and programs, its basic aims
> remained very similar throughout. ... At the height of the
> revival scarcely an aspect of life remained untouched by
> medievalist influence. The very beds people slept in were apt
> to be Gothic. ... The Middle Ages were idealized as a period of
> faith, order, joy, munificence and creativity. ... The Middle
> Ages became a metaphor both for a specific social order and,
> somewhat more vaguely, for a metaphysically harmonious
> world view.
>
> Alice Chandler, 1970, 1

Alice Chandler's description of the mediaeval revival captures perfectly
the ways in which this movement came to permeate and, ultimately,
define certain aspects of the Victorian period. It could be argued,
however, that 'expressions of a medievalizing imagination' (Chandler
1970, 1) were most extensively and self-consciously employed by the
Pre-Raphaelites who, in their paintings and poetry, presented a heavily
idealized view of the Middle Ages. It could also be said that the 'sometimes contradictory ideas and programs' found in the work of the
members of the Pre-Raphaelite Brotherhood stemmed from their
employment, consciously and unconsciously, of two distinct defini-
tions of the term gothic; 'mediaeval as opposed to classical' and
'grotesque'. This second meaning is largely evident in the sub-text of
their writings and visual arts, especially when these are read as veiled
autobiography. With specific reference to William Morris and, to a
lesser extent, Dante Gabriel Rossetti and Edward Burne-Jones, then,

this essay hopes to explore the dual nature of the gothic and, more widely, of Pre-Raphaelite mediaevalism itself.

William Morris's idealized vision of the mediaeval period can be directly traced to the Waverley novels of Sir Walter Scott and, like Scott at Abbotsford, he attempted to *live* the Middle Ages as well as write about them. J.W. Mackail, in his *The Life of William Morris*, vividly describes the gothic household in which Morris grew up:

> At some points there were links with the habits of mediaeval England. ... Just as in the fourteenth century, there was a meal at high prime. ... Morris himself was given a small suit of armor to wear when riding in the park and ... was developing a far more authentic sense of the nation's sylvan past through his explorations of the neighboring Epping Forest. Riding among its shadowy rows of birch trees, clad in his miniature armor, he could imagine himself reliving his favorite scenes from Scott. (Mackail 1932, I,9)

If the image of a young Morris 'clad in his miniature armor' seems a curious one, it seems less strange when placed within its own historical context; throughout the nineteenth century images of The Round Table (and the chivalric code it allegedly lived by and for) were widely manipulated to incite patriotism in the population at large. The now extinct Knights of King Arthur, founded by the Congregational minister William Byron Forbush, for example, combined love of nation with love of dressing up. They were advised by a group of superiors known as 'Merlins' and their manifesto called for the revival of 'the spirit of chivalry, courtesy, recognition of *noblesse oblige*, and Christian daring' (Girouard 1981, 254). In light of the frequency with which such propaganda was used, one is inclined to agree with J.W. Burrow's statement in *A Liberal Descent: Victorian Historians and the English Past* that '... for all its insistence on the "Catholic", there was a marked strain of nationalism in the Gothic revival in its earnest Victorian phase ... neo-medievalism was essentially polemical' (Burrow 1981, 159).

As Morris matured, his formulation of a mediaeval ideal became subject to more powerful literary influences (Henderson 1967, 23).[1] While at Oxford, both he and Edward Burne-Jones steeped themselves heavily in the *Morte d'Arthur*. It has been claimed that 'so great did their love and veneration for this book become, that he [Morris] and Burne-Jones were almost too shy to speak of it, even among their intimate friends' (Henderson 1967, 29). Burne-Jones' wife, Georgiana, also saw fit to remark on the impact of Malory's text in a rather sentimental passage from her *Memorials*:

> I sometimes think that the book never can have been loved as it was by those two men. With Edward it became literally a part of himself. Its strength and beauty, its mystical religion and noble chivalry of action, the world of lost history and romance in the names of the people and places – it was his own birthright upon which he entered. (Burne-Jones 1904, I, 116)

It could just as easily be claimed that the *Morte d'Arthur* was William Morris' 'birthright' as well, even if he did read it from a 'romantically falsified' position (Waters 1990, 57).[2] This particular work determined not only the course which his poetry would take but it also played a significant part in the house he would one day live in, the books he would print, the translations he would undertake and the woman he would marry. Indeed, Morris' only purely pictorial piece is a painting of 1858 depicting Jane Burden Morris as Queen Guenevere (Figure 5.1).

Morris' wife also played the role of a gothic Guenevere in her daily life, as Henry James famously observed:

> Morris read from the second series of his 'un-Earthly Paradise' and Jane, having toothache, lay on the sofa, with a handkerchief over her face. There was something very quaint and remote from actual life, it seemed to me, in the whole scene: Morris reading in his flowing antique numbers a legend of prodigies and terrors ... around us all the picturesque bric-à-brac of the apartment ... and in the corner this dark, silent mediaeval woman with her mediaeval toothache. (Lubbock 1920, I, 17–18)

Jane Burden Morris, 'dark', 'silent', and lurking 'in the corner' is portrayed as a rather sinister figure, a creature of the '*un*-Earthly Paradise' (emphasis mine). As a result, she fuses with the Gothic text, 'a legend of prodigies and terrors', that her husband reads aloud to her. In this scene, the contradictory images of woman projected in the works of the Pre-Raphaelite Brotherhood are placed side by side. On the one hand, Jane's otherworldly beauty and her vulnerability (as signalled by the toothache) are very much in keeping with the highly mediaevalised and highly idealised vision of The Lady as found, say, in numerous passages from Rossetti's translation of Dante's *Vita Nuova*:

5.1   William Morris' 1858 painting of Jane Burden Morris as Queen Guenevere.

My lady looks so gentle and so pure
  When yielding salutation by the way,
  That the tongue trembles and has nought to say,
And the eyes, which fain would see, may not endure.
And still, amid the praise she hears secure,
  She walks with humbleness for her array;
  Seeming a creature sent from Heaven to stay
On earth, and show a miracle made sure. (Rossetti 1892, 74)

This positive image of Jane/woman is seen, however, to co-exist along-side a more misogynistic discourse where women are delineated as predatory, unwholesome, even unregenerate. (Or, to use the term their own contemporaries ironically applied to the Pre-Raphaelites them-selves, 'fleshly' [see Buchanan 1871, 334–50].) The 'basic incompat-ibility' of some of the central tenets of Pre-Raphaelitism become clear here, though it must be remembered that the source of these contra-dictions can be traced back to the Middle Ages.[3] Umberto Eco addresses this, in part, in *Art and Beauty in the Middle Ages*:

> The Medievals inhabited a world filled with references, reminders and overtones of Divinity, manifestations of God in things. Nature spoke to them heraldically: lions or nut-trees were more than they seemed; griffins were just as real as lions because, like them, they were signs of a higher truth. Lewis Mumford has described this as a kind of neurosis – a description which is certainly apposite in a metaphorical sense, for it pinpoints the elements of strain and deformation in the medieval way of looking at things. (Eco 1986, 53)

The 'elements of strain and deformation', indeed, even 'neurosis', in the Pre-Raphaelite 'way of looking at things' are most evident not only in the way they view women (a subject I shall return to later) but also, as has already been suggested, in their particular brand of mediae-valism. They often consciously resisted the darker, more grotesque, elements of their gothic vision in favour of depicting a pure mediaeval past, an age of moral absolutes where good and evil were easily distin-guishable. This has lead Mark Girouard to comment that: 'Their later works lack the peculiar vividness of the work of the 1850s. They move in a world of dreams which seems to have little to do with real people, even real mediaeval people'. (Girouard 1981, 188)

William Morris' translation of *Beowulf*, begun in August of 1892, only four years before his death, is a piece that, as Girouard has suggested of later Pre-Raphaelite works in general, 'seems to have little to do with ... real mediaeval people'. Before he started his *Beowulf* project, Morris had had some success as a translator. Joseph Jacobs, an early editor of his translations of Old French romances, was impressed enough with Morris' efforts to write that they gave 'appropriate English dress ... to classic and mediaeval masterpieces' (Jacob 1970, 152). Regardless of such general praise, Morris' *Beowulf* has always been viewed as something of a flop: many consider it to be his biggest failure as a translator. Fiona MacCarthy, in her acclaimed biography of Morris, sums up the situation well though is rather squeamish about discussing the translation itself in any detail:

> simultaneously with *Chaucer*, Morris was working on his *Beowulf* trans-lation. He was not in any sense an Anglo-Saxon scholar. He worked from the original but with a prose paraphrase supplied by the more expert A.J. Wyatt of Christ's College, Cambridge, which he used as a safety net. ... As he worked through the 3,182 lines of the original he took it week by week to read to Ned and Georgie [Burne-Jones] at the Sunday breakfasts at The Grange. Few people have had a good word to say for Morris' *Beowulf* (least of all in Oxford). I will not attempt one. It is Morris at his most garrulous and loose. The translation is an unex-pected failure since Morris, with his taste for the heroic, might have been expected to respond to the starkness of the setting and the embattlements of giants. (MacCarthy 1994, 648–9)

To dismiss Morris' *Beowulf* so totally, especially without any attempt at real analysis, is to do it a great disservice. Ironically, it is precisely Morris' 'taste for the heroic' that gives the work a certain coherence and moral focus. What has always been overlooked in any examina-tion of the translation, however, is the fact that Morris filtered the Old English poem through his own Victorian gothic lens. The end product was a text informed by his mediaevalism, not his knowledge of the his-torical Middle Ages. A few examples from Morris' *Beowulf* itself should help to substantiate this claim.

   Firstly, however, it is useful to foreground a fact that Morris' critics seldom mention: as an undergraduate, Morris acquired a sound academic knowledge of the Middle Ages. The poet himself confirmed that he 'fell-to very vigorously on history and especially mediaeval history' and began reading ' the books of John Ruskin which were at the time a sort of reve-lation' while at University (Morris 1980, 29). In later life he also wrote a sizeable number of scholarly lectures on the Middle Ages for the Hammersmith Branch of the Socialist League; these included *The Gothic Revival* (1884), *Early England* (1886) and *The Early Literature of the North –*

Iceland. It is clear, then, that Morris knew enough about the history and culture of the Middle Ages to make his *Beowulf* credible as well as readable. So where did he go 'wrong'? Actually, what seems to have happened is that he displaced the text by about five centuries and at least one culture. In other words, his translation of the Old English epic owes more to Morris' idealization of Malory and the conventions of Old French romance than it does to the Germanic warrior society that inspired the original poem. From the moment Beowulf enters the land of the Danes, Morris draws the reader into the world of mediaeval romance.[4] Hrothgar's hall, *Heorot* (which, incidentally, is called *Hart* by Morris) is rendered as a *court,* at the entrance of which Beowulf tells Hrothgar's messenger that he has come to bid a *boon* (352, from OE *ben*) of Hrothgar, 'if to us he will grant it / That him who so good is, anon we may greet' (gif he us geunnan wile / þæt we hine swa godne gretan moton, 346[b]–347).[5] The messenger answers this genteel speech with equal courtesy:

> I therefore the Danes' friend
> Will likely be asking of the lord of the Scyldings,
> The dealer of rings, since the boon thou art bidding,
> The mighty folk-lord, concerning thine errand,
> And swiftly the answer shall do thee to wit
> Which the good one to give thee aback may deem meetest.

(Morris 1966, v. 10, 189)

> Ic þæs wine Deniga,
> frean Scildinga, frinan wille,
> beaga bryttan, swa þu bena eart,
> þeoden mærne, ymb þinne sið
> ond þe þa andsware ædre gecyðan,
> þe me se goda agifan þenceð.

(Klaeber 1950, ll. 350[b]–355)

The tensions which are implicit in the original poem between Hrothgar's sentinel and Beowulf's opposing army do not exist in Morris' translation. They are replaced with a courtly benevolence, courtesy and fair speech – anachronisms central to Morris' mediaevalism and found, consequently, in abundance in his own poetry.[6] Take, for example, the exchange between the Elder of the City (a mediaeval Utopia 'white as the changing walls of faërie / Thronged with much people clad in ancient guise') and The Wanderers in the Prologue to *The Earthly Paradise* (1868):[7]

The Elder of the City

Sit, friends, and tell your tale, which seems to us
Shall be a strange tale and piteous,
Nor shall it lack our pity for its woe,
Nor ye due thanks for all the things ye show
Of kingdoms nigh forgot that once were great,
And small lands come to glorious estate.

The Wanderers

Fair sirs, we thank you, hoping we have come
Through many wanderings to a quiet home
Befitting dying men – Good health and peace
To you and to this land, and fair increase
Of everything that ye can wish to have!

(Morris 1966, *v.* 3, 22)

Morris' tendency to romanticize the world of *Beowulf* is particularly
apparent in the final third of the poem. The original text, admittedly,
becomes more elegiac in mood as it progresses towards its close
but Morris detracts from the real emotional force of these moments
by infusing them with too much sentiment. One striking example
of this is when Beowulf, now an old man about to fight his last
battle, bids farewell to the people he has ruled over for many
years:

Gesæt ða on næsse niðheard cyning;
þenden hælo abead heðrogeneatum,
goldwine Geata. Him wæs geomor sefa,
wæfre ond wælfus

(Klaeber 1950, ll. 2417–2420[a])

Morris translates this in the following manner:

Sat then on the ness there the strife-hardy king
While farewell he bade to his fellows of hearth,
The gold-friend of the Geats; sad was gotten his soul,
Wavering, death-minded.

(Morris 1966, *v.* 10, 252)

The choice to translate *niðheard* (2417[b]) as the rather robust 'strife-hardy', a compound Morris no doubt associated with Arthurian acts of derring-do, is especially telling. *Niðheard* (*nið* = battle, violence; *heard* = hardy, strong, severe) implies much more than Morris allows for; Stephen A. Barney's *Word-hoard: an Introduction to Old English Vocabulary* defines *nið* as 'malice, enmity, violence, persecution, combat' and adds that it is 'not a nice word, but a Beowulfian word' (Barney 1977, 49). The OE word, in context, conjurs up an image of a brooding mind (*geomor sefa*), of a man capable of severe acts of violence, and anticipates Beowulf's behaviour in his bloody, gothic combat with the dragon.

This same type of what we might call 'cultural substitution' occurs in line 2420[a] of the passage as well. Morris' translation of *wæfre ond wælfus* as 'Wavering, death-minded' sentimentalizes it further by suggesting that Beowulf *resists* the idea of his possible death in battle and that this resistance is a direct consequence of his reminiscing with 'fellows of hearth'. Morris implies here that the pleasures Beowulf experiences with his comrades are too great to relinquish even for a heroic end. The intention of the original lines, however, is to show Beowulf becoming inspired during this leave-taking by memories of past glories. As a result, he becomes more *eager* for the fight, 'restless and ripe for death' (Tuso, ed. 1975, 42).

Morris' mediaevalism was his weapon against modernity.[8] Through texts such as *Beowulf* he continued to disseminate his gothic ideal up until the time of his death. By the time he died in 1896, however, the popularity of this type of literature was on the decline and it could be argued that this was largely due to two *fin-de-siècle* phenomena – the vogue for archaeological expeditions and the birth of the Aesthetic Movement. In relation to my first point, Hugh Kenner, in *The Pound Era*, presents a convincing argument for why the 'archaising sensibility' found in much Victorian literature and painting began to dissolve:

This is a crucial fact: it did dissolve, though not quickly, at the touch of several interrelated events. One … was the growing awareness that since about 1870 men had held in their hands the actual objects Homer's sounding words name. A pin, a cup, which you can handle like a safety pin tends to resist being archaized. … Another, which may one day seem the seminal force in modern art history, was the spreading news that painted animals of great size and indisputable vigor of line could be seen on the walls of caves which no one had entered for 25,000 years. They were not 'primitive' in Fra Angelico's way, their vigor might have been put there yesterday. The first response was that they were surely fakes, but by 1895 physical evidence had disposed of any such notion, and a wholly new kind of visual experience caused much change, we cannot say how much; we may take it as an emblem of the change that followed it. (Kenner 1971, 29)

Just as 'a pin, a cup, which you can handle like a safety pin tends to resist being archaized', so Morris resisted any 'physical evidence' which might necessitate a change in his ideological position. He also resisted the influence of Aestheticism.

Morris' disregard, indeed even revulsion, for the aesthetes and decadents who emerged during the *fin-de-siècle* was most forcefully demonstrated in his feelings for Aubrey Beardsley. A row erupted between the two men 'when Morris peremptorily refused his [Beardsley's] frontispiece for *Sidonia the Sorceress*', William Meinhold's popular gothic romance.[9] The novel, sensationally subtitled *The Supposed Destroyer of the Whole Reigning Ducal House of Pomerania*, was translated by Francesca Speranza, Lady Wilde from the German and published by the Kelmscott Press on 1 November, 1893.[10] William S. Peterson, in *The Kelmscott Press: a History of William Morris's Typographical Adventure*, describes how Beardsley's desire to revenge this affront ironically inspired some of his best work and launched his career as an illustrator: '... Beardsley saw Dent's edition of *Le Morte D'Arthur* (1893–94) as a wonderful opportunity to achieve revenge by parodying the Morris–Burne-Jones conventions and modifying them in a sensual, decadent fashion' (Peterson 1991, 283). Beardsley himself addressed the matter and ridiculed what he called the 'Burne-Jones and Morrisian mediaeval business' in a letter to a friend (Calloway 1998, 199):

William Morris has sworn a terrible oath against me for daring to bring out a book in his manner. The truth is, that while his work is a mere imitation of the old stuff, mine is fresh and original. (Calloway 1998, 63)

What Beardsley viewed as a 'fresh and original' approach to Morris' sacred texts, however, Morris believed to be cynical in the extreme.[11] It was the 'knowingness' of decadents like Beardsley and Wilde that troubled him more than anything else; their self-conscious world-weariness posed a challenge to Morris' idealism.

If the *Morte d'Arthur* was instrumental in the formation of Morris' and Burne-Jones' neo-mediaeval ideal, then it could be said that *Sidonia the Sorceress* was a major influence on the more 'gothic-as-grotesque' aspects of Pre-Raphaelitism (Marsh 1985, 124).[12] Ruskin, in *Modern Painters*, asserts that 'the Grotesque [is] divided principally into three kinds':

(a) art arising from healthful but irrational play of the imagination in times of rest

(b) art arising from irregular and accidental contemplation of terrible things; or evil in general

(c) art arising from the confusion of the imagination by the presence of truths which it cannot wholly grasp. (Ruskin 1904, V 130)

In the case of Meinhold's Gothic romance, there were many 'terrible things' to contemplate and Burne-Jones was particularly influenced by them. It all started out, however, as a 'healthful but irrational play of the imagination in times of rest'. This is clear from Fiona MacCarthy's account of what passed as entertainment in the shared London rooms of Burne-Jones and Morris during their bachelor days in London (1856–1859):

...[there was a] rather juvenile cult of spookiness in Red Lion Square where Burne-Jones had a whole repertoire of Gothick horror stories, pulled together from Old French and Gothic sources, tales of white ladies, red knights, black monks and screech owls. (MacCarthy 1994, 124)

MacCarthy also notes here that at some point during these gothic evenings Burne-Jones would murmur: 'He who tells that story often goes mad in the telling of it, and he who hears it *always does*'.[13]

There is certainly enough general 'spookiness' in *Sidonia the Sorceress* to make an impressionable reader go mad. Sidonia, of high birth and unnatural beauty, whose 'eyes glistened like a cat's when she sees a mouse', is the quintessential *femme fatal*. We are told, for example, in a grisly catalogue of gothic events chronicled by the Duchess, a minor character in the novel, that:

Nothing but evil had she brought with her since first she set foot in the castle: she had caused ... sickness; *item*, the death of two young knights by drowning; *item*, the terrible execution of Joachim Budde, who was beheaded at the festival; and had she not, in addition, whipped ... dear little Casimir, which unseemly act had only lately come to her knowledge? And had she not also made every man in the castle that approached her mad for love of her, all by her diabolical conduct? 'No – away with the wretch: she merits her chastisement a thousand and a thousand-fold!' and old Ulrich exclaimed likewise, 'Away with the wretch and her paramour!' (Meinhold 1894, I 168–9)

Meinhold frequently contrasts the behaviour of the 'diabolical' and idle Sidonia to that of the ideal woman, one who is silent, obedient and possessed of some utilitarian value. A local Burgomaster, in a vain attempt to reform the sorceress, chastises her with the help of proverb xxxi:

'A virtuous woman takes wool and flax, and labours diligently with her hands. She stretches out her hand to the wheel, and her fingers grasp the spindle'. Hadst thou learned this, in place of thy costly broidery, me-thinks it would have been better with thee this day. (Meinhold 1894, I 203)

Of course, the reprimand falls on deaf (as well as diabolical) ears and Sidonia continues her reign of terror until, in old age, she is finally captured and executed as a witch. Thus, the ultimate moral of *Sidonia the Sorceress* would appear to be: 'As moths from a garment, so from a woman wickedness' (Meinhold 1894, I 220).

Meinhold stresses throughout his novel that Sidonia caused most men who saw her to suffer 'delerium amatorium' (Meinhold/Wilde 1894, I 211). Burne-Jones appears to have been another of the sorceress' impressionable victims: Jan Marsh claims, for example, that '... the witch-heroine of Meinhold's Gothic romance ... Ned found so wonderful that he never released himself from the spell it cast over his youth'. (Marsh 1985, 186) Indeed, one of Burne-Jones' most provocative paintings (*Sidonia von Bork*, now in the Tate Gallery, see Figure 5.2) is of the 'witch-heroine':

Fanny [Cornforth] was the model for the sorceress Sidonia while Georgie [Burne-Jones], significantly, sat for the picture of her virtuous counterpart and cousin, *Clara von Bork* ... painted at the same time, the images forming a pair of small icons to Ned's two most potent images of woman. Unlike the scheming, seductive Sidonia whose hair and dress are covered with a tangled, symbolic net, Clara is shown as

5.2   Edward Burne-Jones' painting, *Sidonia von Bork*, Sidonia modelled by
Fanny Cornforth.

open, trusting and protective. In her hands she cradles a nest of fledgling doves, keeping them safe from the black cat, Sidonia's familiar, that prowls at her feet. (Marsh 1985, 187)

The images of Clara and Sidonia are spoken of almost religiously (they form 'a pair of icons'), and are shown, most significantly, to signify Burne-Jones' 'two most potent images of woman'. Of further symbolic value is the fact that Burne-Jones' wife sat for the picture of the 'virtuous counterpart' while Fanny Cornforth, a prostitute and long-term mistress of Rossetti's, was chosen as the model for the 'scheming, seductive' Sidonia. This dual representation of woman runs throughout the work of the Pre-Raphaelites and, like their treatment of Gothic images, juxtaposes the ideal with the grotesque.

This juxtaposition is crucial, as it can be argued that it forms the subtext of many paintings and poems produced by the Pre-Raphaelite Brotherhood. This is especially true if the veiled, autobiographical elements of their art are considered. It is a well-known fact, for instance, that Morris initially idealized his wife. She was associated in his mind with the damsels of the *Morte d'Arthur*: 'It was a small step to acting out its legends and it was perhaps inevitable that Morris should fall in love with Janey' (Marsh 1985, 125). For Morris, however, the ideal turned grotesque when Jane embarked upon a very public affair with Rossetti (Weintraub 1977, 159).[14] Stanley Weintraub gives a succinct reading of the situation:

His [Morris'] bluff manic ways could not compete with a mystic rapport of souls, and he wrote bitterly of his frustration, giving the lines to a woman rejecting the poet, despite his kindness and 'hungry eyes', her heart 'grown silent of its grief',

> 'Yea gone, yet not my fauly. I knew of love,
> But my love and not his; nor could I tell
> That such blind passion in him I should move.
> Behold, I have loved faithfully and well!'

(Weintraub 1977, 160)

The chivalric attention *both* men began to lavish on Jane was even documented by Burne-Jones in two humorous sketches, well-known at the time, and published in a contemporary newspaper.

Rossetti's relationship with the other woman in his life, his wife Lizzie Siddal, was also fraught. When she died in 1862 and he notoriously decided, six years later, to exhume her body to retrieve a collection of unpublished poems, things turned truly gothic. If it is true, as Florence Saunders Boos claims in *The Poetry of Dante G. Rossetti: a Critical Reading and Source Study*, that 'Rossetti was concerned equally with the beloved and with the annihilation of identity, with Love and with Death', then these concerns became even more pressing in his poetry and painting after the death of Lizzie Siddal and the eventual exhumation of her body (Boos 1976, 254). These events also contributed to what Michael Wheeler defines as Rossetti's 'obsessive interest in the idealized female form which signifies the transforming, or perhaps transfiguring power of eroticism which issues in death' (Wheeler 1994, 154). It is significant to note here that Rossetti's work, like that of Burne-Jones, was influenced by *Sidonia the Sorceress* and the 'witch-heroine' of Meinhold's novel was, in fact, the inspiration for his poem 'The Card Dealer', a poem that perfectly illustrates this 'obsessive interest'. Boos outlines the history of the poem, and some of the reasons behind Rossetti's fascination with its source, as follows:

> William Rossetti lists 'The Card Dealer' as written in 1849, appear-ing in an early form in the *Athenaeum* of October, 1852, and pub-lished in final form in 1870. Its inspiration was a painting by von Holst of a female figure dealing out cards; the vaguely evil but beautiful single female figure who personifies fatality is almost a Rossettian icon.
>
> Among other precedents 'The Card Dealer' resembles the descrip-tions of the portrait and appearances of Sidonia in Meinhold's *Sidonia the Sorceress*, a work which Rossetti considered one of the greatest he had read. Doubtless Rossetti was attracted not only by the description of the wicked Sidonia's beauty, but by the emphasis on her portrait. Throughout *Sidonia* descriptions of her in various costumes constitute virtual set-pieces, always emphasizing her hair, jewels, and cruelty. There are other works Rossetti admired chiefly for their treatment of the evil, beautiful woman, among them Charles Wells' *Joseph and his Brethren*, which he frequently praised; in a later reprinting with an introduction by Watts-Dunton, Watts-Dunton describes his conversa-tions with Rossetti concerning the play, and they seem chiefly to have concerned the figure of Potiphar's wife, a type of portrayal, that of the sexually aggressive woman, often suppressed in Victorian literature. (Boos 1976, 200–1)

As in relation to Burne-Jones, we again see Sidonia being regarded as an 'icon' of male fantasy. Harold L. Weatherby, in his essay 'Problems of Form and Content in the Poetry of Dante Gabriel Rossetti,' fittingly reads her as one of a legion of female death symbols in Rossetti's work and concludes that this gothic symbol:

> rises to full view in a poem like 'The Card Dealer' in which Rossetti's propensity for juxtaposing realistic detail with supernatural machinery works to good advantage. The atmosphere of a gaming house lends itself quite well to this vision of death whose 'eyes unravel the coiled night / And know the stars at noon,' but the success of the poem does not depend so much upon the technique of correlating realistic with supernatural detail as upon the fact that the reality of death and hence the validity of Rossetti's symbol, is assumed from the outset – just as the heavenly redemptive reality of Dante's Beatrice is assumed. Rossetti believed in the horror which the card dealer symbolizes; the blessed damozel and her heaven are artifice. (Weatherby 1992, 74)

Weatherby also hypothesizes, in a reading that returns us to the issue of Pre-Raphaelite mediaevalism, that Rossetti 'is far more at home with a mysteriously voluptuous woman ... [even if] he was not sure enough about the realities of medieval hierarchies to write convincingly of a Christian heaven' (Riede 1992, 73).

Stanza five of 'The Card Dealer' opens with a question which is then answered by the poet in a variety of ways:

> Whom plays she with? With thee, who lov'st
>   Those gems upon her hand;
> With me, who search her secret brows;
>   With all men, bless'd or banned.
> We play together, she and we,
>   Within a vain strange land:

The following stanza continues:

> A land without any order, –
>   Day even as night, (one saith,) –
> Where who lieth down ariseth not
>   Nor the sleeper awakeneth;
> A land of darkness as darkness itself
>   And of the shadow of death
>
> (Rossetti 1968, 96).

It is incontestable that the Pre-Raphaelites pursued a 'dream of order' (see Chandler above) through their idealized vision of the Middle Ages. Yet, as the life and works of William Morris and Dante Gabriel Rossetti in particular demonstrate, this vision had its nightmarish, grotesquely gothic side. As a result, the members of the self-styled Pre-Raphaelite Brotherhood often found themselves contemplating chaos in a symbolic 'land without any order'.

Notes

1. Henderson elaborates: '... he read *Tracts for the Times*, medieval chronicles, Neale's *History of the English Church*, Milman's *Latin Christianity*, and ... Kenelm Digby's *Mores Catholici*. ... For Morris and Burne-Jones at Oxford, Ruskin's *Modern Painters* was a sacred text. Next to Ruskin in their estimation stood the Carlyle of *Past and Present*, with its angry confrontation of the twelfth and the nineteenth centuries'.
2. Waters explains that this phrase was originally used of Morris' novel *News from Nowhere*: 'One of his [Morris'] critics has claimed that Morris's novel is merely a "recreation of a dead past according to a romantically falsified memory"'.
3. A phrase used by Andrea Roe in her preface to the relatively recent edition of *The Germ: the Literary Magazine of the Pre-Raphaelites* (1992, vi).
4. The best source to consult here is *Malory: Works*, ed. Eugène Vinaver *et al.* (1981).
5. All quotation from William Morris' translation of *Beowulf* is from volume X of *The Collected Works of William Morris, with Introductions by his Daughter May Morris* (1960). Any citation of *Beowulf* in the original is from F.R. Klaeber's edition (1922, rpt. 1950).
6. Morris' *Beowulf* is also characterized by archaic speech. The following are typical examples of the type of vocabulary used throughout the translation: bewounden (OE *bewunden*, 2424[b]); a-drinking (OE *druncon*, 1648[b], etc.); a-ganging (OE *gongan*, 1642[a]); hearkan (OE *hyran*, 10[b]); belocked (OE *locene/gelocen*, 1890[a], 2769[a]); beworthy (OE *weorpode*, 2716[b]).
7. In the introduction to this volume, May Morris praises what she believes to be her father's ability to re-create the atmosphere of an authentic 'romantic chronicle' in *The Earthly Paradise* (xviii).
8. As William S. Peterson explains in *The Kelmscott Press: a History of William Morris' Typographical Adventure*: 'We may perhaps wish to protest that Pugin, Carlyle, Ruskin, Morris and other of their outlook ignored the material benefits of our mechanized civilization; yet we fail to do them justice unless we recognize that the Gothic Revival was not ultimately an attempt to resuscitate a period style of architecture or art but rather a morally powerful protest against the psychological and social disintegration produced by the modern world.

   The K[elmscott] P[ress] was, in effect, the final phase of the Gothic Revival. Burne-Jones compared the Kelmscott *Chaucer* (1896) to a cathedral;

by the same analogy, the smaller books can be regarded as parish churches, each faithfully rendered in quasi-medieval style' (1991, 5).

9. Peterson also provides information regarding the original publication of the Kelmscott Press' edition of *Sidonia the Sorceress*: '*Sidonia the Sorceress* by William Meinhold. Translated by Francesca Speranza, Lady Wilde. Large 4°: Flower (2) paper. 472 pages. Golden type. Black and red ink. Limp vellum binding with silk ties. 300 paper, 10 vellum copies. Colophon dated 15 September 1893. Published by the KP, 1 November 1893, at 4 guineas (paper) and 20 guineas (vellum)' (318).

   All quotation from *Sidonia* is taken from the 1894 edition.

10. Peterson provides a facsimile of the 'Kelmscott Press's first advertising circular, issued in May 1892, with corrections and additions in Morris's hand'. It is comprised primarily of texts informed by Morris' mediaevalism and/or his fondness for the gothic. Included along with *Sidonia the Sorceress* are *The Story of the Glittering Plain; Poems by the Way;* John Ruskin's *Of the Nature of Gothic;* Wilfrid Blunt's *Love-Lyrics & Songs of Proteus & other Poems;* William Caxton's translation of *The Golden Legend; The Defence of Guenevere & other Poems;* Caxton's translation of *The Recuyell of the Histories of Troye; A Dream of John Ball;* and *Sigurd the Volsung.* Peterson adds that 'The *Chaucer,* in a deleted passage, is described as being "in preparation", though it was not to be published until 1896' (1991, 192).

11. MacCarthy relates the following story regarding Morris' 'sacred texts': 'When *The Pall Mall Gazette,* in a Victorian equivalent of *Desert Island Discs,* asked Morris to provide a list of his 100 essential works of literature he included Homer in the uppermost category: 'the kind of book which Mazzini called "Bibles"; they cannot always be measured by a literary standard, but to me are far more important than any literature'. These were books that were in no sense the work of individuals but had 'grown up from the very hearts of the *people*'. With Homer, Morris listed the English Bible; Hesiod; the *Edda; Beowulf;* the Kalevala, Shah-named and *Mahabharata;* collections of folktales, headed by Grimm and the Norse legends; and Irish and Welsh traditional poems' (1994, 562).

12. Marsh cites both Malory's and Meinhold's texts as major influences on Morris and Burne-Jones: 'While students at Oxford, Ned and Topsy discovered and devoured books like Kenelm Digby's *The Broadstone of Honour,* La Motte Fouquè's *Sintram,* Wilhelm Meinhold's *Sidonia von Bork* and Malory's *Morte d'Arthur,* then only recently reissued' (1985, 124).

13. In a review in *The New York Times* of an exhibition of Burne-Jones' work at the Metropolitan Museum of Art called 'Edward Burne-Jones: Victorian Artist-Dreamer', Roberta Smith recounts the gothic moments in the artist's actual life: 'Burne-Jones, like Morris, had loved the Middle Ages since childhood, attracted through poetry and Walter Scott's novels, to its legends, romances and fairy tales. These stories provided escape from a life that was itself a bit gothic: Burne-Jones's mother died within a week of his birth, and his father mourned for years, taking his son on frequent visits to her grave. No wonder love, both lost and found, would be one of the artist's consuming themes, or that his becalmed knights and ladies convey intense if elusive states that include contemplation, grief, reverie and, often, sleep' (June 5, 1998: B32).

14. Stanley Weintraub writes of the very public nature of the affair between Rossetti and Jane Morris: 'Bell Scott ... reported to Alice Boyd that Gabriel's being so fond of Mrs. Top 'was common gossip', and that Gabriel 'understands they are being watched'. Yet with that understanding came little concealment of his ardor'. In light of my essay's concentration on the notion of duality, it is also interesting to note that Weintraub speaks here of Jane's 'dual role as Morris' dutiful wife and Dante Gabriel Rossetti's inamorata and inspiration' (1977, 159).

6
Mary Elizabeth Coleridge, Literary Influence and Technologies of the Uncanny

Alison Chapman

Wanderers, ghosts, and outcasts people the poetry of Mary Elizabeth Coleridge. Contemporary readers such as Sandra Gilbert and Susan Gubar take the dispossessed to be symbolic of her perceived exclusion from the literary heritage of her great-great uncle, Samuel Taylor Coleridge, to whom she is in thrall (Gilbert and Gubar 1979, 15–16).[1] Katherine McGowran takes this further:

> While the 'restless wanderer' may prove a figure of disruption, Coleridge somehow always remains outside, or under the rule of someone else. The great-great uncle is both someone who leads her in the direction of this 'other' world yet also someone who has been there before. He is the host and she is the guest, her identity is confused by the sense of being a visitor in someone else's poem. (McGowran, ed. Leighton 1996, 190)

In this Bloomian reading, Mary Elizabeth Coleridge is doomed to be the weak poet who is 'haunted by the witches and demons of Samuel Taylor's texts' (McGowran 1996, 186). Although her wanderer figures are often read as disrupting the relationship with the dominant precursor poet, the critic slips back into essentializing the dynamic as a monolith: Mary Elizabeth Coleridge is always the outsider, the slave to the master-male poet. But what happens when we reconceive nineteenth-century literary influence as something rather different from the static host-guest model that determines such readings? Indeed, the nineteenth-century discourse of literary influence adopts the evolving paradigms of psychic influence associated with what I term 'technologies of the uncanny' such as telegraphy, electric light, phonograph, radio, the telephone, and, primarily, photography. Such technologies were seen to disrupt and confuse the relationship between a whole range of binary terms: subject/other, viewer/viewed, nature/culture, time/space, inside/outside. Barbara Johnson reminds us that figuring the host/guest model parasitically involves a mutual contamination (Johnson 1980, x–xi). Influence, in other words, works both ways. For Mary Elizabeth Coleridge, this means traversing history and haunting the poetry of her precursor.

That most gothic of psychic effects, the uncanny, shadows her flirtation with chronological time. Both belated and prior, her wandering figures mimic and reverse the traditional relationship between poet and precursor. This straying from the chronological path of literary history has structured the argument of this essay. I begin by sketching Coleridge in the thrall of her male mentors and suggest that her sense of exclusion from the Coleridge poetic lineage liberates her as a subversive wanderer, a type, indeed, of wandering signifier. The essay then spirals out to explain the effect of photography upon the discourse of literary and psychic influence, which posits influence as slippery and dynamic. The photography of Clementina, Lady Hawarden, is turned to in order to elucidate how the camera newly configures of subjectivity. Finally, I turn to Mary Elizabeth Coleridge's poetry, which turns the master/slave binary of poets and precursors into spectrality *par excellence*.

Under the influence

The wanderers in Mary Coleridge's poetry seem adamant that they are forced to be outsiders. The speaker of the poem 'Wanderers' asserts: 'Accuse us not of wandering at our will! / Life's clearest voice it is that bids us roam' (Coleridge 1954, 118). Another of her dispossessed claims to be 'upon no road at all', and to 'wander where men's voices call' (Sichel 1910, 282). Henry Newbolt describes her mind to be 'as sudden and as changeful as the flight of a moth by lantern-light' (Newbolt 1942, 97). Her talk has a certain 'waywardness' (Newbolt 1942, 94) and she is easily susceptible to powerful personalities: 'she was a natural unaffected hero-worshipper and her father's house provided her with glimpses of many heroes – poets, painters, musicians and men of action' (1942, 95). *Gathered Leaves* concurs: 'it was dangerous to bring her within earshot of an egoist, for egoists always captivated her'. This becomes for Sichel a pathological trait: 'the more they made use of her, the more fascinating she thought them. It was partly because she was selfless and enjoyed devotion to others. But it was also because she worshipped vitality and a strong consciousness, the forces she longed for and missed in herself' (1942, 30). In fact, she is represented as inherently open to and passively receiving any influence which comes her way: 'she was a lyre over whose responsive strings every emotion swept, making music' (1942, 31). Implicitly, that music is poetry. Sichel briefly but suggestively translates this into literary influence: 'she was fond ... of powerful or strange effects in literature' (1942, 33).

Although Samuel Taylor Coleridge is the most significant literary influence upon his great-great niece, she was also in the thrall of three other men. William Cory, who left his post at Eton when charged with improper attentions to a schoolboy, tutored Mary and her close circle of female friends, his 'Grecian ladies', in the Classics (Coleridge 1954, 37). She was, in the words of Whistler, a 'disciple' of her teachers and Cory was no exception (35). Sichel, in *Gathered Leaves*, calls Cory 'a great influence' (1910, 5). Coleridge transcribed Cory's 'table talk' during her weekly tutorials, which Sichel publishes in her memoir. This was perhaps not so much a labour of love than a regular exorcism of his influence over her. She writes to Violet Hodgkin on 26 November 1894: 'When Mr Cory died, there came, along with the sense that "there had passed away a glory from the earth", another sense that I was free – that I should never fear anyone again in just that way' (Coleridge 1954, 64). Yet, after death, he nevertheless maintains his grip on her, as she herself admits: 'it is curious, how often I find myself referring and deferring to what I fancy his judgement would have been about some book. And how unsafe to speculate! For one could never tell' (Sichel 1910, 240–1).

Henry Newbolt was another strong male figure who was part of her weekly reading group. He married her close friend Margaret Duckworth in 1889 and went on to correspond frequently with Coleridge when they were apart, to advise her in literary matters and, after her death, to edit her poetry in a volume that guaranteed her posthumous poetic existence. The third figure is Robert Bridges who, in an encounter manufactured by a mutual friend, came across a manuscript book of her poems and cajoled and soothed her way towards the private printing of her first volume of poetry. He also did not hesitate to revise and 'correct' her writing. Whistler's account of their friendship notes that Coleridge was not afraid to 'breezily parry' Bridges' persuasions but also gave him 'homage': 'for Mary he represented the great literary world where her great-great-uncle's shade belonged, and to which she never aspired' (62).

To figure a Victorian woman poet as unambitious, as innately passive, as a receiver rather than creator, is not that unusual. Indeed, the Victorian ideology of female creativity dictates that women could only write what they know, and what they know is restricted to the private sphere of emotions and feelings. For Mary Elizabeth Coleridge, this paradigm of the woman poet is taken to its farthest extreme. Samuel Taylor Coleridge's trope of the creative imagination's relation with outside influences as one of continuous mutuality becomes a static one-way process. Mary Elizabeth Coleridge is depicted as the receptacle who is filled by the influence of other men, a radio who picks up and transmits the signals of others. Although this would seem to result in the ultimate feminine poetry as automatic writing, one of her most influential male friend declares her susceptibility to be inherently flawed. Robert Bridges figures her mind as a wanderer *par excellence* and that this distinctive trait impeded her writing:

> I supposed that she did not recognise the artistic limits of imagination; but I am sure that it was the number and activity of her thoughts that embarrassed her, any one of them seeming to lead anywhere, offering, therefore, a delusive promise of return; and it was in this that her chief difficulty of composition lay. (Bridges 1931 v.6, 224)[2]

Bridges repeats the familiar depiction of her imagination as consciously 'inconsequent' and, although she is good at starting prose fiction she can never see the writing to its end:

> 'Anyone can begin' she writes, in happy disregard of the proverbial difficulty of beginning. She once sent me the beginnings of three separate stories, asking me what could be done with them. Two of them were magically interesting. After puzzling over the problem I was constrained to say that nothing more could be made of them; she had written up to an *impasse*; continuation was impossible, and indeed she found it. (Bridges 1931 v.6, 224–5)

Newbolt tells how writing collaboratively was a game for a reading group they belonged to, affectionately nicknamed 'The Settee', and that Mary Elizabeth Coleridge was 'impossibly brilliant and mysterious' at the beginning, so much so that the project was eventually abandoned 'after following her in the dark for three weeks in succession' (Newbolt 1932, 179). Stephenson was also impressed with her beginnings. After starting her novel *Seven Sleepers of Ephesus*, he comments: 'I confess I am quite in a taking as to how she is going to get out of the muddle. If she does get out, she is devilish ingenious' (Newbolt 1932, 180). Coleridge writes to Newbolt narrating her confession to Bridges that she 'always liked beginning a thing, but never knew what the ends of my beginnings were, and had all the trouble in the world to go on'. Bridges challenges her to begin a story that he cannot continue. She offers him 'three first chapters of nothing ... he was most delighted about them, although he said that he couldn't see "any direction" in them' (Newbolt 1942, 100).

Coleridge's own manipulation of her wandering waywardness, exemplified by her brazen beginnings, is apparent in her choice of pseudonym for her two volumes of poetry, for she had a 'fear of tarnishing the name which an ancestor had made illustrious in English poetry' (Newbolt Preface, Coleridge 1908, v). Her surname was to be assigned to her poems only after her death. The prose did not suffer such a fate. One critic has termed her 'the tail end of the comet S.T.C' (Sichel 1910, 11). Coleridge herself was aware of a sense of exclusion from her poetic lineage: 'I have no fairy god-mother, but lay claim to a fairy great-great-uncle, which is perhaps the reason that I am condemned to wander restlessly around the Gates of Fairyland, although I have never yet passed them' (11). In her diary, she unveils her pseudonym: 'I will christen myself over again, make George Macdonald my godfather, and name myself after my favourite hero, Anodos in *Phantastes*' (24). Anodos, the Greek for 'wanderer' or, more precisely, 'upon no road', is the means by which she escapes what Bridges calls the *'impass'* of her prose and haunts her precursor.

Technologies of the uncanny

> My dear Miss Mitford, do you know anything about that wonderful invention of the day, called the Daguerreotype? – that is, have you seen any portraits produced by means of it? Think of a man sitting down in the sun and leaving his facsimile in all its full completion of outline and shadow, steadfast on a plate, at the end of a minute and a half! the mesmeric disembodiment of spirits strikes one as a degree less marvellous. (Barrett cited in Heron and Williams, eds, 1996, 2)

Recent photographic theory has tended to fix its attention on the veracity of the photographic signifier and on the complex relation of photography to the real. Although the debate has usefully problematized the realism of the medium, it has also left behind something of the awe, wonder and magic of photography's early reception. Barrett marvels at the predecessor to photography, the daguerreotype, which for her uncannily weaves the material world with the occult. Although a man can leave his 'facsimile' on the plate, this is no straightforward imprint of the real, for the fixation of what she calls 'the *very shadow of the person*' is to Barrett Browning a mysterious process, as marvellous as mesmerism. Indeed, early photography was often seen not just as analogous to mesmerism but one and the same operation. The lengthy time and stillness required of the photographic sitter (much longer than the early daguerreotype's minute and a half) may no doubt be conducive to trance. Nathaniel Hawthorne, in *The House of the Seven Gables* (1851), has a male protagonist who is at once a mesmerist, a daguerreotypist, and a writer, associating psychic influence with the visual and with the act of writing (Hawthorne 1986).[3]

Rosalind Krauss turns to the portraitist Gaspard-Félix Tournachon (1820–1910), known as Nadar, to caution against the vulgarization of photography affecting our approach to nineteenth-century visual technology. In his memoir, *My Life as a Photographer* (1900), Nadar argues that photography is the most marvellous invention of the century, for it: 'seems finally to endow man himself with the divine power of creation: the power to give physical form to the insubstantial image that vanishes as soon as it is perceived, leaving no shadow in the mirror, no ripple on the surface of the water' (Krauss in Heron and Williams, eds, 1996, 38). This capturing of the transient depends, for Nadar, upon the intimacy of the event of the photograph. Krauss comments that: 'no matter how any other system of information transfer might work, photography depends on an act of passage between two bodies in the same place' (40–1). She takes this further: photography is predicated upon a collapse of space that allows the act of passage to take place: 'the photographic print, because it is itself a mirror, is thus the only place where an absolute simultaneity of subject and object – a doubling that involves a spatial collapse – can occur' (48). The intimate transaction between photographer and photographic subject is conceptualized by Carol Mavor as a unique dynamic between two subjects, a performance that also involves the viewer of the photographic print (see Mavor 1996).[4] The transaction, for both Mavor and Krauss, is a psychological one: indeed, one of the 'fathers' of photography, Fox Talbot, speculates that the photographic trace can transmit thought and psychological processes (Mavor 1996, 46).

That the interactive relationship between subject and object is bound up with the early desire to photograph is illustrated by Geoffrey Batchen's brilliant study (Batchen 1997). Batchen associates this desire with Foucault's contentious thesis that Western epistemology radically shifted around 1800 and at key moments turns to Samuel Taylor Coleridge as illustration. Batchen argues out that Samuel Taylor Coleridge's friendship with the proto-photographers Humphry Davy and Tom Wedgewood would make it likely that he was involved in their experiments. In fact, Batchen finds Coleridge's conception of nature and visibility to be part of the epistemological shift that also encompasses the desire to photograph:

> Coleridge's early writings are exemplary of a more general shift from an eighteenth-century to a modern view of nature. At the very time that photography was being conceived, nature had become irrevocably tied to human subjectivity; its representation was no longer an act of passive and adoring contemplation but an active and constitutive mode of (self-) consciousness. Nature and culture were inter-constitutive identities. (1997, 62)

In 1817, Coleridge adopts the figure of the camera to describe his poetic ideal: 'creation rather than painting, or if painting, yet such, and with such co-presence of the picture flashed at once upon the eye, as the sun paints in a camera obscura' (cited in Batchen 1997, 84). As with his trope of the mirror, the camera figure connotes an active mind, where the eye engages and interacts with the picture: a 'co-presence' of two subjects, each dependent upon the other.[5] For Batchen, this is an inherently uncanny and provisional process which blurs the distinction between subjects and between binary terms; it is an 'economy of hesitations' which produces 'a newly embodied subject, which in its formation as *doublet* entailed both photographer and photographed, without remaining completely faithful to either' (1997, 101). The binary terms are situated 'as a *differential economy of relations* which is continually divided against itself' (1997, 177). The instant of the Coleridge's flashing upon the eye which produces such an economy might be termed a *photographic moment*, whereby the dynamic and disruptive relationship between two binaries (viewer/viewed, subject/object) is both performed and recorded, a sign and a signifier, at once 'both the subject and object of its own recording'.[6] As such, the photographic moment stages its own haunting; as Batchen comments: 'photography ... is a logic that continually returns to haunt itself. It is its own "medium"' (1997, 216). Coleridge's poetics capture this instant of perception; his great-great niece motivates poetry as her medium, in all senses of the word, to inscribe the photographic moment.

'There was no place for me'[7]

From 1859 to 1864, Clementina, Lady Hawarden, took a series of photographs in rooms on the first floor of her newly built house in 5 Princes Gardens, Kensington. Her title-less plates enigmatically pose her daughters in a sparsely furnished room with large, well-illuminated windows looking out to a balcony and, beyond, to Princes Gardens. All her figures are contained and constricted within the room, whose lack of furniture and adornments emphasize the boundaries of the room, the window, wall and corners. Along with the constriction of the tightly defined space, however, there are uncanny thresholds which suggest a blurring of the limits of the room and of the identity of the sitters. These photographs are the product of, and visually represent, the hesitation of the photographic moment.

The plates employ a variety of devices and props to render the boundaries uncertain and tentative: windows and window ledges, diaphanous net drapes, light and shadow, tables and mirrors, all both define and put into question the space of the room and the containment of the sitters. In Figure 6.1, the figure is caught in the act of stepping into the threshold of the room from the balcony, through the open window.

The contrast between her heavy walking skirts and flimsy top, more appropriate to the indoors, repeat the uncertainty between inside and out. The dark shadows cast diagonally across the floor of the room by the wall between the windows depicts another series of thresholds within the room which the figure must cross to step inside. Although she is illuminated from behind by the strong sunlight, her face is half in shadow and the bare skin of her left cheek, shoulder and arm rendered indistinct by the light, in contrast to the clearly focused chair to her right, the only furniture in the room. Light here does not in itself illuminate; rather, it only makes visible by difference from the shadows. This is repeated with the wall, which are papered with a dark star pattern which serves to emphasize the luminosity of the background white and, indeed, the presence of the wall itself.

6.1 Clementina, Lady Hawarden's photograph of her daughter Clementina in fancy dress in the window of the newly built house at 5 Princes Gardens, Kensington. (Victoria & Albert Picture Library)

In other photographs the trope of the mirror ironically repeats the representational function of the camera. Figure 6.2 centrally positions a woman, who is brushing her hair in a mirror, with her back turned to the photographer.

6.2   Lady Hawarden's photograph of Isabella Grace brushing her hair. (Victoria & Albert Picture Library)

Although the scene is set for a moment of revelation, for the windows to the left are theatrically parted with white net curtains, her reflection is entirely obscured. Indeed, the sitter is both actress and audience. In addition, the photographer, positioned at right angles to the window, further complicates the distinction between viewed and viewer, subject and object. And yet, to stress her liminality, the figure is turned away from both window and camera. Both her reflection and her very figure are withheld.

Julie Lawson notes the disconcerting ambiguity of the function of the room, which sets the scene for the uncanny figure: 'half salon and half studio, it never provides an environment that is entirely at one with the occupants'. The manipulation of the light from the window contributes to the uncertainty about the identity and boundary of the space. Lawson terms the room suggestively a 'light box' which 'allows the light to suffuse and dissolve form rather than to disclose it' (Lawson 1997, 19, 7).[8] The room that functions as Hawarden's studio both makes uncertain the difference between viewer and viewed and entirely collapses the space between them.

In an exhilarating move, this dynamic of dissolution, what Batchen terms an 'economy of hesitation', is performed in Figure 6.3.

The sitter now turns to face the photographer and to display the contents of the mirror. What we see, however, is less than distinct. As

6.3 Lady Hawarden's sitter turned to face the camera. (Victoria & Albert Picture Library)

Lawson comments: 'the sitter who acknowledges the camera ... evades us even as she meets our gaze. The light falls upon her white dress but her face is in shadow: she denies us her secret' (13). The mirror image ironically mimics the photograph's representative function. The white of the reflected net window drapes is repeated in the sitter's voluminous white dress, mirroring the function of the window and the sitter (who holds the mirror at the required angle) as agents of the theatrical display. The discarded props on the table also reiterate the undoing of the photographic scene, as do the torn corners of all of Hawarden's photographs, which were removed when taken from family albums. This plate both performs and records the photographic moment as one which dissolves the space between subject and object and puts radically into question the difference between photographer and photographed. Further, the mirror repeats the self-haunting of the photographic plate, the undoing of its disjunctive relationship to itself. And, within such photographs, the sitter is a threshold figure, a wanderer in a liminal 'no place'.

From aporia to anodos

While photography collapses spatial relationships, it also makes history problematic. Recent poststructuralist commentators on photography have agreed that it does not have a history *per se*, that the origin and narrative of photography cannot be given unity or chronological coherence (see Tagg 1988). *Burning with Desire* convincingly demonstrates, for example, the impossibility of assigning a fixed origin to both photography and to the desire to photograph. Batchen turns to the image cited by Gernsheim and others as the first photograph, a 1827 heliograph entitled *View from the Window at Le Gras* taken by Nicéphore Niépce. This image, long forgotten and dramatically found by Gernsheim in a trunk in 1952, proved impossible to reproduce photographically. The image that he announces as the first photograph is, ironically, extensively painted over in his *Origins of Photography*, so much so that it does not resemble Niépce's plate. Batchen comments:

> the much touted first photograph turns out to be a representation of a representation and therefore, according to photo-history's own definition, not a photograph at all. ... It seems that wherever we look for photography's bottom line, we find this strange economy of deferral, an origin always preceded by another, more original, but never-quite-present photographic instance. (1997, 127)

Photography not only disrupts its own history, but also the notion of temporality within the photographic image. Its apparent similitude, as Barthes famously eulogizes, has more to do with the arrest of time, and, ultimately, with death. The photographic referent 'has been here, and yet immediately separated; it has been absolutely, irrefutably present, and yet already deferred' (Barthes 1993, 77). The arrest of time disrupts photography's relation with the temporal, and, for Barthes as well as for early photographers such as Talbot, impossibly intertwines them both. Batchen elucidates this point:

> The photograph presumes to capture, as if in a vertical archaeologi-cal slice, a single, transient moment from a linear progressive move-ment made up of a numberless sequence of just such moments. Photography apparently figures itself as a progressive linear move-ment from past to future. The present during which we look at the photographic image is but a staging point, a hallucinatory hovering that imbricates *both* past and future. In this paradoxical play between a synchronic and diachronic notation of time, photo-graphy reiterates what Hayden White has called a peculiarly modern time anxiety. (1997, 93)

The collapse of time and space within photography is contempora-neous, Siegfried Kracauer argues, with historicist thinking which acts as a screen to photography's *memento mori* (Kracauer cited in Batchen 1997, 210). I want to perform photography's juxtaposition of synchrony and diachrony here. There is a historical continuum with Samuel Taylor Coleridge's photographic conception of his poetic ideal, Hawarden's photographic aesthetic taken as exemplary of a certain mid-century technique, and Mary Elizabeth Coleridge's grappling with the legacy of her great-great uncle.[9] If uncle and niece are involved in the binaries that determine literary influence – subject/object, precursor/poet, master/slave – the photography of Hawarden might be said to occupy the no-man's land in between. And yet the poetry of Mary Elizabeth Coleridge also initiates a disruption to chronological time, positioning herself as the ghost that haunts her precursor's poetry, while also, uncannily, acknowl-edging her belatedness.

Gilbert and Gubar, in *Madwomen in the Attic*, take Mary Elizabeth Coleridge's 'The Other Side of a Mirror' (1882) to be indicative of her doomed engagement with her precursor and her problematic desire for literary authority and to be emblematic of all nineteenth-century writers' quest for autonomy. The speaker of this poem magically makes present the mirror reflection of a wild woman:

> I sat before my glass one day,
> And conjured up a vision bare,
> Unlike the aspects glad and gay,
> That erst were found reflected there –
> The vision of a woman, wild
> With more than womanly despair.

Coleridge 1954, 88

In Macdonald's *Phantastes*, the protagonist whose name Coleridge adopts for her pseudonym, Anodos, reads the story of his double, Cosmo, who similarly conjures up an image of a woman through black arts. Cosmo recognizes that the mirror represents the ideal of the creative imagination:

> 'What a strange thing a mirror is! and what a wondrous affinity exists between it and a man's imagination! For this room of mine, as I behold it in the glass, is the same, and yet not the same. It is not the mere representation of the room I live in, but it looks just as if I were reading about it in a story I like'. (Macdonald 1905, 161–2)

This repeats the earlier comments of Anodos on the wonder of reflections: 'all mirrors are magic mirrors. The commonest room is a room in a poem, when I turn to the glass' (123). But the woman that Cosmo conjures up is a beautiful Princess, not the wild despairing woman of Mary Elizabeth Coleridge's poem. In fact, her wild woman, who silently shows her 'unsanctified distress' through the 'hideous wound' of her mouth, is more like Anodos's black, malign shadow which dogs him on his journey around Fairy Land. Anodos is warned by an ogre: '"everybody's shadow is ranging up and down looking for him"' (106). Anodos cannot shake off the shadow and finds that it disrupts the chronological history of his adventures in Fairy Land: '"from this time until I arrived at the palace of Fairy Land, I can attempt no consecutive account of my wanderings and adventures. Everything, henceforward, existed for me in relation to my attendant"' (108). He describes his shadow as an uncanny representation of himself, one which both is him and isn't him: '"shadow of me! ... which art not me, but which representest thyself to me as me"' (134). Similarly, Mary

Elizabeth Coleridge's mirror image is a 'shade of a shadow' which both is and isn't her, performing the photographic moment which renders her image magical, static, spectral, specular, and silent:

> And in her lurid eyes there shone
> The dying flame of life's desire,
> Made mad because its hope was gone,
> And kindled at the leaping fire
> Of jealousy, and fierce revenge,
> And strength that could not change or tire.
>
> Shade of a shadow in the glass,
> O set the crystal surface free!
> Pass – as the fairer visions pass –
> Nor ever more return, to be
> The ghost of a distracted hour,
> That heard me whisper, 'I am she!'

The speaker's shadow or mirror image is a malign influence, one which she fears will continue to haunt her after its passing to remind her of the kinship. Anodos, however, associates losing his shadow with death: 'I have a strange feeling sometimes, that I am a ghost' (318).

The significant point about Mary Elizabeth Coleridge's poem, however, is that it seems to substitute her own 'shade of a shadow' in place of her precursor. In other poems, the speakers haunt themselves. In 'Ghosts' she bids 'gentle ghosts' to return 'from that far distant shore', for 'We would not fear you now the day is done'. However, 'One ghost alone I fear, the ghost of one / That lives – but loves and is beloved no more' (Coleridge 1954, 105). Following rather ironically the Victorian tradition of sentimental poetry, this ghost is her own shade.[10] The majority of her lyrics chronicle self-exile, such as 'Delusion', where the speaker is excluded from the 'splendid city' but had to endure watching others enter: 'The gates are shut. I may not enter. Sadly / I run my race / I know not whither' (Coleridge 1954, 85). Significantly, in her journal she termed Macdonald a 'godfather' in an act in which she both engenders herself and names herself (Sichel, 24). Her poems complain of having no place and no name (Coleridge 1954, 103; Sichel 1910, 282), but in her novel *The Lady on the Drawingroom Floor*, her narrator tellingly declares 'I cannot get on without a name' (Coleridge 1906, 73).[11] Coleridge's adoption of Macdonald's wanderer figure performs two functions: firstly, it re-names her and thus disassociates the poetry from the malign shadow of the Coleridge name and frees her from the chronology of genealogy, and, secondly, it engenders the literary lineage as feminine. Although Macdonald is her 'godfather', Anodos's *wanderlust* comes from his fairy blood on the maternal side. On his coming of age, he is given the key to a secret drawer from which a fairy emerges from the threshold. He is attracted to her, and reaches out to touch. She warns him off:

> 'A man must not fall in love with his grandmother, you know'.
>   'But you are not my grandmother', said I.
>   'How do you know that?' she retorted. 'I dare say you know something of your great-grandfathers a good deal further back than that; but you know very little about your great-grandmothers on either side'. (18)

After she promises to show him the way to Fairy Land, he looks into her eyes on her command: 'they filled me with unknown longing. I remembered somehow that my mother died when I was a baby. I looked deeper and deeper, till they spread around me like seas, and I sank in their waters' (19).

The most direct reference to her precursor is to be found in 'The Witch' (1892), in which Geraldine, the lamia from *Christabel*, is given a voice which articulates her desires:

> I have walked a great while over the snow,
> And I am not tall or strong.
> My clothes are wet, and my teeth are set,
> And the way was hard and long.
> I have wandered a' over the fruitful earth,
> But I never came hither before.
> Oh, lift me over the threshold, and let me in at the door!
>
> The cutting wind is a cruel foe.
> I dare not stand in the blast.
> My hands are stone, and my voice a groan,
> And the worst of death is past.
> I am but a little maiden still,
> My little white feet are sore.
> Oh, lift me over the threshold, and let me in at the door!

Coleridge 1954, 145

In these first two stanzas the witch, a wanderer *par excellence*, attempts to seduce Christabel. As Angela Leighton points out, Mary Elizabeth Coleridge transforms the precursor's text into a love poem.[12] And yet the transformation is even more profound. The witch who desires to cross the threshold is, as a quintessential wanderer, a figure for Anodos and therefore the signature of the poet herself. Crossing the threshold entails entering into the precursor's poem. And that poem, represented by the compliant figure Christabel, duly admits her:

> Her voice was the voice that women have,
> Who plead for their heart's desire.
> She came – she came – and the quivering flame
> Sank and died in the fire.
> It never was lit again on my hearth
> Since I hurried across the floor,
> To lift her over the threshold, and let her in at the door.

Like the sitters in Hawarden's photographs, Geraldine crosses the boundary of the threshold which precipitates the poem's closure and the collapse of space between Geraldine and Christabel. This is because the voice of the two women shift between stanzas two and three without any apostrophes or demarcation. In addition, Geraldine describes herself in similar terms to the Christabel of Samuel Taylor Coleridge's poem: she is 'but a little maiden still'. The suspended and abandoned beginning to the habitation of the precursor's poem does not mark an impasse or *aporia* (unpassable road), as Bridges suggests do all her wayward beginnings, but a crossing of the impasse. If this poem is indeed a love poem, as Leighton argues, it the crossing is another kind of deviation: the secret script of incestuous female desire. It is also a passing of the precursor's block to poetic authority that traverses history as well as space. And, as the inscription of a photographic moment, it performs the process that it records while it stages its own haunting of *Christabel*.

To lose one's shadow – the malign influence of the precursor – and to perform the haunting has a disturbing effect on binary terms in other poems. In 'Winged Words' (1888) the movement of swallows, seen here as a type of wanderer, becomes an allegory for the signification process:

> As darting swallows skim across a pool,
> Whose tranquil depths reflect a tranquil sky,

> So, o'er the depths of silence, dark and cool,
> Our winged words dart playfully,
> And seldom break
> The quiet surface of the lake,
> As they flit by.
>
> (Coleridge 1954, 114)

The mobility of the 'winged words' figures language to be, like the migrating swallow, forever a wanderer. As an allegory of signification (suggested by the logical construct 'as ... so'), the image of the 'darting swallows' suggests that words can traverse the space between the 'tranquil depths' and the 'tranquil sky'. Although both swallows and words don't puncture the mirror surface, they both mark and collapse the space between subject and object, mirror and mirrored. This process approaches what Luce Irigaray terms 'specular': the movement across the androcentric looking-glass to a representation of female specificity, in which the female subject has no other (Irigaray 1984, 114–46).[13] Indeed, here the mirror and its image are one and the same: in the timespan of this poem, the photographic moments in which the swallows 'flit', the difference between subject and other is deferred – so much so that there is no other. Perhaps it is from here that a newly configured subject can emerge. Perhaps the camera, and the poetic optical unconscious of which it is a figure, can function as a speculum.

A playful challenge to Wordsworth is issued in a similar poem which collapses the distinction between mirroring surface and sky. In 'To the Writer of a Poem on a Bridge' (1892), Mary Elizabeth Coleridge again desires a subject with no other:

> Dear builder of the Bridge, with thee I stood
> And watched the waters flow
> And heard thy cry of 'Onward' o'er the flood,
> Between two skies, one over, one above.
>
> Whether it was the outward eye that thought,
> The inward eye that saw,
> I know not; into harmony were brought
> The floating image and abiding law.
>
> (Coleridge 1954, 149)

She here revises Wordsworth's sonnet on 'Upon Westminster Bridge' (1802) to again traverse and collapse time (she imagines herself with the precursor) and space (between the Thames and the sky; inner eye and outer eye).

One other poem represents the traversing of the representing surface, 'L'Oiseau Bleu' (1894):

> The lake lay blue below the hill.
> O'er it, as I looked, there flew
> Across the waters, cold and still,
> A bird whose wings were palest blue.
>
> The sky above was blue at last,
> The sky beneath me blue in blue.
> A moment, ere the bird had passed,
> It caught his image as he flew.
>
> (Coleridge 1954, 163)

In this photographic instant, at which the sky and lake dissolve into one another to become 'blue in blue', as the speaker looks down from her vantage point on the hill. When the bird passes it further disturbs the relationship between reflecting surface and reflected object. At the moment in which the sky turns blue, both the reflected sky and the still lake capture the image of the bird. The bird, then, crosses the mirroring surface and collapses the space and time of the instant. The reflected bird's difference from the lake, sky, and from itself, is deferred in an uncanny moment of hesitation that produces a newly configured subject.

Commentating upon both the history of photography and the photograph event, Batchen offers an interpretation which would put the division between key terms – such as photographer/photographed, subject/other, time/space – endlessly in dispute. He argues that: 'photography is a set of relations that carries within itself the trace of a perennial alterity' (177). Such a set of unruly dualisms does indeed mutually contaminate the dynamics of literary influence operating between Mary Elizabeth Coleridge and her great-great uncle, so that she, on no path, is set free to haunt him just as her witch invades his *Christabel*. And yet, within the space of her poetry, operating as a medium to challenge and inhabit the figure of the precursor, there are instances when the traversing of space and time uncannily dissolves the gap between perceiver and perceived. In this photographic moment, the mirror tropes transform into Irigaray's speculum, banishing the shadow of the precursor and the ghost of the poetic signature, representing Mary Elizabeth Coleridge's transgressive desire to herself: as the speaker in 'The Other Side of a Mirror' concludes, "I am she!"'.

Notes

1. Gilbert and Gubar's argument is closer to mine than McGowran's, however, because they assert the ability of Mary Elizabeth Coleridge to defy authority.
2. I have standardized Bridges' spelling.
3. See also Holland (1978, 1–10). For a discussion of mesmeric influence a trope for literary influence, see Chapman (1998, 303–19).
4. See Carol Mavor (1996).
5. Compare the significant opening line of 'Frost at Midnight': 'The Frost performs its secret ministry'.
6. Krauss on the photographic trace as intelligible in a photograph of Debureau (1996, 49).
7. From Mary Elizabeth Coleridge, '"There was No Place Found"' (Coleridge 1954, 103).
8. For useful background information, see Virginia Dodier (1989).
9. An analogous disruption of space is apparent in the so-called 'soft-focus' photography of Julia Margaret Cameron, the most well-known female Victorian photographer (readers are referred to Chapter 7, Marion Wynne–Davies' essay on Cameron). Mary Elizabeth Coleridge as a child would probably have met Cameron. Arthur Coleridge, Mary's father, was a close friend of Tennyson who frequently visited their house. The Coleridges also visited Tennyson at Farringford (Sichel 1910, 25). Cameron was an enthusiastic member of Tennyson's social circle until October 1875 when she moved with her husband to Ceylon. One of Mary's closest friends, Margaret Duckworth (later Newbolt), was related to the Camerons.
10. For an account of the ideology of sensibility and loss in Victorian women's poetry, see Angela Leighton (1992).
11. This novel has as its theme the influence family names have in the construction of personal identity. See also her novel *The Shadow on the Wall: a Romance* (1904) which is also concerned with the power of influence.
12. Leighton also notes that her poetry offers an 'enigmatic script of desire'. See Leighton and Margaret Reynolds, eds (1995, 612).
13. For a discussion of Irigaray's use of mirrors, see Philippa Berry (1994).

7

The 'Anxious Dream': Julia Margaret Cameron's Gothic Perspective

Marion Wynne-Davies

The 'anxious dream' referred to in the title of this essay is taken from the first stanza of Julia Margaret Cameron's translation of Gottfried August Bürger's *Leonora* in which the eponymous heroine waits for her lover, William, to return from the wars:

> Leonora from an anxious dream
> Starts up at break of day:
> 'My William, art thou false or slain?
> Oh! William, why delay?'
>
> Weaver 1984, 146

The first line of the poem, with its allusion to nightmare, anticipates the horrific narrative which will follow and foreshadows Leonora's own grim fate. Thus, when William fails to return with the other knights, the young woman succumbs to despair and ignores the stoical Christian reasoning offered by her mother,

> 'Be calm, my child, forget thy woe,
> And think of God and heaven;
> God, thy Redeemer, hath to thee
> Himself for bridegroom given.'
>
> 'Oh! mother, mother, what is heaven?
> Oh! mother, what is hell?
> To be with William, that's my heaven;
> Without him, that's my hell.
>
> 'Come death! come death! I loathe my life;

> All hope is in death's gloom.
> My William's gone, what's left on earth?
> Would I were in his tomb!'

(Weaver 1984, 148)

Yet, at sunset, William does return for Leonora and carries her off on his horse to their nuptial bed of 'Six boards and two short planks ... still, cool, and small' (Weaver 1984, 149). While the reader immediately recognizes that William is a ghost and that he intends to take Leonora to the grave with him, she remains stubbornly ignorant of her plight, repeatedly inquiring why he persists in referring to 'the dead', and only realizing her danger when he is revealed to her in his true form:

> Now see! Now see! Where is the night?
> What is this horrid ghastly sight?
> All shivering falls the warrior's steel,
> A skeleton from head to heel!

(Weaver, 1984, 151)

As the grotesque figure of death looms over Leonora the horse vanishes into a yawning pit, the earth 'groans' and ghosts whirl about the prostrate maiden singing,

> 'Endure! endure! though break the heart,
>   Yet judge not God's decree.
> Thy body from thy soul both part,
>   Oh! may God pardon thee!'

(Weaver, 1984, 151)

This translation is one of the few extant literary works by Cameron, who is after all best-known for her photography, but it clearly attests to her interest in gothic traditions and demonstrates her familiarity with the common currency of that genre – nightmares (literal and figurative), ghosts, horror, tombs, perverse love, sex and death.

Cameron's translation of the Bürger poem was published as a handsome volume lavishly illustrated by Danial Maclise; Leonora languishes in various poses throughout the text, while evil demons, snake-like vines and grinning skulls shift and leer about her passive form. Today readers of the poem are often surprised to discover that Julia Cameron did not provide the illustrations herself, but it is important to remember that the translation was published in 1847, at least 16 years before she was given her first camera. Moreover, at first glance it seems unlikely that Cameron would have been capable of such overtly gothic sensibilities. For example, in contrasting her work with Rossetti's Helmut Gernsheim comment that,

> Many of her beautiful women have the strange emotional quality and melancholy expression which we find so often in Rossetti's faces but in contrast to his voluptuous types, Mrs Cameron always chose "nice young girls". (Gernsheim 1948, 57)

But while Cameron eschewed the more grisly props of gothic representation she was perfectly capable of illustrating female characters caught in moments of grim passion or dark despair. Her photographic oeuvre, like her foray into translation, demands a central subject, sometimes male but predominantly female, whose face and pose convey deep emotion, the inner-self or inner-truth, of sitter and circumstance. The images may convey a shadow of conventionality, of properly clothed 'nice young girls', but this aspect of the photographic text is no more than the brief reflection of the original material forms as they were exhibited before the lens. Through the use of light, focus and composition Cameron transformed the authentic replication of photography into the atmospheric vision of art.

The transition enacted in the narrative of *Leonora*, from 'anxious dream' to reality to living-nightmare, is replicated in the photographic process where the real sitter is caught on the dreamworld of the plate and then projected back out into reality, not as an accurate replica, but as a synthesis of material source and artistic imagination. Moreover, it is precisely this three-fold combination which imbues Cameron's work with a gothic and dream-like sensibility. When she first exhibited her photographs, however, these same characteristics were castigated as technical inadequacies, as 'smudges' and 'spotty backgrounds', by the dominant critics of the photographic world, those who valued scientific accuracy over artistic sentiment (Roberts 1992, 56 and Hopkinson 1986, 150). Of course, the battle to reinstate Margaret Cameron's position as one of the most important and innovative photographers of the Victorian age, rather than castigating her work as amateurish or unskilled, has long since been won. Yet in some ways the detailed investigations into her photographic techniques that such defences required have produced important information with regard to the effects Cameron was trying to produce. For example, we now know that she never attempted to gain a clear focus rather,

When focusing and coming to something which, to my eye, was very beautiful, I stopped there instead of screwing on the lens to the more definite focus which all other photographers insist on. (Weaver 1984, 155)

In addition, present-day critics have lauded Cameron's use of light and image: Weston Naef comments about her photograph of Carlyle that, 'It's impossible not to observe the audaciousness of the lighting. Dividing the face right down the very middle was unprecedented', while Julian Cox concludes that, 'Cameron's appeal is so strong because her work is dotted with inconsistencies and idiosyncrasies that are evidence of the living process that bespeaks the most serious and daring art' (Cox 1996, 128, 139). It was precisely these revolutionary qualities which allowed Julia Margaret Cameron to transform the 'realist' genre of Victorian photography into the gothic images valued so highly today. The tonal shades, the blurred focus, the blood-like chromosonal effects all contribute to the haunting prints which combine reality and dream, truth and nightmare vision.

As with her translation, the most pungent of Cameron's gothic pictures emerge from a male-authored original; so that, as she reworked Bürger's doomed heroine in ballad metre, so she recast some of the most tragic female characters from English poetry into the shadowed portraits transfixed by her lens. Perhaps one of her most successful studies of gothic women is *Beatrice* (1866; Figure 7.1) drawn from the poignant central character of Shelley's play *The Cenci* (1819).

The dramatic text is based on the true story of Beatrice, who was raped by her father, Count Francesco Cenci, and contrives with her mother to murder him in revenge. Although the general populace feel sympathy towards the women, the Pope insists that Beatrice is punished for her crime and condemns her to death. Mother and daughter were executed in 1599 (Cox 1996, 54). Like numerous gothic novels the play couples salacious detail with an attack upon contemporary morality and the hypocrisy of the church. While Cameron undertook a number of studies for Beatrice the most successful illustration shows her at the moment when she realizes that she must die. This particular plate was based upon a painting attributed to Guido Reni, but the clear lines of the earlier work are eschewed by Cameron for a mist-like backdrop which blurs the division between sitter and setting. For Cameron the face which emerges from the hazy borders is remarkably clear; for example, to the right Beatrice's brilliant white cheek contrasts reasonably well with the shadows of the hair. The face, however, as it tilts contemplatively to the left, becomes driven into the darkness, with the nose, lip and chin

7.1   Julia Margaret Cameron's 1866 portrait depicting the condemned Beatrice Cenci, inspired by Shelley's play *The Cenci*. (Courtesy of the Royal Photographic Society)

sculpted in the deepest black tones, characteristic of Cameron's use of lighting to define facial features. The eyes look down but there is no suggestion that there is an object of their gaze, instead, the implication is of inward contemplation and of a wistful acceptance of fate, of rape, of incest and execution. The whole composition – pose, light, focus – all serve to convey the grim life and sombre destiny of Beatrice Cenci. Cameron's illustration accomplishes a complete transmutation of

Shelley's words into the medium of photography. The central climatic scene of *The Cenci* is reminiscent of Cameron's *Leonora* with Beatrice's nightmare vision and 'anxious dream':

> How comes this hair undone?
> Its wandering strings must be what blind me so,
> And yet I tied it fast. – O, horrible!
> The pavement sinks under my feet! The walls
> Spin round! I see a woman weeping there,
> And standing calm and motionless, whilst I
> Slide giddily as the world reels. ... My God!
> The beautiful blue heaven is flecked with blood!
> The sunshine on the floor is black! The air
> Is changed to vapours such as the dead breathe
> In charnel pits! Pah! I am choked! There creeps
> A clinging, black, contaminating mist
> About me ...'tis substantial, heavy thick,
> I cannot pluck it from me, for it glues
> My fingers and my limbs to one another,
> And eats into my sinews, and dissolves
> My flesh to a pollution, poisoning
> The subtle, pure, and inmost spirit of life!
> My God! I never knew what the mad felt
> Before; for I am mad beyond all doubt!
> No, I am dead! These putrefying limbs
> Shut round and sepulchre the panting soul
> Which would burst forth into the wandering air!
>
> (Shelley 1970, 296–7)

By the end of the play, however, Beatrice has become reconciled to her fate, and it is this moment that Cameron illustrates in *Beatrice Cenci*:

> ... No, Mother, we must die:
> Since such is the reward of innocent lives:
> Such the alleviation of worst wrongs.
> And whilst our murders live, and hard, cold men,
> Smiling and slow, walk through a world of tears
> To death as to life's sleep; 'twere just the grave
> Were some strange joy for us. Come, obscure Death,
> And wind me in thy all-embracing arms!
>
> (Shelley 1970, 333)

Shelley's evocation of this double perception, of graphic horror combined with spiritual resolution, is reproduced by Cameron through the bisected tonal qualities of her photograph, so that the overall gothic quality of both text and image are seen to be riven through with the deepest moral schisms.

The sharp contrast between light and dark in Cameron's work, however, cannot be more in evidence than in *Call and I Follow* (1867; Figure 7.2).

7.2　Julia Margaret Cameron's 1867 portrait, *Call and I Follow*, inspired by Tennyson's poem 'Lancelot and Elaine'. (Courtesy of the Royal Photographic Society)

Here again she drew upon the work of an established male author, in a sense verifying her own artistic achievements through their already recognised genius. The image calls directly upon Tennyson's *Lancelot and Elaine* from *Idylls of the King* where the doomed maiden acknowledges Lancelot's fatal influence upon her:

> I fain would follow love, if that could be;
> I needs must follow death, who calls for me;
> Call and I follow, I follow! let me die.

> (Tennyson 1987, 450)

In Tennyson's poem Lancelot and death develop an entwined identity, so that desire inexorably leads to Elaine's suicide, and female sexuality inevitably culminates in a moment of self-destructive closure. In her path-breaking book *Over Her dead Body* Elisabeth Bronfen argues that,

> The feminine body is used to figure death as the repressed *par excellence* and the displacement of death onto the feminine allows a mitigated articulation of that value otherwise threatening to the stability of the system. (Bronfen, 1992, 165)

Indeed, Tennyson's poetry allows for the passive eroticisation of the female form through the death of Elaine who describes her own death-bed:

> And when the heat is gone out of my heart,
> Then take the little bed on which I died
> For Lancelot's love, and deck it like the Queen's
> For richness, and me also like the Queen
> In all I have of rich, and lay me on it.

> (Tennyson 1987, 453)

However, in the light of these theoretical arguments, Cameron's photograph appears as somewhat incongruous. Indeed, placed alongside the dominant representations of Arthurian women during the mid-nineteenth century, the Elaine of *Call and I Follow* is clearly an anachronism. For example, compared to other pre-Raphaelite images, such as Holman Hunt's *The Lady of Shalott* in which a malevolent and sexualized woman is trapped within the ornate and overly elaborate design of the painting as a whole, Cameron's Arthurian women are a study in stark autonomy. There can be no doubt that Cameron's Elaine is an independent subject, challenging death rather than passively consigning herself to her fate.

Mike Weaver categorizes the Elaine of *Call and I Follow* with Cameron's 'Magdalenes', those women who symbolize an enigmatic combination of moral laxity and redemption, of the secular and spiritual sides of love. In his analysis of the Cameron collection at the J. Paul Getty Museum, *Whisper of the Muse*, Weaver notes that:

> The story of Lancelot and Elaine in Tennyson's *Idylls of the King* is one in which a virginal Elaine adores an adulterous Lancelot. Like Iolande, she is a victim of adultery rather than a perpetrator of it. Yet Lancelot's sin is somehow visited upon Elaine to the point where she is cast in a pseudo-Magdalene role. (Weaver 1986, 41)

The self-aware confidence of this portrait is evidenced from the sharp profile and upward-tilting chin of Cameron's Elaine. Contributing to the powerful effect are the subject's chiselled face and columnar neck, which proffer the only points of light – less than a fifth – to the overall frame. The remainder of the photograph consists of the drapery of gown and hood, barely discernible in the dominant gloom, and the shadowy whispers of hair that flow abundantly, but obscurely out towards the left side of the image. The eyes are half-closed in a heavily-lidded sensuous gaze, which is echoed and intensified by the deep, seductive, unsmiling lips. Indeed, in contrast to the virginal and easily-influenced Elaine of Tennyson's *Idylls*, Cameron's woman is experienced, strong and proud. We get the feeling that this Elaine would have summoned death, and not followed it passively to her doom.

Call and I Follow is one of the key works in Cameron's oeuvre, not only because the subject is pre-eminent in her upholding of an independent female identity, but also because this was one of the photographs that the artist chose to give to the Autotype Company when she returned to Ceylon (Hopkinson 1986, 79–82). There is a certain amount of speculation as to why Cameron, who was so determined in her adherence to the unfocused image, should allow her work to be retouched by the Autotype Company in the process of transforming a selected canon from individual glass plates into the carbon versions necessary for mass commercial printing. The timing of her decision was obviously important, since while her return to Ceylon was both monetarily and emotionally fulfilling, it could not help but remove her from the artistic ideology in which her works were grounded (Cox, 1996, 138). In some sense, therefore, by authorizing repeated printing from her originals, Cameron was able to open up the possibility of a continued recognition of her work in England despite her own personal absence. In addition, the economic precariousness of the Cameron household, which militated against the family remaining in England, was probably also one of the reasons that she chose to establish herself within the photographic market in the first place. As such, her links with the Autotype Company must be recognized as an extension of her need to make a profit from her 'hobby' (Weaver, 1986, 21). Finally, a growing number of Victorian photographers were beginning to question their reliance upon glass-plate negatives as a way of preserving their work and many turned to the carbon prints such as those produced by the Autotype Company (Weaver 1984, 7–8). Today it seems ironic that the tonal shifts made possible by the less resilient glass-plates were abandoned for the sharper carbon prints which reduced depth and detail even as they enhanced longevity. With regard to Cameron's oeuvre we are fortunate that so many glass-plates survived, but at the same time we must acknowledge that her reputation was sustained through the nineteenth-century partly because she allowed her work to be mass-produced in carbon-plate form. *Call and I Follow* thus represents not only the determined independence of the female character represented, but also the autonomy of Julia Margaret Cameron in her resolve to establish her reputation as one of the finest photographers of her age, even if that meant compromising her own stylistic idiosyncrasies.

The combination of death and perverse desire, which characterize Beatrice Cenci and Elaine, are repeated in the character of Ophelia, although with Shakespeare's heroine madness contributes to the overall gothic tone. In *Ophelia* (1875; Figure 7.3) Cameron captures the sense of the subject's instability and despair as the sitter drags her right hand through her long, unkempt hair.

The background is completely black, while the face, arm and upper torso appear luminous and insubstantial in their ethereal white. Adding to this sense of unreality, Cameron pictures Ophelia with leaves adhering to her hair and dress, so that it becomes impossible to place this moment within the play's narrative action. Is this the mad Ophelia with her paean to herbs,[1] or does it capture some unwritten point at which the maiden rises from her tomb in a ghost-like echo of the king? The illusory quality of the image is, however, undercut by the subject's direct gaze at the camera. Her brows knit together, her eyes engage with the viewer's and her lips part slightly as if she is

7.3 Julia Margaret Cameron's 1875 portrait depicting Ophelia. (Courtesy of the Royal Photographic Society)

about to speak. Once again, to anyone familiar with nineteenth-century representations of Shakespearean heroines – most famously Millais's *Ophelia* – Cameron's photograph appears a radical anomaly. Her Ophelia is not a passive object, a victim of the patriarchal power structure, but rather an independent subject who makes direct visual, and seemingly vocal, contact with the viewer.

There is, however, something particularly disturbing about Ophelia's resolute and direct communication. On the one hand, it is quite clear from the pose and lighting that the character is mad and therefore on the margins of the accepted 'norms' of society. But, on the other hand, her gaze forges an association between portrait and spectator which, of necessity, signifies a mutuality of sensation. Consequently, if Ophelia is mad, then, on some level, that same madness inheres within our own subjectivity. The fraught relationship between society's normative values and the concept of madness have been fully investigated by Michel Foucault who argues that,

> Madness is not linked to the world and its subterranean forms, but rather to man, to his weaknesses, dreams, and illusions ... madness no longer lies in wait for mankind at the four corners of the earth; it insinuates itself within man, or rather it is a subtle rapport that man maintains with himself. (Foucault 1971, 26)

Indeed, Foucault goes on to locate Ophelia's madness as a particular aspect of the instability which 'insinuates' itself within us all:

> Then the last type of madness: that of *desperate passion*. Love disappointed in its excess, and especially love deceived by the fatality of death, has no other recourse but madness. As long as there was an object, mad love was more love than madness; left to itself, it pursues itself in the void of delirium. Punishment of a passion too abjectly abandoned to its violence? No doubt; but this punishment is also a relief; it spread, over the irreparable absence, the mercy of imaginary presences; it recovers, in the paradox of innocent joy or in the heroism of senseless pursuits, the vanished form. If it leads to death, it is a death in which the lovers will never be separated again. This is Ophelia's last song. (Foucault 1971, 30–1)

If we transfer this theoretical definition to Cameron's portrait of Ophelia it becomes possible to read the image as a reworking of the traditional representations of women, by male authors and artists alike. Ophelia's otherness cannot be dismissed as relevant only to a marginal gothic sensibility. Instead, Cameron's photograph demonstrates that the gothic image was central to Victorian identity, specifically to the ideology of melancholic and doomed love.

One of the easiest ways of demonstrating the centrality of such 'marginalia' in Cameron's oeuvre is to examine the other photographs taken by her of the same models. *Ophelia* was posed by Cyllene Wilson who also sat for *The May Queen* (1875). There are certain similarities between the two works, for example, the black background and the direct gaze, but the tones differ considerably, since Ophelia's madness has been replaced by the May Queen's serene and virginal stance. In parallel, Mary Hillier who sat for the headstrong Elaine in *Call and I Follow* was Cameron's servant and one of her most regular models, and she is also depicted as a devout and spiritual character. For example, in *The Communion* (1870) Hillier is cast as the Virgin Mary, as well as being pictured as the titular 'Angel' in *The Angel at the Tomb* (1869). Finally, May Prinsep, who was pictured by Cameron as the heroine of Shelley's gothic drama, *The Cenci*, was also given less fraught roles, such as the demure musician in *The Princess* (1874). In each instance the model is transformed by Julia Margaret Cameron into the character determined upon, with as much likelihood that the role would fall into the doomed Leonora-like category as into the 'nice young girls' variety so castigated by the critics.

By choosing to illustrate the gothic tendencies of some of the key tragic heroines in English literature in a manner which foregrounded their independent sexuality and forceful characters, Cameron clearly reworked the conventions of several genres with a distinctly pro-woman bias. But it is not the narrative portraits which stand out as the supreme examples of her gothic sensibilities, instead, the full force of her haunting photographic technique is to be seen in the likenesses taken of her friends and family. One particular relative, who appears several times in Cameron's work, is her niece Julia Jackson, who married Herbert Duckworth in 1867. Julia Jackson/Duckworth was renowned for her beauty and was used by several of the Pre-Raphaelites as a model; for example, Edward Burne-Jones depicted her as the Virgin Mary in his *Annunciation* (1879). Cameron took a set of photographs at the time of Julia's marriage to Duckworth and these depict a strong woman caught in profile during a moment of contemplation. The next extant portraits we have of Julia were taken by Cameron in 1872, two years after Duckworth's death, one of which is *Mrs. Herbert Duckworth/A Beautiful Vision*. In 1878 Julia married again, this time Leslie Stephen. Virginia Woolf was one of their children and the likeness between mother and daughter is immediately apparent when viewing photographs of the two women.

By now, however, Cameron had returned to Ceylon and during her brief visit to England in 1878 she had time only to match-make, unsuccessfully, for Julia, and not to undertake an elaborate series of photographs. What is surprising about the two portrait sequences which do exist is that they portray very different aspects of the same woman. While both groups depict an utterly beautiful woman, the 'vision' of Cameron's title, the clear strength of the younger form is replaced with a ghost-like translucence, a shadowy image replete with melancholy. Julia Duckworth's widowhood shades each of the plates taken in the later session; her eyes look away from the child seated on her lap, her hand rests heavily on an ivy-clad wall, she gazes unseeing at the lens. Here the gothic is not a marginal force which we recognize as an aspect of the real world, instead it overflows from the inner self, from an imaginative perceptiveness, into the lives of actual people, transforming the material whole into a dream-like vision. Julia Duckworth is not a servant or a visitor decked in a costume acting out the tragic fate of a fictional heroine, she is a real woman whose bereavement glistens darkly through the hazy gloom of Cameron's likenesses. Moreover, it is to Julia Margaret Cameron's credit that she recognized the power of such grief and allowed it to stand, unadorned, as one of the most powerful of her gothic images.

Each of the gothic images discussed so far have represented tragic women, either fictional or real, but Cameron's work, although dominated by her female connections, also included portraits of several men. Again she drew upon the groups around her, family, friends, visitors and servants, yet her most well-known likenesses as those taken of the 'great' men of Victorian culture. As such, we are familiar with G.F. Watts, violin in hand, surrounded by the ethereal faces of children; with the deep shadows of Thomas Carlyle's granite-like face; and with William Holman Hunt posing stoically, although with a glint of self-irony, in his fez. However, if there is one Cameron photograph that everyone knows it is *The Dirty Monk* (1865).

After a determined courtship on the photographer's part of three years Alfred Tennyson agreed to be photographed by Cameron. Although she subsequently took numerous likenesses of the poet laureate the most famous is *The Dirty Monk* which Cameron used as a frontispiece to her illustrated edition of *Idylls of the King*. The photograph's title was not, of course, one chosen by Cameron, whose fondness for, and reverence of, Tennyson would never have allowed for such seeming disrespect. Instead, it was Tennyson himself who entitled the picture 'the dirty monk' as it seemed an apt description of the unkempt and tired subject he presented to the camera (Millard 1973, 190–1). Indeed, when this portrait was exhibited in 1868 one critic commented:

[The] portrait of the Poet Laureate (Tennyson) presents him in a guise which would be sufficient to convict him, if he were charged as a rogue and vagabond, before any bench of magistrates in the kingdom. (Roberts 1992, 56)

There can be no question that Cameron colluded in the overall atmosphere of the photograph if not with its common appellation. She posed Tennyson in a dark cloak, wrapped roughly about his shoulders, while in his hand, foregrounded to the right, she placed a heavy book. In terms of character the image suggests a church elder or religious figure from a romantic or medieval past. In addition, Tennyson is caught in profile with his hair straggling over his cloak and his beard untrimmed. The background is light, so that the darkness emanates from Tennyson alone, from the world-weary poet worn by the moral vicissitudes of this earth. The combination of Cameron's haunting tones and Tennyson's chosen name, endows the photograph with a disturbing gothicism. Since the publication of Matthew Lewis's influential novel, *The Monk* (1798) gothic romances had frequently included shadowy religious figures of dubious morality, the salacious horror of their ultimate doom coupled with an attack against the hypocrisy of the Catholic church. Thus, Cameron and Tennyson participate in a double and mutual undercutting of the poet's social standing; she dresses him as a 'rogue and vagabond' while he refers to himself as a villain from a gothic novel. Yet, the bleak vision embodied by her female sitters is absent from Cameron's photographs of Tennyson. The lighting is too monotone, the expression too soft to signify any actual evil. Even Tennyson's title, 'the dirty monk' is more of a jest than a cryptic moment of self-irony. Since he was clearly fond of Cameron, Tennyson would not have felt able to jeopardize her sales, or hurt her feelings, with a more morbid appellation. Nor would she, so conscious of his status and general welfare, have chosen to represent him in the darkest of gothic tones. Indeed, given her kind lighting of Tennyson, we wonder what she felt about Carlyle whose photograph is shrouded in an absolute black.

There is, however, a final area of Cameron's work that contained gothic elements: her photographs of children. There has been a considerable amount written about the differences between Victorian and more modern perceptions of childhood, not least about the seemingly overt sexuality of the nineteenth-century poses. For example, one of the most commonly reproduced images in this debate is C.L. Dodgson's *Alice Liddell as a beggar girl* (c. 1859) in which Alice, half-clothed in rags,

appears to flirt with the camera. Julia Margaret Cameron also photographed Alice Liddell several times, but in no instance is there the least
suggestion of sexual availability; instead Liddell is presented as somewhat
serious and forbidding. It is clear from her work that Cameron was not
interested in the sexual aspects of childhood. Instead Cameron was
fascinated by the grief ensuing upon infant mortality and the fate of the
innocent dead souls.

In a letter to H.H. Vaughan written in 1859, Cameron offers consolation on the death of his child:

> Sweet little one – ! might we not all have seen that it had an angel's
> soul already blessed – I was always struck with the majesty of that
> child-beauty – I did not then read the meaning of it as now I do – &
> yet I felt all its preciousness to you in unfolding the many mysteries
> of Earth – of baby Life – of Parent Life – and Parent Love – of inno-
> cence – mysteries your beautiful & ardently impressible nature loved
> to dwell upon ... [but] had it continued on Earth its immortal
> nature might have been *dimmed* and *obscured* by sin – by assault by
> temptation – now it lives in its own native air of heaven in bright
> realms where it will watch over you, and pray for you, and see and
> feel those tears ... shed daily for its long absence and your utter loss
> of present bliss. (Weaver 1984, 152)

Whether or not such extravagant and incoherent words comforted
her niece's husband is not known, but the presence of dead children,
bereaved children, as well as infant angels in her photographic
canon, attest to the fact that for Cameron such concerns extended
beyond a particular moment of grief to a whole ideology of child-
death. One of the most poignant, but also macabre, of these infant
portraits is *The Nestling Angel* (1870: Figure 7.4) in which a winged
child inclines its head to the left, the cheek retreating into shadowed
obscurity.

The face is bleak and although the eyes are open the whole tone
suggests a death-like trance. Indeed, even as the image echoes the
'angel soul' described in Cameron's letter, the gothic elements of
death, the supernatural, claustrophobic dream, and gloomy background demand that the photograph be recognized as an exaggerated
symbol of morbid melancholy. If Cameron endowed her female sitters
with an independent subjectivity, she transformed her children into
depersonalized objects of a dark, gothic sentimentality.

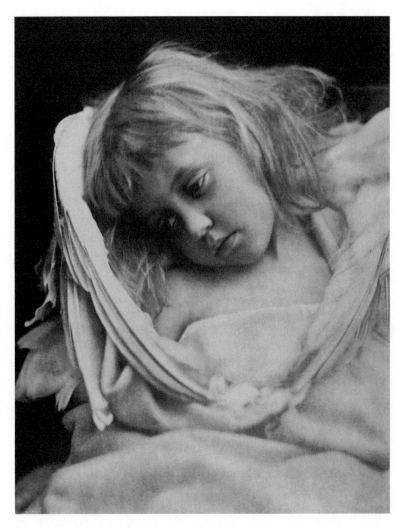

7.4   Julia Margaret Cameron's 1870 infant portrait, *The Nestling Angel*.

Julia Margaret Cameron might well have been at odds with her contemporaries in the field of photography, eschewing verisimilitude for atmospheric effect, but she was faithful to the Victorian fascination with the gothic, from her early translations through to the doomed heroines, sombre male figures and departed children of her photographic canon. Still, Cameron's renditions were not always an accurate reflection of either text, sitter or current cultural curiosity. Take, for example, the last stanza of Bürger's poem which in the German reads,

> 'Geduld, geduld. Wenn's Herz auch bricht!
> Mit Gottes Allmacht hadre nicht!
> Des Leibes bist du ledig;
> Gott sei der Seele genädig!'

(Bürger, 1932, 71)

The modern English translation gives the stanza as,

> Patience, patience. Even if your heart breaks!
> Quarrel not with God's omnipotence!
> You are free of your body;
> God have mercy on your soul.

(translation courtesy of Carol Williams)

while Walter Scott's translation, which Cameron had access to when making her own, reads,

> 'E'en when the heart's with anguish cleft,
> Revere the doom of Heaven!
> Her soul is from her body reft;
> Her spirit be forgiven!'

(Scott, 1992, 61)

In each instance there can be no question of Leonora's death. Compare these with Cameron's version (already quoted at the start of this essay):

> 'Endure! endure! though break the heart,
>   Yet judge not God's decree.
> Thy body from thy soul both part,
>   Oh! may God pardon thee!'

(Weaver 1984, 151)

The repetition of 'endure' in the first line of the stanza suggests that the ghosts encourage Leonora to cling to life, and this questioning of her death is confirmed by the complex syntax of the third line which fails to make the nature of her ending clear. Of course, this mistranslation might simply mean that Cameron's command of German was inadequate for the task she set herself. Yet, she certainly knew Scott's translation and would have had ready access to both John Herschel's and William Whewell's versions of the same text, so that she would have been free to compare different renditions of the original before compiling her own. To accuse Julia Margaret Cameron of translative incompetence is, therefore, akin to the attacks upon her photographic techniques made by her contemporaries. As such, we may only conclude that if Cameron renders Leonora's fate ambiguous, then we must accept it as a deliberate construct and not construe it as a linguistic inadequacy. Moreover, Cameron's mutation of the gothic heroine's denouement is paralleled by her transformation of the other male-authored heroines discussed in this essay. As Leonora is called upon to 'endure', so the images of Beatrice, Elaine and Ophelia all reveal a powerful assertion of female independence. So that, in a final twist of these 'anxious dreams', Cameron reworked the dominant patriarchal ideology of the her age in order to liberate female subjectivity, and in so doing, to lay claim to a radical feminized version of the Victorian Gothic vision.

Note

1. "There's fennel for you, and columbines. there's rue for you; and here's some for me. We may call it her-grace o'Sundays. O, you must wear your rue with a difference. There's a daisy. I would give you some violets, but they withered all when my father died" (Shakespeare 1987, 307–8).

8
Trance-Gothic, 1882–97

Roger Luckhurst

My thesis is that the waves of production of gothic fictions are bound up with the cyclical history of trance-states as they have been theorized within modernity. Identifiable clusters of gothic activity – the late eighteenth century, the 1840s, and the late nineteenth century – map onto three phases of great public and scientific interest in trance extremely well. The first is the rapid rise of Anton Mesmer's theory and practice of 'animal magnetism' across Europe in the 1780s and its intermittent falls and revivals through to the 1810s; the second wave starts from the dismissal of Elliotson from University College in 1839 over his mesmeric treatments, and the emergence in the 1840s of a mesmeric counter-orthodoxy which included Bulwer Lytton, Dickens, Thackeray and Harriet Martineau (an American mesmeric gothic appears contemporaneously); finally, there is the sanction by 'official' science of the hypnotic state as a result of the eminent neurologist Jean-Martin Charcot's report in 1882, which was followed by twenty years of intense dispute over the pathological status and even existence of hypnotic susceptibility.[1] One could argue that the critical industry that has proliferated around the gothic in the last decade or so is also linked to the most recent cyclical recurrence of hypnosis after its long suppression by the very different suspicions of psychoanalysis and cognitive psychology. Mikkel Borch-Jacobsen has proposed that the history of psychology 'has been nothing but a fantastic objectivisation of trance phenomena' (1993, 113); such objectivizations, I want to suggest, often take gothic form.

For Robert Miles, the cyclical interest in the genre is due to the fact that 'the Gothic has found itself embroiled within a larger, theoretically complex project: the history of the "subject"' (1993, 2). The modern subject is founded, according to Foucault, upon a number of constitutive demarcations and acts of exclusion, one of which is to define reason against delirium. Delirium ('from *lira*, a furrow; so that *delirio* actually means to move out of the furrow, away from the proper path of reason' [James cited in Foucault 1971, 99–100]) includes those states of dream, distraction and reverie marked by the suspension of the will (or 'abulia'). This is the terrain explored by the first cycle of the gothic, in which, for instance, merely to listen and sympathize with a noctambu- list's tale, as in *Edgar Huntley, or the Memoirs of a Sleepwalker,* is to *become* one, and be compelled to repeat the disordered and occluded acts of the entranced (Brown 1984). Huntley is contaminated by *narrative*, but Hogg's justified sinner is caught in a rapport explicitly derived from mesmeric accounts: 'I felt a sort of invisible power that drew me towards him, something like the force of enchantment which I could not resist. As we approached each other, our eyes met and I can never describe the strange sensations that thrilled my whole frame' (Hogg 1995, 116). Supernatural or telepathic powers were often held to be products of this strange rapport, so when Robert's 'most secret thoughts' (125) become transparent to Gil-Martin this is faithful to the claims of the exponents of 'magnetic sleep'. This structure of repetition, of becoming other, of sexualized surrender to the occult double, marks out abulic reverie and rapport as *loci* of terror for an emergent Protestant individualism. The gothic shadows the abjection of trance-states con- sistently expressed by 'Enlightened' thought from Lord Kames to Henry Maudsley.[2]

However, Terry Castle has proposed that just as the modern subject is constructed as self-willed and rationalist, it is undergoing a simultaneous *spectralization* in the late eighteenth century. For Castle, Ann Radcliffe's *The Mysteries of Udolpho* displays an expunging of ghostly superstition whilst staging the emergence of a newly haunted subjectivity at another level, in which nostalgic memories of the mourned or absent beloved construct 'inner pictures' in which 'one becomes more and more transfixed ... lost, as it were, in ... romantic reverie' (Castle 1987, 244). Here, dreaminess or trance is not abjected, and is a space of memorial retention rather than amnesic dispersal of the self. Elsewhere, then, and more radically, Castle has proposed:

> The rationalist attitude, it might be argued, inevitably depends on this primal internalisation of the spectral. For as long as the external world is populated by spirits ... the mind remains unconscious of itself, focused elsewhere, and unable to assert either its autonomy or

its creative claim on the world. ... The post-Enlightenment language of mental experience is suffused with a displaced supernaturalism. (Castle 1988, 29–30)

This liminality or reversability of reverie, at once the other of the modern subject and its foundational state, suggests it will recur as gothic theme, not least because trance is always transgressive, not so much an object as 'a *passage* between terms' (Borch-Jacobsen 1993, 101). My aim here is to read the late Victorian gothic revival as intrinsically linked to the furious debates over hypnosis from 1882, and this as part of a further stage of spectralization of the modern subject. This will provide a different trajectory from the current critical focus on 1890s gothic fiction as a vehicle for anxieties over degeneration, or as a repository for articulations of racism, sexism and homophobia, the reversionary bodies of its villains 'technologies of monstrosity' for a pathological, 'gothicized' society.[3] Certainly, hypnotic or mesmeric power is part of the repertory of the fin-de-siècle monster, and certainly representations of hypnosis are traversed by racial stereotyping (Svengali's Jewishness), degenerate criminality (Moriarty, even John Buchan's Medina), and sexual terrorism (Dracula, and a host of exotic women mesmerists demoralizing plucky Englishmen).[4] Indeed, one of the central reiterated tropes from this phase of the genre that needs analysis is the *remote controlled* person, involuntarily dragged, like the justified sinner, towards the horrifying other. Trance states do continue to invoke horror, but I want to retain the sense in which the gothic is also a space for investigating new states of subjectivity in ways which contested the supposed authority of degeneration at the time. It is easy to forget that the late Victorian gothic has more modalities than horror, that it can, in fact, debunk conservative scientific elites and ageing positivist ideologies, and can point the way towards a modern, dynamic subjectivity which breaks the determinist chains of Victorian materialism.

'Something about it "no canny"': Hypnosis returns[5]

It is a complicated task to offer a history of hypnosis in the late nineteenth century, not least because the 'new' phenomena catalogued by researchers often repeated those of 1840s mesmerists. The suppression and marginalization of mesmerism by official medical bodies at the mid-century has become a text-book example in the history of science for demonstrating the ways in which scientific demarcations were tied to anxieties of professionalisation (Parssinen 1979, 103–20). Mesmerists believed trance-states and the cures effected therein were the result of a 'magnetic' influence passing along 'a universally distributed and continuous fluid ... of an incomparably rarefied nature' (Mesmer 1967, 808). From the first official committee investigation in 1784 the existence of this fluid was denied, although condemnation derived more from concerns over its danger to public (and particularly women's) morals and the alarmingly democratic openness to claiming mesmeric powers. So virulent was the response to this demonised popular 'quackery' that when in 1842 a Manchester doctor, James Braid, dismissed the existence of fluid yet confirmed the objectivity of a state he termed neurypnology or hypnosis, a nervous sleep which was physiologically induced by a monotonous stimulus, his theory was vilified merely by association and ignored by mainstream science until re-surfacing in France in the 1880s.

J.-M. Charcot's fame rested on his neurological researches; his secular positivism made him a political icon of a modern, anticlerical Third Republic France. His inquiries into artificial somnambulism, begun as early as 1877, had confirmed Braid's findings in 1878, and his paper to the Academie des Sciences in 1882 sanctioned the study of hypnosis. Charcot viewed hypnosis as 'an artificially produced morbid condition. ... This neurosis discloses itself almost always on the soil predisposed by hysteria' (Charcot and de la Tourette 1892, 308). This was a comforting nosology, following the same stages he outlined for hysteria; it was purely physiological and restricted susceptibility to the *already* weak-willed. Hypnosis, in other words, was only a symptom; it held no curative value, and might indeed actively provoke incipient hysteria. Openness to suggestion, two of Charcot's team confirmed, was the result of 'accumulated hereditary degeneration' (Binet and Féré 1891, 356). However, in the same year of Charcot's pronouncement, Hippolyte Bernheim, a professor of medicine at Nancy, visited a country doctor who had held an open clinic for a largely peasant constituency in which he had employed 'mesmeric' (or, more accurately 'Braidist') cures for over twenty years. Dr Liébeault converted Bernheim to a practice in which an induced hypnotic state rendered the patient open to therapeutic suggestions. This 'suggestive therapeutics' became the theoretical basis of the Nancy school, and was in direct conflict with Charcot's view: it centred on the curative effects of suggestion, and hypnosis was considered non-pathological and susceptibility near universal. This medical dispute raged for over ten years, was bitter, highly public, overcoded with metropolitan/provincial tensions, and was staged through sensational displays of hypnotic phenomena, reported enthusiastically by a partisan press.

Charcot's view that any sign of hypnotic susceptibility was a mark of morbidity perfectly conformed to the broadest nineteenth-century conceptions of selfhood, in which the active surrender of will (other than to the will of God) was anathema.[6] His hysterization of morbid hypnotic phenomena thus contained *abulia* relatively safely to an extreme minority, whose theatricalized performances reiterated demarcations of the normal and the pathological. This was meant to be a rationalist de-mystification of magnetic marvels although, as Anne Harrington has pointed out, Charcot and his doctors at Salpetrière spent much of their time placing patients in trance and using magnets to 'transfer' symptoms from one side of the body to another, and even to carry symptoms from one *patient* to another. These were old mesmeric displays (Harrington 1988, III 226–46).

The Nancy school, meanwhile, often regarded as the source for much modern psychotherapeutics, caused its own panic through their universalization of hypnotic susceptibility. Liégeois, a professor of law at Nancy, ceaselessly warned that suggestibility might produce a wave of criminal activity. Women might be the passive and amnesic victims of hypnotic seducers; others might find themselves acting in trance or post-hypnotic suggestion to rob, murder or rape; jurisprudence would have to confront the paradox of innocently guilty agents, robbed of any memory or responsibility for their crimes. A mere handful of legal cases in which hypnosis was invoked, often unsuccessfully, nevertheless resulted in spiralling claims between press reports, medical theorists and (as we shall see) fiction.[7]

Both the Paris and Nancy schools, therefore, aimed to de-mystify but often only engendered *re*-mystifications of trance phenomena. This slippage between scientific and mystical aspects is another element of the liminality of trance. In Harrington's words:

> Some medical men might have used science to 'pathologise' the supernatural, but there was nothing within the rules that forbade others from setting the equation up the other way – and using French psychiatry's appropriations of the bizarre world of hysteria and hypnosis as a pathway back to the supernatural. (Harrington 1988, 239)

Such a process is evident in the British reception of hypnotic phenomena. The Society for Psychical Research was founded in London in

1882 to investigate the 'nature and extent of any influence which may be exerted by one mind upon another, apart from any generally recognised mode of perception' (1882–83, 3). Evidence for thought-reading or telepathy was pursued through mediumistic trance, re-assessments of Mesmeric claims of trance-inducement over distance, and hypnotic experiments. Initially the group strictly divided mesmerism from Braid's hypnosis, the latter 'confined to phenomena which may be produced without any special influence or effluence passing from the operator to the subject'.[8] Rapidly, though, key members of the group – Edmund Gurney and the brothers Frederick and Arthur Myers – became leading experts of the new Continental psychology. They visited Nancy and Paris, and were conducting 'telepathic hypnotism' experiments with Pierre Janet in 1886 (Janet 'succeeded' in hypnotizing a patient from over a mile away [Myers 1886–87, 127–88]. They theorized that 'abnormal' mental states might be 'supernormal', increasing psychic abilities to project telepathic messages and apparitional phantasms. Given the kinds of activity sanctioned by Charcot, the psychical researchers were hardly marginal eccentrics; indeed, many psychologists of the time (Flournoy, Binet, William James, *et al.*) made explicit their debt to Frederick Myers' theory of subliminal consciousness.[9] The reports of the Society imitated measured, empiricist methods, and often checked inflated claims, one early report reassuring readers that 'persons in a normal state seem to be little if at all liable to have their will dominated, or their actions dominated against their will, by the silent determination of another' (1884, 13). Rather bizarrely, a society established to scientize the supernatural, was at one level making far more cautious claims than either the Nancy or the Paris schools.

The group were mocked, principally for their spiritistic materialism (the *Saturday Review* always referred to the 'Spookical Society'). But they were also attacked, I think, because they came to value an *inverted* model of the Victorian self. Myers regarded willed, waking life as a tiny band on a vast spectrum of potential consciousness; he considered reverie, sleep, dreams, altered states and hypnotic trance as revealing glimpses of new evolutionary advances in the powers of the mind, of which telepathic communication was the leading edge. With further affront to psychiatric orthodoxies, Myers included hysterics in this category, and in opposition to degenerationist theory, he asserted: 'our 'degenerates' may sometimes be in truth *progenerate*; and their perturbation may mask an evolution which we and our children needs must traverse when they have shown the way' (Myers 1903, 56).

Neither these views, nor the supernaturalized aura around trance, would enamour British medical authorities of hypnosis. The debates concerning it began seriously in 1889. When Lloyd Tuckey published his short book, *Psycho-therapeutics*, he claimed that, other than the Psychical Society, 'there is in English no literature on the subject' (Tuckey 1889, x). After a demonstration at the annual British Medical Association meeting in September 1889, however, the medical and general press move from virtual silence to saturation within a year. This shift was promoted, no doubt, by the First International Congress on Hypnotism held in Paris in August 1889, and, through 1890, a sensational murder case which came to court in December, at which Gabrielle Bompard claimed she had been hypnotically compelled into complicity with murder by her lover.[10] *The Lancet*, having been central to hounding Elliotson from his post in 1839, was suspicious of the whole revival, a leader warning 'common experience teaches that, the will mastered, and not once but often, by another, is less potent' (May 24 1890, 1133). Its pages gave space to reporting dismissals of hypnosis by Sir Andrew Clark as 'a gross distortion and perversion' and later, Norman Kerr's long attack at the BMA meeting of 9 August, 1890 (Clark 1890, 1202). What *The Lancet* had to report on this occasion, however, was an audience largely favourable to establishing an investigative committee, which was promptly set up. The *British Medical Journal*, meanwhile, was more amenable to carrying reports, although the editor, Ernest Hart, often avowed his admiration for Charcot. This meant that while he accepted its objective existence, he regarded as susceptible only those with a 'neuropathic constitution' (1890, 1264). He held it 'a dangerous mental poison' (Hart 1891, 723) and later very publicly and very successfully trounced the remarkable claims of 'transfer' and hypnosis-at-a-distance made by the gullible Parisian Dr Luys in the pages of *The Times* and *Pall Mall Gazette*, and became an ardent critic of the 'futile and inane' pursuit of telepathy (Hart 1982, 27).

Hart was probably most concerned that such respected journals were publishing work by Luys, who claimed, amongst other things, to have proved receptivity in certain sensitives to visible magnetic flows, the auras of humans, and the traces of passing thoughts and emotions left imprinted on objects. It was neither the observer errors nor the atavistic nature of these claims that led Hart to deliver speeches and write de-bunking articles. It was, I think, a recognition that positivistic science had *itself* produced the legitimation for a re-supernaturalization of psychology. Ralph Vincent could complain that 'the playwright and the novelist have both apparently been at pains to write the greatest amount of nonsense in the shortest possible space, and they have been at liberty to write with no knowledge and little understanding', yet four pages later, Vincent was claiming that, purely by suggestion, a hypnotist could will a 'fatal syncope' in the heart of a patient (Vincent 1897, 236, 240). This is a typical juxtaposition of the time, since trance-states were erasing demarcations and locally suspending the operations of 'normal science'. And since the gothic investigates transgression, seizing opportunistically on anxiously insecure borders, hypnosis was to be an inevitable site for 'a play of ambivalence, a dynamic of limit and transgression that both restores and contests boundaries' (Botting 1996, 9).

Trance-gothic fictions: Arthur Conan Doyle and others

The prize for immediacy might well be awarded to J.E. Muddock, whose 1889 collection, *Stories Weird and Wonderful*, contained a Paris-based tale in which an adulterous dandy takes advantage of his wife's 'fragile form and dreamy eye' to entrance her and suggest the murder of his mistress's husband. This murder and her own compelled 'suicide' is only exposed by a servant. Whatever liberties are taken with detail are perhaps registered by the name of the murdered man: Monsieur Charcot. The story is rather jokingly framed as a second-hand report of gossip, to which the Parisians, in that 'city of original crimes', are indifferent (Muddock 1889, 296, 294).

As early as 1884, however, a young doctor and keen *Lancet* letter pages contributor in Southport, had composed a tale which was to become a template for the gothic inflection of hypnotic rapport. Conan Doyle's 'John Barrington Cowles' (Doyle, ed. Redway 1888, III 260–302)[11] is narrated by a medical student, and is a re-construction of events leading up to Cowles's death. Cowles had been engaged to a Miss Kate Northcott, who has a 'classically perfect countenance' (1888, 263) yet somewhat obscure colonial parentage. She has been previously engaged to two men, one of whom committed suicide just before the wedding, the other breaking off to indulge in 'a long course of intemperance [which] had affected his nerves and brain' (270). The narrator's suspicions of Northcott harbouring 'some mystery ... some dark fatality' (280) are enhanced by her cruelty to her chaperone, and he writes to an uncle who had served in India, inquiring after Northcott's father. The link is established: the uncle answers the man 'had some strange theories, I remember, about the power of the human will and the effects of mind upon matter' (282). The set-piece is the arrival of the stage performer, Dr Messinger, expert in animal magnetism, who is the didactic vehicle for theory:

> A strong will can, simply by virtue of its strength, take possession of a weaker one, even at a distance, and can regulate the impulses and actions of the owner of it. If there was one man in the world who had a very much more highly-developed will than any of the rest of the human family, there is no reason why he should not be able to rule over them all, and reduce his fellow-creatures to the conditions of automatons. (284–5)

As the wedding approaches, Cowles returns from a private interview with Kate, having broken the engagement over her 'too dreadful – too horrible – unutterably awful' revelations (290). Cowles appears to recover from a long illness over the ensuing months, but on his last night hallucinates the beckoning image of Kate. The narrator gives chase – 'I could catch a glimpse of his dark figure, running rapidly in a straight line, as if to reach some definite goal' (298) – but he cannot prevent his friend from throwing himself from cliffs.

This is a paradigmatic tale for a number of reasons. Susceptibility is rendered here as occulted, orientalized and a channel for sexual terror. At once an exotic and rarefied knowledge, it is yet accessible to popular stage performers: the sureties of medical science, in other words, slip between the esoteric and folkloric, leaving official knowledges impotent without extending their boundaries. It is precisely this interstitial trembling between scientific and occult frameworks that the late Victorian gothic begins to exploit.

'John Barrington Cowles' is paradigmatic in other ways, most particularly in the gender reversal of the sexualized rapport at the centre of the story. A female mesmerist inverts societal norms of weaker feminine will-power, norms reflected by mesmeric theory. From the first accounts of Mesmer's treatments it was the risk to women at the hands of male charlatans that was the key anxiety. Indeed, the first official report on Mesmerism in 1784 had a private addendum, in which women's 'more mobile nerves' and 'more easily excited' imaginations were cited as dangers. Given the description of the trance state and the curative 'crisis' into which women were sent, it is difficult to misinterpret the source of this anxiety:

> When this kind of crisis is approaching, the countenance becomes gradually inflamed, the eye brightens ... the eyelids become moist,

the respiration is short and interrupted, the chest heaves rapidly, convulsions set in, and either the limbs or the whole body is agitated by sudden movements.[12]

While it was argued that it was the very passivity and amnesiac state of trance that left women open to ravishment (in conformity, too, with melodramatic conventions), doctors were also concerned that the 'voluptuous feelings' associated with trance could lead to women patients inventing accusations of rape from their disorderly and sensual trains of thought. This displacement of desire is typical, but the full inversion in 'John Barrington Cowles' reads rather more symptomatically. Kate's sexuality is hinted at confusedly by 'wehr-wolves' and dark transformations, but her 'unutterably awful' secret marks a textual blank that typifies the occluded representations of female sexuality at the fin-de-siècle. An active female desire is figurable through a mesmeric will that renders men subordinate, but it is the rhythm of the gothic to allow this transgressive play only to re-draw the limit. Here, Cowles dies, but when Doyle returned to the same plot in 'The Parasite', it is Miss Penclosa who is killed.

'The Parasite' (Doyle 1992, 55–91), initially subtitled 'A Mesmeric and Hypnotic Mystery', was published in 1894, and is a condensation of scientific theories of trance available since the discursive explosion of 1889. It is narrated by a Cambridge professor of physiology, a materialist whose scientific machismo is asserted almost in defiance of his own constitution: he had been 'a nervous, sensitive boy, a dreamer, a somnambulist, full of impressions and intuitions' (55). This plainly signals Gilroy's latent susceptibility to the newest mesmerist, a Miss Penclosa, introduced to Cambridge circles by his colleague and psychical researcher, Wilson.[13] Penclosa's crippled, feral, Trinidadian exoticism is marked against Gilroy's fiancée, Agatha, the Aryan ideal. Gilroy's views begin in accord with Charcot (mesmerists can affect only those with 'abnormal organisms' [58]), but after a demonstration in which Penclosa successfully plants a temporary post-hypnotic suggestion in Agatha – that she should break off her engagement – Penclosa explains to him the power of suggestion and rapport. Penclosa's power is constructed between criminal suggestion as discussed by the Nancy school, and the older mesmeric language of distant willing, a parasitism in which, for Agatha, a 'second soul had stepped in, as it were, had pushed her own aside, and had seized her nervous mechanism' (62).

Once Gilroy agrees to submit to a series of mesmeric experiments, the novella becomes saturated with the language of sexuality. Gilroy describes himself as involuntarily addicted to the sessions with Miss Penclosa, unable to resist her will that he attend nightly. The one subjective description of entry into trance is figured in terms of a descent; when he awakes, barely suppressing an avowal of love for the repulsive mesmerist, he theorizes he has reached 'some lower stratum of my nature – a brutal primitive instinct' (69). This triangulation of trance, sexual urge and primitivism expresses the dominant medical view that to disengage conscious self-control is to risk mental and moral degeneration. Typically, though, this parasitic rapport provides a displacement which allows Gilroy both to experience and deny sexuality, rendering it simultaneously self and other:

> I must do as she wills. Worst of all, I must feel as she wills. ... There is some consolation in the thought, then, that these odious impulses for which I have blamed myself do not really come from me at all. They are all transferred from her. (71–2)

The last pages telescope sensational stories of criminal suggestion together; after retrieving sufficient will to express his revulsion, he is subject to a series of public humiliations, carrying out criminal acts and violent assaults, all unconsciously. His final act is to 'awake', alone, awaiting Agatha with a bottle of acid in hand; this return to consciousness corresponds to Penclosa's death. It is unclear if she has over-exerted her psychic force, or if Gilroy's own willful assertion ('your next outrage will be your last' [88]) manifests some residual occult power of his own.

This dense freighting of the hypnotic relation in 'The Parasite' is considerably more complex than Doyle's earlier tale, yet 'John Barrington Cowles' plainly continued to exert an influence over other gothic writers of the period. Riccardo Stephens's *The Cruciform Mark* borrows the Edinburgh medical setting for the activities of a murderously alluring female mesmerist (Stephens 1896). The narrator, Richard Tregenna, reports on a series of accelerating suicides of students and university staff, all of whom hallucinate the haunting image of a female face 'calm and cold, beautiful and yet hideous, with eyes that spoke of undreamt horrors' (14). This is a gothic text which attempts to satirize New Woman fiction (reading a novel, one character complains 'the heroine, you know, just shudders and palpitates and vibrates and shivers and squirms on every page' [42]), and yet is itself full of men committing suicide or on the edge of nervous collapse, either hallucinating or entranced, whether by the strokes of Miss Verney's mesmeric passes, crystal-gazing, opium cigarettes, monitory dreams or devilish music. In a splendidly incoherent conclusion, Miss Verney, trained by Charcot and Virchow no less, is revealed as an unconscious serial murderer, her impulses for murder and arguably her mesmeric powers deriving from an old brain lesion and tumour. This late example of the 'explained supernatural' ('All done by suggestion! Jendrassik and Krafft-Ebing tell of this, but I never saw it before' [338]) in no way explains the occult rag-bag of phenomena it conjures up, yet it clearly regards hypnosis as a privileged model of explanation.

George du Maurier's *Trilby* and the attendant Trilby-mania of 1894 familiarized a far wider constituency into the dramatic possibilities of hypnotic phenomena; however, much mesmerism acts as a *retrospective* explanation in the novel, appearing only in its final pages. Its melodrama re-reversed the sexual dynamism, too, returning to models of the dangerous, foreign masculine influence, in this case anti-Semitically derived (see Pick 1998, 105–25). Yet even Ernest Hart praised du Maurier for 'having produced, for the first time, a literary masterpiece in which the conditions of hypnotism are used with the power of genius, and in which their limitations and nature are correctly indicated' (Hart 1982, 210). In the latter half of the 1890s hypnotism was culturally pervasive. Mesmeric power was an essential device for the villain (Dr Nikola, for instance), it filtered into periodical detective fiction, and comic tales of misdirected hypnotic or suggestive power manifested a jokey over-familiarity by the turn of the century.[14] Nevertheless, there is one element of trance-gothic that retained its potency, and was central to two of the most effective gothic novels of the 1890s.

Remote control: *The Beetle* and *Dracula*

Richard Marsh's *The Beetle* and Bram Stoker's *Dracula* (both 1897) have moved from relative obscurity to become exemplary texts not so much of the gothic revival as the fin de-siècle *itself*.[15] Critics have focused on the extremity of their racial panic, gender inversions and sexual polymorphousness, but have tended to ignore that these are also *trance texts* through and through, and that the somnambulic, mesmeric and hypnotic states circulating within them are complexly coded both with and against the grain of gothic 'horror'.[16]

The Beetle (Marsh 1994), structured in four books, each narrated by a different actor in the plot, only exits from susceptibility to entrancement in its final narrator, the confidential agent Champnell. Before his overseeing of the fortuitous destruction of the liminal man-woman-goddess-beetle-Thing, three others narrate different encounters with trance. Robert Holt's is the most abject and ultimately deathly. From the very opening pages of his account his 'mental organisation had been stricken by a sudden paralysis' (10) and he is reduced to an abulic 'automaton' (12) by an uncategorizable Oriental figure he disturbs in a suburban house: 'I realized that he had exercised on me a degree of mesmeric force which I had never dreamed that one creature could exercise on another' (23). From this uncanny opening, in which Holt is left in cataleptic trance, uncertain if he is alive or dead, Marsh constructs one of the most bizarre sequences in 1890s fiction. Holt is re-animated and mesmerically propelled at speed through mysteriously de-populated London streets from the suburbs to the fashionable centre, stripped down, with bleeding feet, on a criminal mission that is less 'suggested' than compelled by occult force – 'as if some strong magnetic current had been switched on to me' (45). He is then reeled back to the suburbs at impossible speed. Remotely controlled in body, even to the extent of ventriloquy, Holt experiences 'dual personality' (30), a splitting between automatic response and mute complaint. Holt's eventual end is to be discovered in a Limehouse slum, vampirically sucked dry of vital fluids by the Beetle; a physical rendering of his psychic enslavement.

Sydney Atherton, in contrast, is an upper-middle-class scientist, and breeding counts. He recognizes the 'mesmeric quality' in his Oriental visitor, 'one of those morbid organisations which are oftener found, thank goodness, in the east than in the west', and airily notes 'the sensitive something which is found in the hypnotic subject happens, in me, to be wholly absent' (64). At the second encounter, however, he is nearly toppled:

> I was conscious that it was only by an effort of will that I was able to resist a baleful something which seemed to be passing from his eyes to mine. ... I could understand how, in the case of a nervous, or a sensitive temperament, the fellow might exercise ... an influence of a most disastrous sort. (99)

Atherton succeeds by countering mesmeric force with electrical 'magic': 'the visitor was treated to a little exhibition of electricity. The change in his bearing was amusing. ... He salaamed to the ground' (102). Marsh is operating in this scene within a generically 'comic' colonial encounter, in which the native's primitive superstition is exploited by the westerner. What is perhaps more surreptitiously acknowledged is the *proximity* of mesmeric and electrical forces, *both* of which were discussed in 'occult' frameworks well into the late nineteenth century.[17] The hidden Egyptian cult of Isis behind these demoralizations of English will-power works by mesmeric hook-ups; the Beetle itself is destroyed in a train crash, having been cornered by criss-crossing telegrammatic and telephonic messages between our English heroes. Atherton has, after all, patented his design for a System of Telegraphy at Sea, which the Admiralty has purchased (68). This circulation of terminologies between mesmeric remote control, telepathic hypnotism and tele-technologies, and the intermixing of oriental arcanae and occidental modernity, is also central to *Dracula*.

Finally, Marjorie Lindon describes her trance experiences in her section of the narrative. These are of a different order, being clairvoyant visions: 'As with a sort of second sight, I saw out of the room in which I was, into another, in which Paul was crouching on the floor, covering his face with his hands, and shrieking' (160). It is Marjorie's decision to marry Paul that renders atmospheres 'electrical' (148). This very attachment between Marjorie and Paul opens the visionary channel: Marjorie experiences what the Society for Psychical Research had termed a *telepathic phantasm of the living*, an apparition thrown out with huge psychic energy to the most beloved one at moments of crisis (Gurney, Myers and Podmore 1886).[18] The gendering of this type of trance-vision is a result of the common view that women possess 'finer nerves'; Grant Allen's typical words, for instance, are not many steps from supernaturalization:

> Her frame is made up of sounding boards. She has a greater number of nervous resevoirs ... and in moments that conspicuously call forth this energy, one can see her whole bodily form vibrating to the particular chord that happens for the time to be touched by circumstances. (1890, 334)

Marjorie's accesses to vision (there is another, more hallucinatory scene, in which the house becomes overrun by beetles) in fact mark her out as *pro*generate, of an advanced sensibility, correctly gender aligned. It makes her worthy of capture by the agents of the Isis cult, and equally worthy of rescue by our heroic band of men. If Paul Lessingham risks, at times, 'approximating the condition of a hysterical woman' (247), it is because his own past transgressions lie behind these oriental infractions. The secret core of events is his hypnotic seduction by an alluring singer in Egypt, an ecstatic surrender becoming cataleptic imprisonment by the Children of Isis, where he witnesses 'a phantasmagoric display', including white women 'subjected to every variety of outrage' (197).[19] Such a secret renders *The Beetle* ultimately a somewhat normative allegory of the fantasmatic dangers of miscegenation and pre-nuptial sex, exploiting the syphilitic dangers broadcast by social purity campaigners. The novel, however, displays the ways in which popular fictions and audiences of the time were conversant with different categories of trance.

Dracula is of an entirely different order of elaboration (Stoker 1979, 51). That it is a remarkable condensation and fusion of fin-de-siècle discourses is often noted, and this is especially the case in its insistent use of trance states. There is Harker's 'dreamy' and disordered fantasy, leaving him initially uncertain whether it is the women vampires or his own erotic reverie that is producing 'voluptuous' objects and 'languorous ecstasy' (the familiarity of one vampire suggests confabulation [51–2]). There is his experience of Dracula's mesmeric eyes 'in all their blaze of basilisk horror', which 'paralyses' him (68), eventually sending him into prolonged delirium. Stoker's portrait of the decline of Lucy Westenra follows a rigorous pattern, from over-sensitivity due to an implied hereditary weakness from her father ('Lucy ... feels influences more acutely than other people do ... I greatly fear that she is of too super-sensitive a nature to go through the world without trouble' [109–10]), through the development of somnambulistic trances, with attendant eroticism ('at night I hear her gasping for air'[118]), ever increasing the dominance of her 'half-dreamy state' until she enters a full alternating personality (described as oscillating between waking and lethargic states [192–3]). Her subjective descriptions of the trance-state are later echoed by Mina's first hypnotization at the asylum, a sequence which rigorously moves Mina through Charcot's three stages of the hypnotic state. It begins with 'lethargy creeping over me', develops into catalepsy, in which 'I was powerless to act; my feet, and my hands, and my brain were weighted' (308), and ends with a full somnambulistic state, in which new forms of susceptibility develop, in accord with the psychiatric literature ('I closed my eyes, but could still see through my eyelids' [309]). For much of the remainder of the novel, Mina is in a peculiar state of trance, and *Dracula* comes to be predominantly concerned with trance-dependent tele-communications of natural and supernatural kinds.

David Glover acutely observes that Stoker's speculative gothic 'starts from some contemporary branch of learning, a set of observations or a stray theory, and uses it to elaborate a blatantly phantasmagoric order of possibilities' (Glover 1996, 17). It is precisely on the question of hypnosis that Van Helsing insists Seward step beyond 'normal science' (see Greenway 1986, 213–30):

> then you understand how [hypnosis] acts, and can follow the mind of the great Charcot – alas that he is no more! – into the very soul of the patient that he influence. No? … Then tell me – for I am a student of the brain – how you accept the hypnotism and reject the thought-reading. (230)

It is the phase of 'extraordinary science' around the phenomena of trance that Stoker effectively exploits for his gothic: it remains so in *The Jewel of the Seven Stars*, a text saturated with catalepsis, reverie and hypnotic forces, in which ancient Egyptian magical powers of will are explained via Rontgen's discovery of one of the new 'forces of light' – X-rays (Stoker 1996, 121).

If Stoker absorbed his popular science, he also had privileged access to other cultural resources. As Henry Irving's theatre manager, Stoker witnessed hundreds of performances of Irving's most famous role, in *The Bells*. In this popular melodrama, Mathias's wealth derives from the murder of a Polish Jew, his crime only revealed in a dream in which a court orders a mesmerist to entrance him and compel him to act out the murder. The actual staging of a dream sequence made the play a major success, and was continually revived by Irving, well into the 1890s (Mayer 1980). Stoker later included Mesmer in his *Famous Impostors*, somewhat ambivalently noting the scientific acceptance of his 'astonishing discovery', yet arguing its use was 'surrounded with the atmosphere of imposture' and that mesmeric techniques 'combined to wreck the moral and mental stability of those present' (Stoker 1910, 93, 97).

Stoker echoes more than one hundred years of cultural anxiety over the effects of trance-states here, and in the novel Lucy's decline induced by the mesmeric Dracula plainly overcodes susceptibilty with degenerate weakness and the operator with every available anti-Semitic and racially abjecting stereotype. Once again, though, there is a certain reversability to trance that can make it difficult to code. As Mina realizes, Dracula has manifested himself through her dreamy state, he intones: 'When my brain says "Come!" to you, you shall cross land or sea to do my bidding' (343). Just as they belatedly realize Renfield serves as 'a sort of index to the comings and goings of the Count'

(269), Mina has entered that terrifying state: the remote-controlled Victorian. Stoker looks set to replay the other major source for the novel, Bulwer Lytton's occult masterpiece, *A Strange Story* (1861–62), in which the dreamy Lilian is mesmerically pulled through a landscape towards a rendezvous with the mesmeric, orientalized magus, Margrave.[20] But in *Dracula* this is only the beginning of a very strange closing sequence of the novel.

Friedrich Kittler's brilliant reading of the novel focuses on Mina's technological capacities as typist, transcriber, archivist and timetable fiend: he calls her 'the central relay station of an immense informational network' (Kittler 1990, 353).[21] She is indeed a switching point, but what also needs to be tracked is the way in which the telegrams and other communication technologies are insistently doubled by telepathic and occult connections. Although Lucy believes, in her very first letter, that Seward has a 'wonderful power' and 'a curious habit of looking one straight in the face, as if trying to read one's thoughts' (71–2), it is Mina who will be the telepathic receiver and transmitter of distant thoughts. Seward bows to her greater abilities, when she renders Renfield lucid: 'If this new phase was spontaneous or in any way due to her unconscious influence, she must have some rare gift or power' (279). This may be mere (feminine?) 'nerves', but those too are accentuated after her 'contamination' by the Count. Her telegram that Dracula is on the move (361) is followed by a more successful command to Van Helsing: 'He must hypnotise me before dawn, and then I shall be able to speak' (370).

From this point Mina can tap distantly into the physical status of Dracula, travelling in reverse along the mesmeric hook-up. For Van Helsing, Mina is a telephone, picking up the 'magnetic or electric … occult forces' that exist in Dracula's 'vital principle' (380). This telephonic image should not be surprising, given that the famous journalist W.T. Stead opened his occult magazine *Borderland* with samples of his own automatic writing, proclaiming his body was a 'bifurcated telephone' picking up messages 'without the employment of any wires or any instrument. … Distance does not affect the messages'. Stead was 'using my hand as a writing telephone' (Stead 1893, 4, 6).[22] Mina needs to be dialled up to get the Count, the international exchange working irregularly only at the liminal times of dawn and dusk. It seems to take an inordinate time for Van Helsing to discover that a telephone transmits as well as receives: 'If it be that she can, by our hypnotic trance, tell what the Count see and hear, is it not more true that he who hypnotise her first … compel her mind to disclose him that which she know?' (384). They sever the connection for a while, but Van Helsing re-connects, using what seems to be an occult power that mirrors that of his arch-enemy directly: 'he seems to have power at these moments to simply will, and her thoughts obey him', Harker observes (396). The pursuers later begin to worry about the regularity of the hypnosis, not because her will might decay, but because she begins (accurately again to the psychiatric literature) to move from straight description to acting out and the risky confabulations of 'imagination' (410). Since this mesmeric link is a tele-effect – that is, one of distance – it begins to falter the closer they get to Dracula. In a final reversal, Van Helsing is only saved from hypnotic entrancement himself by the 'soul-wail of my dear Madam Mina' (440). This wake-up call is her last act as an occult telephone.

However much Lucy is punished for her somnambulistic eroticism, and Renfield killed for his passive receptivity, the coding of Mina's susceptibility to trance is different. Like Marjorie Lindon, her trance-states and telepathy work *for* the powers of modernity and progress, doubling the effectiveness of the information systems that trap the Count. Fin-de-siècle attitudes to trance therefore reach one of their most complex popular expressions in *Dracula*. The *abuliae* of somnambulism, insanity and moral weakness are abjected, but hypnosis is also regarded as a potentially curative force, and one that opens onto vast possibilities beyond the limited determinist dreams of positivist science. This is perhaps the central point to assert about the gothic in the fin-de-siècle: it never simply confirms the ideology of degeneration, as so much reiterative contemporary criticism risks asserting. The gothic has always been a space for expansive thrills as well as reactive terrors; by the 1890s, the real ghost stories were no longer always about monstrosity, but 'the suggestion recently made by hypnotists and psychical researchers of England and France, that each of us had a ghost inside him' (Stead 1897, 1).[23] Rightly, then, fin-de-siècle gothic should be regarded as a crucial place for cultural articulations of emergent dynamic psychiatries – but particularly those available *before* Freud, the theorist whose inability to master the *mystisch* elements of hypnotism led him to expel it from his system.

Notes

1. The principal sources used here for the history of mesmerism and hypnotism are Adam Crabtree (1993) and Alan Gauld (1992).

2. Compare Lord Kames in 1751, 'a reverie is nothing else but a wandering of the mind through its ideas, without ... the perception of self' (cited in Miles 1993, 64) and Maudsley in 1883, who regards any lessening of will-power, that 'latest and highest product of social evolution', as signalling degeneration (Maudsley 1883, 243).

3. See Daniel Pick (1989), Kathleen Spencer (1992, 197–225), William Greenslade (1994), Judith Halberstam (1995); Kelly Hurley (1996). See also H.L. Malchow, who aims to explore 'the gothicisation of race and the racialisation of the gothic' (1996, 3).

4. See Daniel Pick, (1998, 105–25). John Buchan's *Three Hostages* was published in 1924, yet the Latin-Irish criminal Medina, a 'ghastly throw-back', uses hypnosis to steal the souls of his captives in a dastardly fin-de-siècle manner (1995, 139).

5. Dr Gairdner's response to a hypnotic display: 'While he did not doubt that there was a great psychic force here, still he had the strangest feeling ... that there was something about it "no canny"' (1890, 308).

6. See John R. Reed (1989) for cultural, scientific and theological overview.

7. For this specific aspect, see Laurence (1988).

8. This early distinction represents the influence of the physicist William Barrett, whose idea the Society was. He firmly believed mesmeric phenomena were the result of a physical force, whose existence advanced physics was on the verge of discovering.

9. For a re-assessment of F.W.H. Myers' importance, see Crabtree (1993).

10. See Ruth Harris (1988, II 197–241). This case was the very public stage on which the theories of Nancy and Paris did battle. Liégeois performed disastrously, and Bompard was declared 'morally blind', any evidence of hypnotizability already a sign of her criminal tendencies.

11. Doyle's are the only named contributions; as the editor notes, he is 'a member of a distinguished family'(I, viii).

12. Addendum cited in Binet and Féré, *Animal Magnetism*, 18 and 21.

13. Miss Penclosa appears to be modelled on the Italian medium Eusapia Palladino, and Wilson on Myers. It may be the views expressed about psychical researchers ('He has lost sight of human beings. Everything to him is a case and a phenomenon' [79]) that led Doyle to suppress this tale.

14. Guy Boothby, *A Bid for Fortune, or, Dr Nikola's Vendetta* (1895), in which Nikola mesmerizes the hero on two key occasions. In detective fiction, see, for example, C.L. Pirkis, 'The Ghost of Fountain Lane', one of *The Experiences of Loveday Brooke, Lady Detective* (1986) or L.T. Meade and Clifford Halifax, 'The Adventures of a Man of Science VI', *Strand Magazine* (July-Dec 1896). For comic tales, see H. Tomlinson, 'How I Committed My Murder', *Strand Magazine* (July–Dec 1902) and the story by Richard Marsh in his *Marvels and Mysteries* (1900) – 'By Suggestion'. My thanks to Chris Willis for sharing her knowledge of fin-de-siècle detective fiction.

15. As late as 1980, David Punter felt *Dracula* 'greatly underrated', and that it 'has not been taken seriously; yet it deserves to be' (1980, 256). For *Dracula's* predominance now, see works listed in note 3 above, and, in addition, David Glover (1996).

16. However, see Garrett Stewart (1994, 1–18).

17. See my own chapter, '(Touching on) Tele-Technology' (1996, 171–83), for more extended discussion of this point.
18. The results of the Society's 'Census of Hallucinations', concerning phantasms and hallucinatory experiences, had been released in 1894.
19. Marsh would probably not have known that there *was* a sect in London that met in the 'Isis–Urania Temple'. By 1900 its secret was out, and readers of *The Humanitarian* could learn of the magicians Mina and Samuel Mathers' attempts to revive the worship of Isis, this time in Paris. The Chiefs of the Hermetic Order of the Golden Dawn, however, made it clear they did not accept 'persons accustomed to submit themselves as Mediums to the Experiments of Hypnotism, Mesmerism, or Spiritualism; or who habitually allow themselves to fall into a completely passive condition of Will'. As the pleasingly mad history of the Order shows, there was a disappointing lack of sex, and magicians tended to petty displays of willfulness, rather than any occult manifestations of the Will. For details, see R.A. Gilbert, *Revelations of the Golden Dawn: the Rise and Fall of a Magical Order* (1997), 23.
20. Many other parallels include narration focused through a rigidly materialist doctor, who has to adjust his views to encompass the metaphysical and the occult under the tutelage of a Faber, a clear model for Van Helsing.
21. See also more extended comments in his 'Dracula's Legacy', *Stanford Humanities Review* 1 (1989).
22. The journal ran until 1897.
23. This is a revised edition of the special Christmas issue of the *Review of Reviews* for 1891, whose 100,000-copy print-run sold out in one week.

9
'Withered, Wrinkled, and Loathsome of Visage': Reading the Ethics of the Soul and the Late-Victorian Gothic in *The Picture of Dorian Gray*

Kenneth Womack

As a literary phenomenon, the Victorian gothic manifests itself in *fin-de-siècle* literature both as a subversive supernatural force and as a mechanism for social critique. Envisioning the world as a dark and spiritually turbulent tableau, the fictions of the late-Victorian gothic often depict the city of London as a corrupt urban landscape characterized by a brooding populace and by its horror-filled streets of terror. In *The Three Impostors* (1895), for instance, Arthur Machen offers a desolate, hyper-eroticized portrait of London and its invasion by a chemically altered degenerate race of pagan beings. In one of the more chilling portrayals of London's citizenry, Marie Corelli's *The Sorrows of Satan* (1896) narrates the Devil's progress through the city's ethically bankrupt environs as he searches for someone – indeed, *anyone* – with the moral strength to resist his temptations. He does not succeed. At the conclusion of *The Sorrows of Satan*, the Devil ascends the steps of Parliament, walking arm-in-arm with its acquiescent ministers. The characters in Richard Marsh's *The Beetle* (1897) encounter a similarly troubled London cityscape. In the novel, a desperate and lonely Robert Holt wanders the city in search of lodging only to confront the supernatural insect, metaphor for London's spiritual vacancy in the form of a giant beetle. Finally, in *The Lodger* (1923), Marie Belloc Lowndes depicts the mean streets of 1880s London in her fictional account of Jack the Ripper's murderous exploits in the city's notorious East End. The novel's chilling atmosphere of suspense, fear and horror – as with other works in the genre – underscores the manner in which the Victorian gothic provides a critique of the moral and spiritual value

systems of London and its forlorn inhabitants. Each volume also narrates – in one form or another, human, insect or otherwise – the corruption of the soul.

In *The Picture of Dorian Gray* (1890), Oscar Wilde likewise investigates the ethics of the soul through his own well-known portrait of
aesthetic narcissism and *fin-de-siècle* decadence. Yet in the novel's
Preface, Wilde writes that 'no artist has ethical sympathies. An ethical
sympathy in an artist', he coyly adds, 'is an unpardonable mannerism
of style' (1991, 69). During the novel's initial serialization, the
popular press severely rebuked *The Picture of Dorian Gray* for its osten-
sible lack of moral import. A reviewer in the 30 June 1890 edition of
the *Daily Chronicle* described the novel as 'unclean' and a 'poisonous
book' with 'odours of moral and spiritual putrefaction'. In a 5 July
1890 notice in the *Scots Observer*, yet another reviewer complained
about the novel's 'false' morality, 'for it is not made sufficiently clear
that the writer does not prefer a course of unnatural iniquity to a life
of cleanliness, health, and sanity' (cited in Beckson 1998, 271). Wilde
swiftly replied to the growing horde of critics, arguing, rather ironically, that *The Picture of Dorian Gray* was in fact *too* moral: 'All excess,
as well as all renunciation', Wilde soberly concluded, 'brings its own
punishment' (cited in Ellmann 321). While the novelist's contradictory stances regarding his narrative's ethical properties seem
purposefully beguiling, few critics deny the moral fable that functions
at the core of *The Picture of Dorian Gray*. Although Colin McGinn, for
example, evaluates the novel in terms of its humanist agenda in
Ethics, Evil, and Fiction (1997), he neglects, as with other Wilde critics,
to consider the role of the Victorian gothic as the mechanism via
which Wilde achieves his moral aims regarding the soul and its
function as the repository for humanity's notions of goodness and
evil – the essential qualities that define our perceptions about the
interpersonal fabric of the self.[1]

An ethical reading of Wilde's novel reveals the ways in which the
novelist exploits the fantastic elements inherent in the Victorian
gothic as a means for fulfilling his decidedly *moral* aims in *The Picture
of Dorian Gray*. Ethical criticism, with its reliance upon contemporary
moral philosophy, affords readers with a paradigm for considering the
contradictory emotions and problematic moral stances that often mask
literary characters. Ethical criticism also provides its practitioners with
the capacity for positing socially relevant interpretations by celebrating
the Aristotelian qualities of living well and flourishing. As Martha C.
Nussbaum reminds us in *The Fragility of Goodness: Luck and Ethics in*

Greek Tragedy and Philosophy, the ethical study of literary works offers a powerful means for interpreting the ideological and interpersonal clashes that define the human experience. The ethical investigation of literature, she writes, 'lays open to view the complexity, the indeterminacy, the sheer difficulty of actual human deliberation'. Such humanistic criticism, she adds, demonstrates 'the vulnerability of human lives to fortune, the mutability of our circumstances and our passions, the existence of conflicts among our commitments' (1986, 1314). By focusing our attention upon the narrative experiences of literary characters, ethical criticism provides a powerful mechanism for investigating the interconnections between the reading experience and the life of the reader.

An ethical reading of Wilde's novel – concerned, as it is, with the soul and our perceptions regarding the nature of goodness – demands that we devote particular attention to these issues and their relevance to such a reading of *The Picture of Dorian Gray*. In her important volume of moral philosophy, *The Sovereignty of Good*, Iris Murdoch elaborates upon the concept of goodness and the ways in which our personal configurations of it govern human perceptions regarding the relationship between the self and the world. Murdoch's paradigm for understanding goodness functions upon the equally abstract notions of free will and moral choice. 'Good is indefinable', Murdoch writes, 'because judgments of value depend upon the will and choice of the individual' (1985, 3). Postulating any meaning for goodness, then, requires individuals to render personal observations about the nature of this precarious expression and its role in their life decisions. Although Murdoch concedes that goodness essentially finds its origins in 'the nature of concepts very central to morality such as justice, truthfulness, or humility', she correctly maintains, nevertheless, that only individual codes of morality can determine personal representations of goodness (89). 'Good is an empty space into which human choice may move' (97), she asserts, and 'the strange emptiness which often occurs at the moment of choosing' underscores the degree of autonomy inherent in the act of making moral decisions (35). Individuals may also measure their personal conceptions of goodness in terms of its foul counterpart, evil, which Murdoch defines generally as 'cynicism, cruelty, indifference to suffering' (98). Again, though, as with good, evil finds its definition in the personal ethos constructed by individuals during their life experiences in the human community.

Because such ontological concepts remain so vitally contingent upon personal rather than communal perceptions of morality, Murdoch suggests that their comprehension lies in the mysterious fabric of the self. 'The self, the place where we live, is a place of illusion', she observes, and 'goodness is connected with the attempt to see the unself, to see and to respond to the real world in the light of a virtuous consciousness' (93). In Murdoch's philosophy, goodness manifests itself during the *healthy* pursuit of self-awareness and self-knowledge. The soul, as the product of such an intrapersonal quest, functions as the repository for goodness and evil, as well as the essential material that comprises the self. Moral philosophers often conceive of the soul as a vast entity that consists of our innate emotional senses and desires. In *Love's Knowledge: Essays on Philosophy and Literature*, Nussbaum elaborates upon the concept of the soul, which she sees as 'shaped and structured by the needs and interests of an imperfect and limited being. Its characterization of what truth and value are is distorted by the pressure of bodily need, emotional turmoil, and the other constraining and limiting features of our bodily humanity' (1990, 248). The soul operates as a conflation of sorts between bodily desires and individual value systems, and the harmony between these two elements produces a kind of moral beauty. Robert E. Norton describes the soul's capacity for moral beauty as 'both the motivation and manifestation of virtue' (1995, 48) and associates 'moral purity and goodness with a kind of beauty of soul' (1995, 96). As the essence of a given individual's humanity, then, the soul consists of spiritual and emotional components that define the sensual and virtuous qualities of our selves.

'To choose a style', Nussbaum writes in *Love's Knowledge*, 'is to tell a story about the soul'. For Wilde, the literary style of *The Picture of Dorian Gray* manifests itself in his appropriation of the Victorian gothic as his novel's narrative means. 'Form and style are not incidental features', Nussbaum argues. 'A view of life is *told*. The telling itself – the selection of genre, formal structures, sentences, vocabulary, of the whole manner of addressing the reader's sense of life – all of this expresses a sense of life and of value, a sense of what matters and what does not, of what learning and communicating are, of life's relations and connections' (1990, 259, 5). In this manner, the Victorian gothic's supernatural elements make possible Wilde's narration of Basil Hallward's artistic rendering of Dorian Gray, the painting of whom functions as the basis for the ethical debate that undergirds much of the novel: should we, as human beings, pursue our id-driven desires for sensual gratification and external beauty for the price of a hideous soul? Wilde employs the paradoxical Lord Henry Wotton as the voice of *The Picture of Dorian Gray*'s moral deliberations and Dorian's soul as the object of Lord Henry's intellectual whimsy. In addition to calling into question the ethics of the aristocracy in his novel, Wilde avails himself of the Victorian gothic as a means for engendering a philosophical discourse on good and evil, as well as on the mysterious properties of the human soul.[3] An ethical reading of *The Picture of Dorian Gray* not only allows us to speculate about Wilde's moral aims in his depiction of Dorian's increasingly repulsive soul, but also to interrogate the Victorian gothic as an ethical construct in itself.

As with the novel itself – which John Stokes describes as being from 'that bottomless pile of Gothic stories' (1996, 37) – the character of Dorian Gray combines elements of aesthetic decadence with the Victorian gothic. As he roams through the 'dim roar' of the novel's desolate London setting, Dorian vacillates between states of pronounced ennui and musical euphoria (Wilde 1991, 71). As Basil completes the portrait, for instance, the eternally posing Dorian complains of boredom: 'You never open your lips while you are painting', he tells the artist, 'and it is horribly dull standing on a platform and trying to look pleasant' (1991, 83). Conversely, Wilde punctuates Dorian's most intense life experiences, particular his aesthetic ones, with musical images. Talking to Dorian, Wilde writes, 'was like playing upon an exquisite violin. He answered to every touch and thrill of the bow ... with all the music of passion and youth' (1991, 99). Dorian's beauty informs every aspect of his *persona*, from his external appearance to his capacity for inspiring confidence in every person he encounters: 'Yes, he was certainly handsome', Wilde writes, 'with his finely-curved scarlet lips, his frank blue eyes, his crisp gold hair. There was something in his face that made one trust him at once. All the candour of youth was there, as well as youth's passionate purity. One felt that he had kept himself unspotted from the world' (1991, 83). As an exquisite combination of youthful good looks and a pleasant outward demeanor, Dorian enjoys the worship of nearly everyone he meets, especially Basil and Lord Henry.

While Dorian ultimately subscribes to Lord Henry's ontology of new Hedonism, Basil proffers the moral philosophy that the young aesthete clearly – given the novel's tragic conclusion – *should* have accepted. Devoted both to his craft as well as to his subject, Basil espouses a theory of moral beauty simply too realistic for Dorian to imbibe, stricken, as he is, with his ostensibly fleeting good looks. In sharp contrast with the *fin-de-siècle* decadence that surrounds him, Basil's philosophy of the soul argues for a healthy balance between our inner and outer selves, between our spiritual centres and the external images that we present to the world.

'The harmony of the soul and the body', Basil cautions, 'we in our madness have separated the two, and have invented a realism that is vulgar, and ideality that is void' (1991, 79). In his portrait of Dorian, Basil clearly attempts to strike a balance between these two vital elements, so much so that he initially refuses to exhibit his latest creation and unleash it upon an aesthetically absorbed late-Victorian society. Basil fears, correctly, that the painting will consume 'my whole nature, my whole soul, my very art itself' (1991, 75). Perhaps even more troubling, the artist confesses that Dorian's 'personality has suggested to me an entirely new manner in art, an entirely new mode of style' (1991, 78). This all-encompassing sense of artistic style, a kind of decadence in itself, frightens the painter even more, for he perceives the unsettling wave of aestheticism that characterizes *fin-de-siècle* London, particularly evidenced by Lord Henry's mindset.[4]

Unlike Basil, who champions a theory of moral beauty founded upon a balance between body and soul, Lord Henry advocates the separation between these two forms of experience. Lord Henry, in the words of Amanda Witt, 'cultivates the attitude of observing his own life, rather than actually living it' (1991, 91). At times a caricature of the disinterested upper class, Lord Henry subscribes to a range of effected homilies and aphorisms. In one instance, he proudly proclaims that 'there is only one thing in the world worse than being talked about, and that is not being talked about'. The philosophy of new Hedonism that he delineates in the novel – and which Dorian, to his detriment, literally and figuratively absorbs – can only function by separating fully the spiritual from the corporeal self.[5] 'Beauty, real beauty', Lord Henry remarks, 'ends where an intellectual expression begins' (1991, 72), adding that 'Beauty is a form of Genius – is higher, indeed, than Genius, as it needs no explanation' (1991, 88). Lord Henry's decadent philosophy challenges its subscribers to elevate their desires for aesthetic experience and fulfillment over interpersonal consequences, to achieve a total separation between their ethical obligations to their community and their needs for self-indulgence: 'I believe that if one man were to live out his life fully and completely, were to give form to every feeling, expression to every thought, reality to every dream', Lord Henry observes, then 'I believe that the world would gain such a fresh impulse of joy that we would forget all the maladies of mediævalism, and return to the Hellenic ideal – to something finer, richer, than the Hellenic ideal' (1991, 85).

Lord Henry's late-Victorian philosophy of new Hedonism also proposes a striking counterpoint to notions of goodness as espoused by such contemporary moral philosophers as Murdoch, Nussbaum, McGinn and others. In Murdoch's ethical paradigm, the concept of goodness relates to a given individual's capacity for perceiving the 'unself', or that person living within us who attempts to approach the world with a 'virtuous consciousness'. Such a lifestyle possesses the possibility of producing a beautiful soul. In Lord Henry's philosophy, however, what matters is 'one's own life', as opposed to the lives of the others with whom we live in community. New Hedonism, at least in Lord Henry's postulation, urges its adherents to pursue pleasure at any cost. 'Individualism', Lord Henry argues, 'has really the higher aim' than endeavouring to share in the ethical codes of one's society (1991, 134). The philosophy of new Hedonism also eschews morality in favour of pleasurable experience. Although some experiences initially may be spiritually distressing or ethically unsatisfying, Lord Henry contends that their iteration should produce nothing but pleasure once the individual has inured his or her conscience to the soul-purging qualities of such experiences, no matter how sinful they may prove to be. 'Moralists had, as a rule, regarded it [experience] as a mode of warning, had claimed for it a certain ethical efficacy in the formation of character, had praised it as something that taught us what to follow and showed us what to avoid', Lord Henry remarks. 'But there was no motive power in experience', he adds. 'All that it really demonstrated was that our future would be the same as our past, and that the sin we had done once, and with loathing, we would do many times, and with joy' (1991, 118).

Delivered with the confidence and verbal precision of his station, Lord Henry's aesthetic philosophy proves too enticing for the naïve and impressionable Dorian to ignore and serves as the catalyst for the Faustian bargain that he strikes in the novel. 'A new Hedonism', Lord Henry tells the young aesthete, 'that is what our century wants. You might be its visible symbol. With your personality there is nothing you could not do. The world belongs to you for a season' (1991, 88). Yet Dorian, inspired by Lord Henry's philosophy, dares to possess the world for more than a mere season. While staring at his portrait, 'the sense of his own beauty came on him like a revelation. He had never felt it before' (1991, 90). Fearing the day when time finally robs him of his youthful good looks, Dorian initially vows to kill himself when he grows old. For Dorian – with Lord Henry's theory of beauty still ringing in his ears – living in anything other than a state of exalted beauty seems simply unfathomable:

> There would be a day when his face would be wrinkled and wizen, his eyes dim and colourless, the grace of his figure broken and

deformed. The scarlet would pass away from his lips, and the gold steal from his hair. The life that was to make his soul would mar his body. He would become dreadful, hideous, and uncouth. (1991, 90)

Dorian soon finds himself unable to distinguish between himself and the picture, describing it as 'part of myself' and the 'real Dorian' (1991, 93–4). Unbeknownst to himself at the time, Dorian enters into a super-natural bargain of sorts when he wishes he could change places with the picture: 'If it were only the only the other way!' he pleads. 'If it were I who was to be always young, and the picture that was to grow old! For that – for that – I would give everything!' (1991, 90).

The ethics of his Faustian transaction and of his absorption of Lord Henry's philosophy only become known to Dorian after his brief asso-ciation with Sybil Vane, an aspiring young working-class actress from London's East End. Night after night, Dorian watches as she performs in various Shakespearean plays, taking on a myriad of fictional identi-ties while remaining, in Dorian's envious words, 'more than an indivi-dual' (1991, 115), a beautiful soul in her own right. Unconcerned with her lower-class origins, Dorian falls in love with the youthful actress: 'Sybil is the only thing I care about', he tells Lord Henry. 'What is it to me where she came from? From her head to her little feet, she is absolutely and entirely divine. Every night of my life I go to see her act, and every night she is more marvelous' (1991, 114). In short, Dorian admires Sybil for her ability to create genuine, beautiful souls upon the stage. He reveres her capacity for taking fictional characters and imbuing them with the physical and spiritual aspects of real life that Dorian, whose external beauty depends on stasis for its endurance, simply cannot grasp. Yet Dorian's love for Sybil collapses after she gives a lifeless performance in *Romeo and Juliet*. After the play, Sybil appears 'transfigured with joy' because her incipient relationship with Dorian had freed her 'soul from prison'. Before encountering Dorian, the only reality that she knew existed on the stage; after meeting Dorian, however, 'suddenly it dawned on my soul what it all meant', she explains, vowing to give up the theatre and its artificiality (1991, 140–1). Dorian subsequently chastises Sybil for her change of heart, for her implicit denial of Lord Henry's philosophy.

After he leaves a distraught Sybil in her dressing room, Dorian strolls alone among London's desolate gothic streets: 'He remembered wandering through dimly-lit streets, past gaunt black-shadowed archways and evil-looking houses', Wilde writes. 'Women with hoarse voices and harsh laughter had called after him. Drunkards had reeled by, cursing, and chattering to themselves like monstrous apes. He had seen grotesque children huddled under doorsteps, and heard shrieks and oaths from gloomy courts' (1991, 143). When he returns home after experiencing his dark night of the aesthetic soul, Dorian perceives a change in Basil's portrait of him, 'a touch of cruelty in the mouth' that had not existed there previously (1991, 144). Suddenly remembering his wish for eternal youth and its spiritual consequences, Dorian decides to return to Sybil in order to forestall the spiritual demolition of his soul. As he bathes in the warm glow of his romantic feelings for the young actress, Dorian repeats her name over and over again to the music of singing birds. 'I want to be good', he later tells Lord Henry. 'I can't bear the idea of my soul being hideous' (1991, 149). After he learns of Sybil's suicide, however, Dorian chooses to devote himself entirely to a lifestyle of hedonism in the tradition of Lord Henry's philosophy. Having already tasted the pleasures of decadence, Dorian resolves to avail himself of sin with the knowledge that he can do so without being challenged by a guilty conscience: 'Eternal youth, infinite passion, pleasures subtle and secret, wild joys and wilder sins – he was to have all these things', Wilde writes. 'The portrait was to bear the burden of his shame' (1991, 157). In this fashion, the picture becomes Dorian's ethical *doppelgänger*, his wilful sacrifice for a decadent lifestyle and the means via which he will preserve his youth.

Dorian embarks upon his life of debauchery with the aid of a book given to him by Lord Henry. Essentially a handbook for decadent living, the volume – a yellow, paper-covered French novel – influences Dorian's progress toward total spiritual and ethical ruin.[6] 'The whole book seemed to him', Wilde writes, 'to contain the story of his own life, written before he had lived it' (1991, 174). With his new Hedonist education at the hands of Lord Henry complete, Dorian engages in a protracted life of crime and corrosive sensuality in gothic London. At the age of 25, Dorian's aristocratic social standing begins to erode when an exclusive West End club threatens to blackball him. In addition to consorting with thieves and coiners, Dorian brawls with foreign sailors in the Whitechapel area. Suddenly the subject of numerous rumours and upper-class gossip, Dorian becomes associated with scandals involving the suicide of a 'wretched boy in the Guards' (1991, 193); the disappearance of Sir Henry Ashton, who fled England in disgrace; and the diminished reputations of the young Duke of Perth and the son of Lord Kent. 'Women who had wildly adored him, and for his sake had braved all social censure and set convention at defiance', Wilde writes, 'were seen to grow pallid with shame or horror if Dorian Gray entered the room' (1991, 186–7).

In addition to his chosen life of crime and social iniquity, Dorian feeds his exaggerated licentious desires during his search for new arenas of sensual fulfillment. In one instance, he considers joining the Roman Catholic communion, not for spiritual reasons, but rather, because the 'Roman ritual had always a great attraction for him' (1991, 178). Dorian also becomes an avid collector of beautiful objects and searches for yet other venues for assuaging his aesthetic needs. At one juncture in the novel, Dorian devotes himself entirely to the study of music, constructing an elaborate room with a vermilion-and-gold ceiling and walls of olive-green lacquer in which to serenade himself with the pleasing strains of Schubert, Chopin and Beethoven. As a collector of sensual objects, Dorian accumulates perfumes from the Far East, painted gourds from Mexico, rare and expensive jewellery, tapestries and embroideries once housed in the palaces of Northern Europe, and various ecclesiastical vestments. Dorian assembles his orgy of material possessions to provide himself with a 'means of forgetfulness', Wilde writes, with 'modes by which he could escape, for a season, from the fear that seemed to him at times to be almost too great to be borne' (1991, 185). Hidden in the attic above his palatial London home lies the picture, which grows even more ghastly as Dorian's evil exploits continue to mount. At 38, Dorian soothes his fears in opium dens in remote London, where 'the heavy odour of opium met him', Wilde writes. 'He heaved a deep breath, and his nostrils quivered with pleasure' (1991, 224). All the while, Dorian earns glowing praise for his decadent lifestyle and his lack of meaningful social or artistic endeavour from Lord Henry, his hedonist master and tutor.[7] 'You are the type of what the age is looking for, and what it is afraid it has found', Lord Henry tells him. 'I am so glad that you have never done anything, never carved a statue, or painted a picture, or produced anything outside of yourself! Life has been your art. You have set yourself to music. Your days are your sonnets' (1991, 248).

Dorian's life of debauchery begins to collapse, however, with the confluence of his murder of Basil and his dogged pursuit by James Vane, Sybil's vengeful brother. Dorian kills Basil after the artist insists that the aesthete show him the picture of Dorian's rotting soul. Basil reacts in horror as he glimpses the portrait of Dorian's foul inner life being slowly corroded by 'the leprosies of sin' (1991, 199). After he stabs the artist to death for condemning his evil lifestyle, Dorian stares disinterestedly at Basil's lifeless body as a woman on the street sings in a hoarse voice. By murdering Basil, Dorian attempts to rid himself once and for all of the artist's irritating moral influence. As Stephen Arata observes in *Fictions of Loss in the Victorian fin de siècle*, 'The contrast between the lovely Dorian and the hideous portrait can be taken to stand for the difference between Henry's ethic and Basil's' (1996, 64). In this instance, Henry's hedonistic philosophy wins out yet again. Dorian finally begins to re-evaluate his decadent existence after experiencing James's stubborn effort to exact revenge for the untimely death of his sister. After spotting him in a London opium den, James follows Dorian to a social occasion at the home of the Duchess of Monmouth. James startles Dorian into a 'death-like swoon' after pressing his face against the window of the conservatory. 'The consciousness of being hunted, snared, tracked down, had begun to dominate him', Wilde writes (1991, 233–4), and Dorian conceals himself in the Duchess's house.

After the Duchess's brother accidentally kills James during a shoot-ing-party the next day, Dorian experiences a 'cataleptic impression' – a cognitive, philosophical phenomenon that, according to Nussbaum in *Love's Knowledge*, 'has the power, just through its own felt quality, to drag us to assent, to convince us that things could not be other-wise. It is defined as a mark or impress upon the soul' (1990, 265). Relieved to have survived James's efforts at revenge, Dorian resolves to devote himself to goodness. 'I wish I could love', he tells Lord Henry. 'But I seem to have lost the passion and forgotten the desire. I am too much concentrated on myself' (1991, 238). Despite Lord Henry's con-siderable protests, Dorian demonstrates his intentions to adopt an ethical lifestyle by opting not to destroy the innocence of Hetty Morton, a girl in the village near the Duchess's estate. Shocked by his sudden change of heart, Dorian 'determined to leave her as flower-like as I had found her' (1991, 243). As Dorian symbolically rises from the piano – the producer of the sensual music that served as the sound-track for his evil life – he confesses to Lord Henry that 'I am going to be good' and that 'I am a little changed already' (1991, 249). Yet when he later checks the picture for evidence of his ethical renewal, he discovers 'no change, save that in the eyes there was a look of cunning, and in the mouth the curved wrinkle of the hypocrite', Wilde writes. 'The thing was still loathsome – more loathsome, if possible, than before' (1991, 252).

Rather than being the product of a genuine shift in moral attitude, Dorian's aspirations toward goodness result from his own vanity, as well as from his apprehension regarding the potential loss of the self that he adores above all others in his community. In this manner, the novel's *faux* cataleptic impression confronts readers – and perhaps

Dorian himself – with an unusual ethical construct, the anti-epiphany. Stultified by his own hypocrisy and his 'mask of goodness', Dorian chooses to destroy his decaying soul: He 'would kill the past, and when that was dead he would be free', Wilde writes. Dorian 'would kill this monstrous soul-life, and without its hideous warnings, he would be at peace' (1991, 253). Taking up the knife that he used to murder Basil, Dorian stabs at the picture. After servants hear an agonized cry and a 'crash', they enter the attic and discover a splendid portrait of their master in all 'his exquisite youth and beauty. Lying on the floor', Wilde writes, 'was a dead man, in evening dress, with a knife in his heart. He was withered, wrinkled, and loathsome of visage' (1991, 254). By attempting to eradicate the picture that serves as a record of his unethical life, Dorian succeeds in destroying himself. While the novel's *deus ex machina* conclusion, a virtual cliché of gothic fiction in general, suggests a number of narrative possibilities,[8] Dorian's supernatural demise nevertheless results directly from his Faustian bargain and the ethically vacuous existence that he deliberately pursues.

In *The Picture of Dorian Gray*, Dorian's adherence to Lord Henry's hedonist philosophy clearly manifests itself in his spiritual and physical destruction. Dorian's soul expires, William Buckler astutely observes, because of the 'inevitable consequence, not of aestheticism, but of an ugly, self-deceiving, all-devouring vanity that leads the protagonist to heartless cruelty, murder, blackmail, and suicide' (1991, 140). Wilde employs the Victorian gothic as the express means through which he characterizes the corrosion and ultimate demise of Dorian's soul. Because Wilde relies on the supernatural and the grotesque as means for narrating Dorian's spiritual digression in *The Picture of Dorian Gray*, the Victorian gothic clearly operates as an ethical construct in Wilde's novel. Ethical criticism, with its interest in exploring the trials and tribulations of human experience and their intersections with the act of reading, simply affords us with a mechanism for recognizing a given writer's humanistic agenda. In *The Realistic Spirit: Wittgenstein, Philosophy, and the Mind*, Cora Diamond argues that through ethical criticism 'we can come to be aware of what makes for deeper under-standing and an enriching of our own thought and experience; we can come to have a sense of what is alive, and what is shallow, sentimental, cheap'. The ethical critique of literature reminds us, moreover, that 'it is our actions, our choices, which give a particular shape to the life we lead; to be able to lead whatever the good life for a human being is *is* to be able to make such choices well' (Diamond 1991, 303, 373). In *The Picture of Dorian Gray*, Wilde avails himself of the Victorian Gothic in a stunning depiction of what transpires when human beings make ineffectual choices and sacrifice their own senses of moral beauty by elevating the aesthetic pleasures of the body over the spiritual needs of the soul.

Notes

1. In 'Ethics and Aesthetics in *The Picture of Dorian Gray*', Michael Patrick Gillespie offers yet another ethical critique of Wilde's novel, although, as with McGinn, he fails to consider the role of the Victorian gothic as the engine of the novelist's moral debate regarding the sanctity of the human soul, opting instead to read the novel in terms of the ethical nature of its aesthetic elements: 'Through the actions of its characters', Gillespie writes, *The Picture of Dorian Gray*'s 'discourse establishes within us a sense of the wide-ranging aesthetic force that ethics exerts upon a work of art. Furthermore, Wilde's novel gives us the opportunity to enhance the mix of our aesthetic and ethical views by extending our sense of the possibilities for interpretation beyond those delineated by our immediate hermeneutic system' (1994, 153–4).
2. For a useful definition of 'ethics' and discussion of its emergence as a viable reading paradigm during the past decade, see Geoffrey Galt Harpham's chapter on 'Ethics' in Frank Lentricchia and Thomas McLaughlin's *Critical Terms for Literary Study* (2nd edn, 1995). 'Understanding the plot of a narrative', Harpham writes, 'we enter into ethics. Ethics will always be at the flashpoint of conflicts and struggles', he continues, 'because such encounters never run smooth' (1995, 404). As Wayne C. Booth observes in *The Company We Keep: an Ethics of Fiction*, 'the word "ethical" may mistakenly suggest a project concentrating on quite limited moral standards: of honesty, perhaps, or of decency or tolerance'. In Booth's postulation of an ethical criticism, however, 'ethical' refers to 'the entire range of effects on the "character" or "person" or "self". "Moral" judgments are only a small part of it' (1988, 8).
3. In *Fictions of Loss in the Victorian fin de siècle*, Stephen Arata rejects the notion that Wilde appropriates an ethical rhetoric in *The Picture of Dorian Gray*, contending that 'here as elsewhere Wilde rejects humanistic notions of the organic and autonomous individual' (1996, 61). Yet a comparison of Wilde's divergent characterizations of the competing ethics of Lord Henry and Basil suggests otherwise. Wilde clearly derides Lord Henry's ambiguous philosophy of new Hedonism through its expositor's pompous and malformed discourse, while arguing in favour of Basil's theory of moral beauty through the devastation, and ultimately the death of, Dorian's soul.
4. In this instance, Basil clearly fears the rise of aestheticism because he senses the erosion of the ethical and cultural value systems of his community, a process that William Greenslade describes as 'degeneration' in *Degeneration, Culture, and the Novel, 1880–1940*. 'Such fears at the *fin de siècle* were at work shaping institutional practices – medical, psychiatric, political – and their assumptions', Greenslade writes. 'Degeneration facilitated discourses of

sometimes crude differentiation: between the normal and the abnormal, the healthy and morbid, the "fit" and "unfit", the civilized and the primitive. Degeneration', he adds, 'was, in part, an enabling strategy by which the conventional and respectable classes could justify and articulate their hostility to the deviant, the diseased, and the subversive' (1994, 2). Despite his espousal of a new Hedonism, Lord Henry also registers anxiety about the lower classes and the disenfranchised in *The Picture of Dorian Gray*. As an anti-Hedonist, Basil ironically demonstrates little affinity for the practices of degeneration and proves to be remarkably tolerant of the lower classes, particularly evinced by his enthusiastic approval of Dorian's relationship with Sybil.

5. In *Oscar Wilde and the Poetics of Ambiguity*, Gillespie reminds us of the illogic inherent in Lord Henry's philosophy, an anti-ethical system with little concern for consistency or reason. 'As the novel progresses', Gillespie writes, 'one finds that each of these points of view contributes to a more detailed illumination of the discourse and in doing so blunts inclinations to privilege any one of these perspectives over the others. New Hedonism in fact defines itself only through the symbiotic support of multiple systems of values, and any effort to view it in isolation would prove reductive' (1994, 61).

6. In *Oscar Wilde*, Richard Ellmann speculates about the book's identity. At his trial, Wilde conceded that the mystery book was Joris-Karl Huysmans's *À Rebours* (1884), although it also has thematic similarities to Walter Pater's *Studies in the History of the Renaissance* (1873). According to Ellmann, in the first draft of *The Picture of Dorian Gray* Wilde entitled the book *Le Secret de Raoul*, by Catulle Sarrazin. 'This author', Ellmann writes, 'was a blend of Catulle Mendès, whom he had known for some years, and Gabriel Sarrazin, whom he met in September 1888, and the name of 'Raoul' came from Rachilde's *Monsieur Vénus*' (1988, 316).

7. In *Oscar Wilde: Myths, Miracles, and Imitations*, John Stokes notes the interesting similarities in the interpersonal dynamics of the relationships between Lord Henry and Dorian and between Wilde and Lord Alfred Douglas, the novelist's youthful lover and aesthetic protégé (1996, 11).

8. For a thorough analysis of *The Picture of Dorian Gray*'s sudden and mysterious conclusion, see McGinn's *Ethics, Evil, and Fiction*. 'What Wilde has done is to condense the general theme of his book into this final scene', McGinn argues, 'giving it literal expression, so that Dorian's odd ambiguous status, suspended between life and art, is represented' (1997, 135).

10
Apparitions Can Be Deceptive: Vernon Lee's Androgynous Spectres

Ruth Robbins

... this uncanny is in reality nothing new or alien, but something which is familiar and old-established in the mind and which has become alienated from it only through the process of repression.

Sigmund Freud, 1990, 363–4

When you meet a human being, the first distinction you make is 'male or female?' and you are accustomed to make the distinction with unhesitating certainty. ... Science next tells you something that ... is probably calculated to confuse your feelings. It draws your attention to the fact that portions of the male sexual apparatus also appear in women's bodies ... and vice versa in the alternative case ... an individual is not a man or a woman, but always both. ... you ... must conclude that what constitutes masculinity or femininity is an unknown characteristic which anatomy cannot lay hold of.

Sigmund Freud, 1986, 413–14

The limit and transgression depend on each other for whatever density of being they possess; a limit could not exist if it were absolutely uncrossable, and reciprocally, transgression would be pointless if it merely crossed a limit composed of illusions and shadows. ... Transgression ... is not related to the limit as black to white, as the prohibited to the lawful, the outside to the inside, or as the open area of the building to its closed spaces. Rather, their relationship takes the form of a spiral which no infraction can exhaust.

Michel Foucault, 1977, 34–5

What might be thought of as the dominant tradition of nineteenth-century criticism in art and literature is a tradition which takes 'seeing clearly' as its prime metaphor and method for the achievement of the critical objectivity which is its declared ideal. For Ruskin, 'the greatest thing a human soul ever does in this world is to *see* something, and tell what it *saw* in a plain way. ... To see clearly is poetry, prophecy, and religion, – all in one' (Ruskin 1983, 15). And more famously, for Matthew Arnold, the function of criticism was 'to see the object as in itself it really is' (Arnold 1970, 130); the artist should 'see life steadily and see it whole' (Arnold 1972, 149), and he should pursue 'sweetness and light' (1994). What poet and critic should try to achieve is a 'total impression', not 'detached expressions ... [or] a shower of isolated thoughts and images' (Arnold 1972, 32–3). This reliance on 'seeing' speaks of a faith in sense impressions, that what is perceived by the senses, primarily by sight, is what is actually there. The solidity and reliability of the real world is guaranteed by sense impressions, and in the arts, especially narrative and pictorial arts, there is the belief that seeing is knowing. This tendency in criticism is intimately related to realist modes of representation.

However, this was not, of course, the only way of thinking about representation in the nineteenth century. The Ruskinian and Arnoldian will-to-knowledge through the eye can be revealingly juxta-posed against the Paterian aesthetics of decadence in which seeing is hardly a guarantee of anything except individualized and isolated experience. Pater famously wrote of the senses as giving us only fleeting impressions, an atomized experience, entirely at odds with seeing things steadily and whole. Moreover, his tortuous syntax drama-tizes an anti-Ruskinian position: Pater never tells anything that he saw in a 'plain' way. In his works, knowledge is contingent and not neces-sarily expressible. His is an anti-realist position, and in Pater's ideas one finds a complex matrix of associations that suggest that seeing is sub-jective and internal, not objective or external.

Pater's writing is motivated by his position as a spectator implicated in a Victorian regime of seeing and knowing; but his writing actually produces and reproduces the spectral rather than the objectively known. The word spectre, coming from its Latin root (*specere* = to see), and aligned thereby with 'seeing', is precisely the figure that can be seen and yet which inhibits knowledge. Seeing a spectre both is, and is not, knowing. In many of the essays of *Studies in the History of the Renaissance*, Pater invokes a fascination with looking in which seeing does not guarantee that the thing seen is what is objectively there.

Curiosity (in the sense of 'curiousness'), strangeness, incompletion and fascination are some of his key words.[1] What is curious, strange or fascinating is that which is not immediately discernible. What is incomplete is not seen steadily or whole. If the dominant tradition of English Victorian criticism was a tendency towards objectivity and realism, Pater's reworking of that tradition is a founding moment of late-nineteenth-century gothic formulations and of an alliance between aestheticism, decadence and the gothic.

The key moment is perhaps in Pater's chapter in *The Renaissance* on Leonardo da Vinci. His description of the Mona Lisa is probably his most famous passage, but it still merits quotation and re-examination:

> The presence that thus so strangely rose beside the waters is expressive of what in the ways of a thousand years man had come to desire. Hers is the head upon which 'all the ends of the world are come', and the eyelids are a little weary. It is a beauty wrought out from within upon the flesh, the deposit, little cell by cell, of strange thoughts and fantastic reveries and exquisite passions. Set it for a moment beside one of those white Greek goddesses or beautiful women of antiquity, and how they would be troubled by this beauty, into which the soul with all its maladies has passed! All the thoughts and experience of the world have etched and moulded there, in that which they have of power to refine and make expressive the outward form, the animalism of Greece, the lust of Rome, the reverie of the middle age with its spiritual ambition and imaginative loves, the return of the Pagan world, the sins of the Borgias. She is older than the rocks among which she sits; like the vampire she has been dead many times, and learned the secrets of the grave; and has been a diver in deep seas, and keeps their fallen day about her and trafficked for strange webs with Eastern merchants; and as Leda, was the mother of Helen of Troy, and, as Saint Anne, the mother of Mary; and all this has been to her but as the sound of lyres and flutes, and lives only in the delicacy with which it has moulded the changing lineaments and tinged the eyelids and the hands. The fancy of a perpetual life, sweeping together ten thousand experiences, is an old one; and modern thought has conceived the idea of humanity as wrought upon by, and summing up in itself, all modes of thought and life. Certainly Lady Lisa might stand as the embodiment of the old fancy, the symbol of the modern idea. (Pater 1980, 98–9)[2]

Taken in isolation, this passage speaks of multiple transgressions, not least of the ideal role of the critic. Pater positions himself as one gazing at Leonardo's picture, but what he sees is not only the picture itself, but also an image of his own making. The metaphor of seeing usually has the implications of perspective and distance that go with the ideal of objectivity. It implies also a concentration on the object itself, 'as in itself it really is'. Pater is bringing other kinds of knowledge to bear on his description, so that Pater's and Leonardo's Mona Lisas are not quite the same things. He sees more than is immediately there to be seen. His knowledge is contextual as well as textual, hence the references to Leda and St. Anne, both of whom Leonardo had also depicted, using a face that is recognizably the same face as that of *La Gioconda*. That contextual evidence operates to place the painting in terms of Pater's own definition of the Renaissance, not so much a period as an attitude which emphasized 'the care for physical beauty, the worship of the body, the breaking down of those limits which the religious systems of the middle age imposed on the heart and the imagination' (Pater, ed. Hill 1980, xxii–xxiii). For him, the Renaissance meant a kind of deconstructive play between apparently self-evident or naturalized binary oppositions: body and soul; ancient and modern; pagan and Christian; oriental and occidental (those Eastern merchants with their strange webs); purity and danger; strangeness and beauty. For Pater, great art depends on the mingling of those elements.

It is important, however, not merely to take the passage in isolation. Part of its force comes also from its own context in the chapter as a whole, in which Pater describes Leonardo's art as powerful because of its 'mystery' (not its sweetness and light); his work contains 'something enigmatical ... that ... fascinates, or perhaps half repels' (Pater 1980, 77). Before he gets to *La Gioconda*, he has lingered awhile on Leonardo's *Medusa*, which he reads as a gothic image, 'the head of a corpse, exercising its power through all the circumstances of death' and possessing 'the fascination of corruption [that] penetrates in every touch its exquisitely finished beauty' (Pater 1980, 83). If this is beauty, it is not easily read as beauty, and the moral message beloved of Ruskin is not present. 'Curiosity and the desire of beauty – these are the two elementary forces in Leonardo's genius', says Pater; 'curiosity often in conflict with the desire of beauty, but generating, in union with it, a type of subtle and curious grace' (Pater 1980, 86). And the element of strangeness comes from the androgyny of his faces, from the inability of the viewer to know precisely what s/he is seeing – dead or alive? male or female? He takes also one of the Louvre drawings ascribed to Leonardo, and discusses it as the very type of Leonardo's female beauty, although the picture appears to be of a man: 'It is', he says, 'a face of doubtful sex, set in the shadow of its own hair, the cheek-line in high light against it, with something voluptuous and full in the eyelids and lips' (Pater 1980, 90–1). And again, he describes Leonardo's John the Baptist as a figure whose 'delicate brown flesh and women's hair no one would go out into the wilderness to seek, and whose treacherous smile would have us understand something far beyond the outward gesture or circumstance' (Pater 1980, 93). If you did not know the pictures in question, you could pass over Pater's implicit argument – an argument by juxtaposition rather than by strict logic; he quietly suggests that the faces of these apparently male figures map very precisely onto the features of Lady Lisa herself. Perhaps it is she who is only apparently female. Pater's position as the spectator of art is haunted by the indeterminacy of Leonardo's androgynous spectres. In this aesthetic, seeing is not knowing; seeing is precisely what displaces knowledge.

The chapter on Leonardo is one of the places in which Pater's writings become almost openly aligned with both decadence and the gothic, themselves linked terms, as Eve Sedgwick has noted. She suggests that the allure of gothic writing lies in 'its promise of initiatory shortcuts to the secret truths of adulthood', especially secret sexualities (Sedgwick 1985, 90).[3] The gothic depends on *not* being able to see things clearly and whole; Victorian representations of sex, especially in gothic texts, are distorted, disjointed and lack perspective too. And anatomized, disjointed experience, following Pater, is what also defines decadence. As Arthur Symons was to write, in his article 'The Decadent Movement in Literature' (1893), decadence was 'a new and beautiful and interesting disease', whose symptoms included 'an intense self-consciousness, a restless curiosity in research, an over-subtilizing refinement upon refinement, a spiritual and moral perversity' (Symons 1893, 858). His description of Paul Verlaine as the decadent poet *par excellence* is both a clear description of the gothic, and a stylistic homage to Pater (whom he also identified as a decadent writer in this article): 'To fix the last fine shade, the quintessence of things; to fix it fleetingly, to be a disembodied voice, and yet the voice of a human soul: that is the ideal of Decadence' (1893, 862). This is a spectral ideal.

What I want to investigate in the light of these ideas are the intersections and disjunctures between the real and the fantastic, between the senses as guarantors of an objective reality and the senses as disrupters of the real, in the ghost stories of Vernon Lee, pseudonym of Violet Paget

(1856–1935). Lee's stories, I want to suggest, drawing on Pater's aesthetic model, articulate the decadent and the gothic as they collapse apparently stable oppositions, between life and art, between male and female, between past and present, between moral commitment and sensuous pleasure, and between reality and fantasy.

Lee's typical haunting figure is an apparitional androgyne, a term adapted from Terry Castle's book, *The Apparitional Lesbian: Female Homosexuality and Modern Culture*. Vernon Lee's own erotic preferences were indeed probably for other women. She lived a life filled with passionate female friendships, and her works eschew satisfactory heterosexual consummations. If, as Castle argues, 'lesbian fiction resists any simple recuperation as "realistic"', and 'stylizes and estranges' the real, presenting the world 'parodistically, euphuistically, or in some other rhetorically heightened, distorted, fragmented or phantas-magoric way' (Castle 1993, 90), there is certainly an argument for seeing Lee's fiction as lesbian fiction. Writing of a story Lee published in *The Yellow Book*, Burdett Gardner, for example, connected Lee's style, 'everywhere loaded with an unhealthy excess of color and jewelled ornament' with what he called her 'lesbian imagination' (Gardner 1987, 21). But alongside those stylistic features, Castle also suggests that any theory of lesbian fiction must also acknowledge the specific erotics of lesbianism – that lesbians are women who are physi-cally attracted to women: she warns that we mustn't let the sex slide out of the discussion. And if Lee did not write satisfying heterosexual relationships, nor did she write about the joys of female same-sex desire.

This may of course be a product of the historical period in which she was writing (she was at her most productive between 1880 and 1914, and wrote her most famous stories in the 1880s and 1890s, a period that included the homosexual panic induced by the Wilde trials of 1895). It may also be, on the Queen Victoria principle of lesbian non-existence, as Castle terms it, that Lee could not imagine an embodied lesbian desire – though I rather doubt that. My own position is that the androgynous spectre in Lee's stories might well stand as a code-figure for lesbian desire, despite the fact that the figures are not generally the ghosts of women's bodies. It is a way of both articulating and displac-ing desires that contemporary readers would have understood – if they understood them at all – as perverse. Spectral desire may be disem-bodied; it is often also, in Vernon Lee's stories, romantically fatal to those who enter its world. But it is imaginable – an eros of images more than of bodies, that takes place in the imagination and gives the reader a thrill precisely because of the curiosity, strangeness, incompletion and fascination with which Pater had also loaded his emotionally charged prose for his coterie audience of beautiful young men in his literary seductions without literal consummations.

Vernon Lee had certainly read Pater. She met him and admired him, and in turn, he wrote appreciatively of her work in psychological aesthetics. It is at least likely that it is Pater's fascination with sexual indeterminacy that haunts her work in the period that Elaine Showalter identifies as one of 'sexual anarchy' (Showalter 1991). Her fictions are populated by characters who disrupt categorical norms of the period – women who usurp masculine power, men who glory in – but who also fear – their own effeminacy, and pre-pubescents whose sexual identities and genders are ever open to question. Pater admired the tendency of Greek art to 'merge distinctions of sex' (Pater 1980, 263),[4] and saw in the suspension between 'growth and completion' in the 'moulding of the bodily organs' an ideal in Greek sculptures of adolescent male figures (Pater 1980, 174). Lee develops that indeterminacy and writes it into her fictions. Her androgynous and ambiguous figures are haunted by varieties of impossible desire. The stories present a threat to dominant models of heterosexuality and fixed sexual identities. They skirt the edges of homoerotic potential; but because of the gothic genre of the ghost story, they also mark a retreat from that potential, in the stories' endings, and their various retreats to the real.

In three stories from her 1890 collection *Hauntings*, Lee's writings display a close relationship with the Paterian gothic. Because the stories are not very well known, I want briefly to introduce the plots before going on to discuss their significance.

The first of Lee's successful ghost stories was a novella entitled 'The Phantom Lover: A Fantastic Story', also known as 'Oke of Okehurst'.[5] The narrator is an articulate artist, who is invited to Okehurst in Kent to paint the Lord and Lady of the manor. He tells the story of the Okes to a visitor to his studio who has noticed a particular picture stacked against the wall, and has presumably asked questions about it. The story opens with his explanation of the picture, which then leads to the ghost story (im)proper:

That sketch up there with the boy's cap? Yes; that's the same woman. I wonder whether you could guess who she was. A singular being, is she not? The most marvellous creature, quite, that I have ever met: a wonderful elegance, exotic, far-fetched, poignant; an artificial perverse sort of grace and research in every outline and movement and arrangement of head and neck, and hands and fingers. ... Look at the strange cheeks, hollow and rather flat; well, when she smiled she had the most marvellous dimples here. There was something exquisite and uncanny about it. Yes; I began the picture, but it was never finished. (109–10)

The commission to paint the Okes had not at first greatly interested the painter. His impression of William Oke is one of utter banality, and he predicted that the wife would be equally normal and dull, 'a bouncing, well-informed, model house-keeper, electioneering, charity organising young lady, whom such an individual as Mr Oke would regard in the spirit of a remarkable woman' (144). The reality is pleasingly, and ultimately disturbingly, different. Alice Oke is 'the most graceful and exquisite woman I have ever seen, but with a grace and exquisiteness that had nothing to do with any preconceived notion of what goes by these names' (122). Mrs Oke is not conventionally beautiful. She is too tall, too thin, and has a stoop. Her charms defy both linguistic analysis, and the pen of the artist, because they are 'altogether a question of movement' (110).

Whatever her physical presence, Alice Oke also fascinates the painter because of her mind, which he sees as perverse. She believes that she is the reincarnation of one of her ancestors, one Alice Pomfret, who married an earlier member of the Oke family in the early-seventeenth century. This belief is reinforced by her pronounced resemblance to an old family portrait of her namesake. The present-day Alice Oke plays on the likeness by wearing what turn out to be the original Alice's clothes, preserved by the family through the generations.

William Oke disapproves of this infatuation with the past because his ancestors were implicated in the scandal of a love affair and a murder. A cavalier poet named Christopher Lovelock, with the signs of effeminacy about him – he has long flowing hair and gorgeous apparel – had become the lover of the seventeenth-century Alice Oke. For no real reason, the original Alice had conspired with her husband to waylay the poet and to kill him. It was the original Alice, dressed as a boy, who had fired the fatal shot. The present-day Alice preserves Lovelock's writings and his memory, until her obsession begins also to haunt her husband. He becomes maddened with jealousy for the dead poet. With the painter as his unwilling witness, he bursts into his wife's room, insisting that Lovelock is with her, though the painter can see no one. Thinking to shoot the ghost, he actually shoots his wife, and 'a pool of red' forms on her gown, the very dress which the original Alice had worn as a wedding gown. Maddened, Oke then shoots himself. A locket is found on Alice Oke's body; it contains a lock of hair which does not belong to her husband. The painter comments that he is 'quite sure that was Lovelock's' (191).

The second story is entitled 'A Wicked Voice'.[6] The story narrates the haunted madness of a contemporary (1880s) Norwegian composer who writes Wagnerian music, but who is terrorized, while holidaying in Venice (the site of many kinds of terror, including sexual terrors) by a mysterious voice which he finds both compelling and repugnant. The composer dislikes the human voice in general because it blurs the line between flesh and art: it depends on a human body for its production, but is disembodied and intangible: 'O cursed human voice, violin of flesh and blood, fashioned with the subtle tools, the cunning hands, of Satan! O execrable art of singing' (127). The composer presents his disgust to himself as an intellectual problem predicated on the belief that life and art are separate categories, a belief that singing undermines. His punishment for his attitude is to be haunted by the strange singing of the ghostly voice of an eighteenth-century *castrato* named Zaffirino.

The composer's obsession with Zaffirino begins when he accidentally comes across an engraved portrait of the singer, an image which compels both his attention and his disgust, presumably because it is an androgynous image:

> That effeminate fat face of his is almost beautiful, with an odd smile, brazen and cruel. I have seen faces like this, if not in real life, at least in my boyish romantic dreams, when I read Swinburne and Baudelaire, the faces of wicked vindictive women. Oh yes! he is decidedly a beautiful creature, this Zaffirino, and his voice must have had the same sort of beauty and the same expression of wickedness ... (135; ellipsis in original)

The composer learns more of the singer from an old Italian count who claims that Zaffirino's voice had killed his great aunt. The singer's boast was that no woman could resist his singing. His first song 'could make any woman turn pale and lower her eyes, the second make her madly in love, while the third song could kill her off on the spot, kill her for love, there under his very eyes, if he felt inclined' (132). The count's aunt had scorned his boast, but, having once heard him sing, she had begun to pine away. Her family, as she lay dying, had brought the singer to her bedchamber, where he had sung her three songs. After the first, she began to revive, after the second, she appeared quite cured, but with the third song, she fell back down, dead.

The composer speaks his contempt for this story, but immediately begins to be haunted by a voice coming to him across the Venetian waters. He is not the only person to hear the voice; other people are equally fascinated by it, drawn by their inability to decide whether it is a man or a woman singing: it is 'a man's voice which had much of the woman's, but more even of a chorister's, but a chorister's voice without its limpidity and innocence' (144–5). The composer tries to forget the voice, but he begins to hear it everywhere, even when others do not hear it, and especially when he is working on his own Norse opera, 'Ogier the Dane', when he finds himself writing 'scraps of forgotten eighteenth-century airs' which are entirely inappropriate to his Wagnerian subject. Eventually he consults a doctor, and is prescribed rest in the country.

He goes to a villa at the invitation of the count who had originally told him Zaffirino's story. Only when it is too late does he realize that this is the very villa in which the count's great-aunt had been sung to death. The voice gets louder here and more insistent, seeming to come from one of the rooms in the old house; its sensuousness provokes a strong bodily response in the composer – a terrifying ecstasy in which he fears he is about to disappear. The indeterminacy of the singer's gender identity threatens the composer with the inability to 'lay hold of' his own gendered body: 'I felt my body melt even as wax in sunshine, and it seemed to me that I too was turning fluid and vaporous, in order to mingle with these sounds as the moonbeams mingled with the dew'. The crisis comes when the voice sings a particular *cadenza* phrase, which the composer recognizes as the phrase that will kill him: 'I understood ... that this singing *must* be cut short, that the accursed phrase *must* never be finished. I understood that I was before an assassin, that he was killing ... me ... with his wicked voice' (156 emphasis in original). He stops the voice by bursting violently into the room where the singing appears to be coming from; but in his terror at apparently having come face to face with the metonymic evidence of a ghost (a broken chandelier, a destroyed harpsichord), he rushes out into the night, and contracts a marsh fever from which he almost dies. Although he recovers his bodily health, he is never able to compose again because Zaffirino's voice still haunts him with its effeminate eighteenth-century music:

> I live the life of other living creatures. But I am wasted by a strange and deadly disease. I can never lay hold of my inspiration. My head is filled with music which is certainly by me, since I have never

heard it before, but which still is not my own, which I despise and abhor: little trippings, flourishes and languishing phrases, and long-drawn, echoing cadences. (158)

Like 'A Wicked Voice', 'Amour Dure; Passages from the Diary of Spiridion Trepka' is also set in Italy with all its implications of un-English and unmanly eroticism and exoticism, though this time the ghost is a Lucrezia Borgia figure from the Italian Renaissance. Spiridion Trepka is a Polish academic, researching the history of Urbania in the Vatican library. Trepka becomes obsessed with a sideline in his researches, a sixteenth-century duchess named Medea da Carpi, whose miniaturized portrait he has found apparently by accident (though the story hints that his obsession with her predates his arrival in Rome [90]). Trepka presents himself in the pages of the diary which make up the narrative as a man committed to dry academic study, while at the same time, he is also romantically disappointed that his objective research does not really put him in touch with the past as it was actually lived. When he finds Medea's portrait, however, he becomes obsessed with tracing her story, and the past begins to live in the present; Medea's ghost haunts him and dominates his research.

Medea's story is one of murder and mayhem. She has directly and indirectly caused the deaths of five men, husbands and lovers, through her ferocious powers of attraction. Her reign of murder is only ended when she meets her match in a former Cardinal who captures her in battle. The victor, ex-Cardinal Robert, does not have Medea put to death, but he refuses to see her, fearing her mythically fatal beauty. Only when Medea starts to plot against him does he act. He has her secretly strangled by women who have murdered their own children – women are not swayed by her looks. His fear of her power is so great that he does not even allow her a priest, and she dies unshriven.

Spiridion Trepka, having seen the portrait of Medea da Carpi, becomes obsessed with her fatally attractive Paterian face:

The face is a perfect oval ... the eyes grey, large, prominent, beneath exquisitely carved brows and lids just a little too tight at the corners; the mouth also, brilliantly red and most delicately designed, is a little too tight, the lips strained a trifle over the teeth. Tight eyelids and tight lips give a strange refinement, and, at the same time, an air of mystery, a somewhat sinister seductiveness; they seem to take, but not to give. The mouth with a kind of childish pout, looks as if it could bite or suck like a leech. ... A curious, at first rather conventional, artificial-looking sort of beauty, voluptuous yet cold, which, the more it is contemplated, the more it troubles and haunts the mind. (96–7)

Trepka forgets his real research, and begins to research Medea. He discovers, amongst other things, that Duke Robert, when he had his statue made, had had placed inside it a silver statuette of his familiar genius or soul, believing that this act of superstition would enable him to rest in peace until the day of judgement. The diarist makes nothing of this, but simply allows the image of Medea da Carpi to dominate his thoughts. Her influence over him causes him to lose all sense of academic perspective: 'we must put aside aside all pedantic modern ideas of right and wrong', he tells himself: 'Right and wrong in a century of violence and treachery does not exist, least of all for creatures like Medea. Go preach right and wrong to a tigress, my dear sir!' (100). He concludes that she was neither cruel nor immoral, but merely that she was magnificent, and deserved the tribute of death that various people paid her:

> The possession of a woman like Medea is a happiness too great for a mortal man; it would turn his head, make him forget even what he owed her; no man must survive long who conceives himself to have a right over her; it is a kind of sacrilege. And only death, the willingness to pay for such happiness by death, can at all make a man worthy of being her lover; he must be willing to love and suffer and die. (102)

This is what he believes is the meaning of her heraldic motto, 'Amour dure, dure Amour' – love that lasts, cruel love.

After many months spent nurturing his obsession, Trepka receives a letter, apparently written in Medea's hand, on antique paper with ancient ink, which invites him to a tryst at an old derelict church. It is the church of St. John the Baptist, and one of the altar paintings depicts the dance of the biblical *femme fatale*, Salome herself. He goes there at the appointed time, and finds a service in progress (despite the fact that the church has been abandoned for more than a hundred years); the congregation is dressed in the clothes of the sixteenth century. There he sees the apparition of Medea who beckons him to follow her, though she never allows him to reach her. When he leaves the church in pursuit of the phantom, she has disappeared. He goes back to the church on two further occasions, with the same result, and leaves convinced on the third 'meeting' that Medea has promised him her love – though the apparition has never actually spoken. After this third meeting, he finds another letter from Medea, giving him instructions to break open Duke Robert's statue, and to destroy the silver statuette that is in it. As a reward for his obedience, 'she whom thou lovest will come to reward thy fidelity' (120).

Trepka is under no illusions as to the fatality of his love for Medea. 'The love of such a woman is enough, and is fatal – I shall die also' (122). But he goes to meet his death anyway, buying a hatchet and an axe, and making his way to Duke Robert's statue. On the way there, he meets three lost souls, the ghosts of men who died for Medea, or at her hand, who try to prevent him from fulfilling his quest. His diary describes his mutilation of the statue, and his return home to await Medea's coming. Her footstep is heard on the stair, and then the diary breaks off, and the story ends with a note appended to the diary in a different type face.

> Here ends the diary of the late Spiridion Trepka. The chief news-papers of the province ... informed the public that on Christmas morning of the year 1885, the bronze equestrian statue of Robert II had been found grievously mutilated; and that Professor Spiridion Trepka ... had been discovered dead of a stab in the region of the heart, given by an unknown hand. (126)

These three stories all have Paterian pictures at their centres, Paterian in a double sense. First, the descriptions of the pictures map very closely onto the features that Pater identified with the great art of the Renaissance – they are enigmatic, strangely attractive, indeed, attractive because of their strangeness, and therefore ambiguous; they are also androgynous images, sexually unclear. Second, the effects of these pictures are internalized by the viewer. They are not objectively known or knowable, but subjectively interpreted. The readings of the paintings are an index of the 'spiritual and moral' perversities of the viewer, at least as much as of the objects viewed. This is compounded by the fact that they are all also 'frame stories' in which the life-story of the ghost is embedded in the story of its spectrality.

The portrait appears often, like the double and the mirror, in Victorian gothic, as the representation of self and other, of selfhood implicated in spectral otherness. The most famous example is probably Wilde's *Picture of Dorian Gray* (1890, 1891),[7] which itself possibly derives from Edgar Allan Poe's 'Oval Portrait'. But *Dorian Gray* differs markedly from Vernon Lee's perverse portraits. As Rosemary Jackson comments, it is closer to faery than to fantasy (1988, 112); it lacks the indeterminacy of the Freudian gothic in which not quite knowing what one sees is a defining characteristic. In Wilde's novel, the magic is manifest. The portrait 'really' changes and the changes are available for anyone to see, hence Dorian's terror and anxiety to prevent the picture's disclosures. In contrast, Lee produces portraits whose objective messages are never disclosed. The pictures are always seen through the eyes of one who is implicated in the ghostly events that are narrated. In 'A Wicked Voice' and 'Amour Dure', the narrators are themselves the haunted figures, and may, in fact, be mad; in 'The Phantom Lover', it is hard for the reader to get a proper view of the narrator, to know whether he is to be trusted in his descriptions, particularly because he himself casts doubts on his ability to represent and comprehend the events he tells.

The narrator of 'The Phantom Lover' is himself a painter, so that the concentration on pictorial art is not a surprise: that is his own obsession. The story begins with his own failure to depict a figure whose attractions depend on movement: Alice Oke cannot be seen steadily and whole; she always flickers ambiguously. That uncertainty is mirrored in the story's telling, in conversational tones, the present tense enveloping the narrative past as if it were not yet quite over. His style suggests at once the eye-witness's credibility – 'I was there, I saw with my own eyes' – and the unreliability of one implicated in the events he narrates. Indeed, one of the themes of the story is the inadequacy of the codes of representation to give a proper picture of the real. The painter complains, for example, that pencil and brush cannot adequately reproduce Alice, and that words can give only the 'vaguest notion' because they possess only an 'impotent, conventional association' ('The Phantom Lover', 124). His lack of faith in language codes – both verbal and iconic – alerts the reader to the possibility that his own narrative is perhaps unreliable. He speaks, for example, of not having been in love with Alice Oke, merely fascinated with her: 'I pursued her, her physical image, her psychological explanation, with a kind of passion which filled my days, and prevented my ever feeling dull' (127). Perhaps he protests too much.

There are, however, two other portraits in the story: that of the seventeenth-century Alice Oke, and that of her supposed lover, Christopher Lovelock. The picture of her ancestress provides impetus for the obsessions of the present-day Alice. It shows a family resemblance between the two women:

The lady was *really* wonderfully like the present Mrs. Oke, at least so far as an indifferently painted portrait of the early days of Charles I. can be like a living woman of the nineteenth century. There were the same strange lines of figure and face, the same dimples in the thin cheeks, the same wide-opened eyes, the same vague eccentricity of expression, not destroyed even by the feeble painting and conventional manner of the time. One could *fancy* that this woman had the same walk, the same beautiful line of nape of the neck and stooping head as her descendant. (131, my emphasis)

As the narrative implies, however, the relationship between what is really there in the portrait, and what might be imagined or fancied by the viewer is not easy to sort out. What is actually there is elided with what *might* be there and that might be entirely in the spectator's imagination.

The portrait of Lovelock is described very briefly in the text, but its appearance is nonetheless significant, for it appears as a religious icon, behind a curtain on a kind of altar, 'the sort of thing behind which you would have expected to find a head of Christ or of the Virgin Mary' (147), associating the picture with the unhealthy exotic world of Roman Catholicism as well as emphasizing its period associations with Jacobean tragedy. It is thus also linked with both decadence and the gothic, both of which in turn often take Catholicism and the early seventeenth century as part of their décor. The picture is a miniature, 'representing a young man, with auburn curls and a peaked auburn beard, dressed in black, but with lace about his neck, and large pear-shaped pearls in his ears: a wistful, melancholy face'. Mrs Oke's attitude to it is also religious; this is an image that she worships, and her attitude is to be understood as profane, making the painter feel nervous: 'She seemed to me, suddenly, perverse and dangerous', he comments, once she has shown him the picture (148). The metonymic evidence of the poet's existence, his poems and his picture, prove his existence to Alice Oke, and suggests, moreover, his continued presence in the house. That apparent presence (though Lovelock's ghost never quite appears) has wrecked the relationship between Alice and William. William is quite unmanned by it. From having been a soldier, a sportsman, a perfect Victorian man of action, William Oke has become a mere cipher for a man. He does his duty by his tenants; but is uncommitted to action. There is also a strong hint that the couple do not have sexual relations; there are no children to the marriage, thus ensuring the end of the Oke line, of which they are the last remnants. Whatever sexuality is in the house, then, is unproductive, and the late nineteenth century (mirrored in the responses of the painter, who expects 'five or six little Okes – that man certainly must have five children' [114]) would have seen it as perverse.

The uncertainty engendered by the story is about more than whether or not there is 'really' a ghost. It proliferates outwards to the question: if there is a ghost, who is it – Alice Oke or Christopher Lovelock? And Alice generates further uncertainties. As has been said, he cultivates a resemblance to her ancestor, even wearing her original clothes as well as inhabiting her rooms. She is an androgynous figure. In the murder story, the original Alice was dressed as a boy; at a masquerade, the present Alice wears old Alice's male clothes and looks very much the part (165); in the present day, Alice wears a boy's cap, and drives herself in a coach like a daredevil, as well as having a physique which linguistic description and painterly skill 'cannot lay hold of': her tall slim body can easily be mistaken for that of a boy, which is presumably precisely the point of fascination for the painter. She cannot be fixed, even in gender terms, except fleetingly.

The relationship between Zaffirino's portrait and Pater's Mona Lisa is very marked, even down to the famous enigmatic smile. And it is the face that obsesses the composer, though he is haunted by the voice. The story clearly hints that the composer brings his own already-formed obsessions to bear on the singer's picture, since the images the engraving recalls are those of his own 'boyish romantic dreams, when [he] read Swinburne and Baudelaire, the faces of wicked, vindictive women' (135). His emphasis is always on the gender ambiguity of the face – a man's face, but also 'a wicked woman's face' – and on the smile: 'a wicked cynical smile ... a mocking fatuous smile' (136). He is trapped between two interpretations, as he will later be by the ghostly voice: is it a man or is it a woman? He cannot tell by looking, or by listening. The senses do not guarantee the status of the real.

For Spiridion Trepka, unlike the composer, the spectre is an emanation of his own desires, not the realization of his fears about the unfixity of identity. Trepka is dissatisfied with modern civilization, and has come to Italy with a mission to uncover the past. His role as a historian is academic and realistic; but alongside his professional role, he nurtures a romantic ideal of the past. He says he is 'wedded to history, to the Past', and there is no modern woman for whom to 'play the Don Quixote'; no modern woman 'out of whose slipper to drink, and for whose pleasure to die' (100). Instead of present pleasures, he is haunted by Medea da Carpi. Like Pater's ideal, her face in the miniature Trepka finds is 'the ... most admired by the late Renaissance' (96). He comes across another portrait which might almost be *La Gioconda* again:

> The face is the same as in the other portraits: the same rounded forehead ... the same beautifully curved eyebrows, just barely marked: the same eyelids, a little tight across the eyes; the same lips, a little tight across the mouth. ... She looks out of the frame with a cold, level glance; yet the lips smile. (108)

The pictures and the written evidence of Medea's life seek out Trepka's weak points. He wants dangerous romance, so that is what he finds in both her story and in her image. He has to gaze on her image because it is somehow unresolved; he has to think about her story because it absolves men from their supposed responsibilities, and absolves them of their masculine agency. Trepka wonders to himself, as the obsession takes hold, whether he is losing his grip on the real, the very thing that defines his profession as a historian: 'Am I turning novelist instead of historian? And still it seems to me that I understand her so well; *so much better than my facts warrant*' (100, my emphasis). The will to comprehend the image, the will to know it, and to fix it with a single particularized meaning (seeing clearly and telling what he saw in a plain way), is what undoes him. Medea's story stands out against the totalizing version of history that Trepka has set out to write. She unmans him by robbing him of his professional masculine status, and then, apparently, of his life. She is not herself womanly, according to modern lights, since she has an aggressive sexuality and masculine power. She compels attention precisely because she is curious, strange, unfixed. For the modern man to become unfixed is probably tantamount to his becoming unhinged. Trepka may be mad, his narrative hints. He ends up dead too.

The spectre depends on the senses, most commonly the eye, but the other senses can come into play too. What the gothic suggests about those senses is that they are always subject to interpretation. There is a displacement between the so-called thing itself and the experience of that thing mediated through the senses. All reality is thus contingent – not known or knowable, not even necessarily there. Realism and the modes of criticism which support it disguise and naturalize the indeterminacy of reality. The gothic emphasizes the contingency of ontologies and epistemologies: it asks us to wonder whether we ever 'really' see what is really there, and whether we can ever precisely tell what we saw.

The late-Victorian gothic has its own historical specificity. Its own particular preoccupations with sexual anarchy are one of the symptoms of that, though sexual ambiguity is very often a gothic code sign. The gothic of the 1880s and 1890s is perhaps characterized by combining the fears and fantasies of gendered indeterminacy with the loss of perspective – the inability to see clearly – that Pater's critique advocates and that Lee's stories dramatize. Not for nothing did Lee introduce the word 'empathy' (feeling into) into English critical language. In her works on psychological aesthetics, deriving in part from Pater's essay on Wincklemann in *The Renaissance*,[8] she tried to test physical and mental responses to aesthetic phenomena, telling not what she *saw*, but what she and her collaborator *felt*, in mind and body, about what they saw.[9]

Pater's criticism represents a retreat into subjectivity, away from the real; Lee's stories do the same. The narrators are more or less unreliable, but they provide us with our only access to the haunting events that the tales tell. The epigraphs to this chapter, from Freud and Foucault, tell of the return of the repressed, of the fear of sexual ambiguity – of not 'knowing' through 'seeing', and of transgression. When Lee's narrators feel into history and empathize with their spectres, are they feeling what is there, or do they feel what they always felt but knew to be forbidden? That we cannot answer that question is the symptom of late-Victorian gothic, defined by its movements away from object towards subject, and from seeing towards feeling. The feelings may be inspired by sight or by the other senses; but Lee's characters see what is not quite there.

Notes

1. Isobel Armstrong identifies a number of other words in Pater's work which unsettle the foundations of objective knowledge. 'Intense, fervent, sharp, enthusiasm, excitement, delight, blitheness, sensuous form, pure form, penetrate, penetrative, restraint, unity, are key words in the nervously subtle arpeggios of his prose', she writes (1993, 388).
2. I have quoted the 1873 variants given by the editor of this edition, Donald Hill, rather than the 1893 text – in this case they are quite small variations

which were largely carried over into the editions of 1877 and 1888, the editions that Vernon Lee is most likely to have read.

3. Sedgwick also notes that the words gothic and decadent might easily be glossed by the word 'homosexual' for the late nineteenth century.

4. This comment appeared in the first edition of *Studies in the History of the Renaissance*, but was later suppressed by Pater.

5. The story was first published in 1886, by W. Blackwood and Sons, in a volume by itself. It was reprinted in *Hauntings: Fantastic Stories* (1890) with the title 'Oke of Okehurst'. Parenthetical references are to the 1890 edition.

6. This story first appeared in the 1890 edition of *Hauntings*. The edition of *Hauntings* to which I was able to refer was badly damaged by ink, and had a number of pages missing. Therefore, both this story and the subsequent story ('Amour Dure: Passages from the Diary of Spiridion Trepka'), which have been recently reprinted are referenced in a different edition, Vernon Lee, *Supernatural Tales*, ed. Irene Cooper-Willis (1987). For readers interested in following up Lee's writings, this is the only edition of her collected stories that is still in print; but it is a good place to begin.

7. One might also mention Wilde's 'The Picture of Mr W.H'. which is also about a fatal, haunting portrait.

8. The Winckelmann essay is possibly Pater's most 'scandalous' piece in *The Renaissance*. Amongst the vagaries of Winckelmann's career, his conversion (or perversion) to Rome, and his death as a murder victim, Pater insists that he *touched* the statues he commented on, breaking down the cordon sanitaire between art and life that the metaphor of seeing tends to erect. See Pater (1980, 146–7).

9. See, for example, Vernon Lee, *Beauty and Ugliness and Other Studies in Psychological Aesthetics* (1912).

11
Gothic and Supernatural: Allegories at Work and Play in Kipling's Indian Fiction

Peter Morey

It becomes clear ... that the social and literary functions of the supernatural are one and the same: it is a question of breaking the law. Whether it occurs within social life or within a narrative, the intervention of the supernatural element always constitutes a rupture in the system of established rules, and this is its justification.

Tzvetan Todorov

All literary works are determined by their relation to an ideology ...: the excellence of the novelist lies not in his ideology but in the fact that he confronts an ideological utterance with a fictional utterance.

Pierre Macherey

A number of recent works of colonial cultural criticism have questioned the unidirectionality of the power–knowledge axis described in Edward Said's ground-breaking work. However, when one comes to study those stories concerning questions of the gothic and the supernatural in India which Kipling scatters among the more realistic tales of Anglo-Indian life, it is important to comprehend the subtle change which takes place in the nature and function of knowledge. Where a supernatural economy of power is shown to operate, knowledge, for the Anglo-Indian protagonist, ceases to be a mark of power. It becomes instead a general understanding or enlightenment as to the altered realities of his position as a victim of supernatural or unknowable phenomena. It becomes a source of instability and lack of power. In this sense, the knowledge that something is supernatural acts as a subversion of power through knowledge, an ironic commentary upon it. Moreover, in certain tales one might claim that this supernatural absence-of-power constitutes part of an allegory depicting the unseating of the white man from his position of sovereign authority in India. That rationalism which has been the guiding light of Western intellectual development is suspended in a supernatural economy as the phenomena witnessed are not subject to empirically established laws of nature. To know that something which apparently exists is beyond the realm of human knowledge is, at the same time, a form of knowledge and a recognition of the inadequacies of that *sovereign-knowledge* by which England rules India: one simply knows that one does not know.

In this essay I propose to examine certain stories in which a supernatural or gothic economy operates, and to scrutinize the author-narrator's attempts to restrain the development of that economy to a point where it is no longer reclaimable through realistic teleological conventions. Kipling achieves this more successfully in some texts than in others. The stories to be focused upon are 'The Return of Imray' and 'The Mark of the Beast' (both from *Life's Handicap*, 1891), and 'The Strange Ride of Morrowbie Jukes' (*Wee Willie Winkie and Other Stories*, 1895).

The Orient as a land of mystery and strangeness is a long-established, if reductive, Orientalist tenet. Kipling's supernatural and gothic stories take this somewhat clichéd idea as their base and use it to explore issues of imperial control and, I would claim, enact the struggle of colonizer versus an Ultimate Other in the formal qualities – the hesitations, lacunae, selections and omissions of the texts themselves. However, at the outset, two key questions present themselves. What is the importance of the distinction between the gothic tradition and what may be termed the raw supernatural? And what are the qualities which allow the supernatural to be read as a radical commentary on political relationships? The answer to the first question exists in the malleability of the gothic genre. There is no obligation on gothic texts to explain their resolution through the supernatural. For example, in works such as *The Mysteries of Udolpho* and *The Italian*, Mrs Radcliffe provides rational explanations for events that have appeared preternatural. The implications of such coy resolutions for a reading of the gothic as subversive through its irrationality are immediately clear. Any event can be reclaimed for rationalism through an authorial will-to-power of the kind to which Kipling resorts again and again in the Indian tales of horror. This tendency of gothic can be used to impose a consoling, one might say conservative, ending on what had appeared a wilful and radical text, as Rosemary Jackson argues: 'Gothic is a complex form situated on the edges of bourgeois cultture, functioning in a dialogical relation to that culture. But it also conducts a dialogue within itself, as it acts out and defeats subversive desires. Hence the difficulty of reading Gothic as politically subversive' (1988, 96). Thus, if it is the author-narrator's intention to use situations of horror as allegories depicting inversions of political power – as does Kipling in 'The Return of Imray' and 'The Strange Ride of Morrowbie Jukes', for example – it is then simple to restore the previously existing balance, or imbalance, of power. He merely has to explain in some way that the phenomenon described is an exception to established rules and display the eventual victory of those rules. The supernatural is not so easily assimilable, for if the author-narrator leaves a supernatural explanation in place he has effectively burned his bridges: whatever conclusions may be drawn, the fact of the unexplainable exists like a hole in his narrative.

The pliable nature of the gothic convention makes it a convenient vehicle for the kind of disturbing yet ultimately conservative political allegory Kipling favours. Yet these qualities, at the same time, draw attention to the more irrevocable tendencies of the supernatural, and provide an answer to our second question. One can claim that the supernatural tales display a potential for independence from reactionary determinism, an antithetical allegorical potential, since an oppositional reading may see in them a coding of the breakdown of that rationalism on which imperial power is based. Potential allegories are those tales where the outlandish events narrated refuse to yield to the consoling schemes of teleological certainty. They remain recalcitrant, elusive tales in which ordinary Aristotelian narrative – the trumpet of imperial discourse – is choked off, and where resolution remains unattainable. The supernatural is always *beyond*, always inscrutably Other. As *super-nature*, the events described in these narratives are above and beyond the realm of the natural; that which is framed within nature and its laws as they have come to be understood through Western empirical observation. Francis Hutchins has described the late-nineteenth-century attempt by British imperial discourse to represent English rule over India as natural or *orientalized rule*. Yet if British rule is *natural*, anything – like the supernatural – which contravenes or transcends nature consequently calls into question the power and permanence of that rule. In this way the supernatural stands as a surrogate Other, a form of allegorical subversion, and must be combatted in the stories by *knowledgeable* figures such as Strickland, the police inspector. Whether it is made manifest in the form of a doppelgänger, through ghosts or by bestial regression, the attack by the Other on the role of Western rationalism performed in the supernatural possesses a power of contribution to the decolonization process since its phenomena refuse the parameters defined for them both by imperialist rationalism and the attempted containment operation enacted by the author as he constructs the narrative. Those narratives which employ what I have termed the gothic and that may therefore be read as straight allegories include 'The Return of Imray' and 'The Strange Ride of Morrowbie Jukes'. They depict temporary inversions of racial and imperial power relations: in the first case between master and servant, and in the second between the colonizing and colonized races. In stories where the supernatural remains undiluted, and which display allegorical potential – such as 'The Mark of the Beast' – power is problematized and the text itself, the mechanics of the telling, forms a site of struggle which is only resolved through premeditated authorial action, and which reveals the inadequacies and contradictions of privileged narrative positions. What one must bear in mind is that the straight allegories are consciously such and Kipling as author and ultimate authority is empowered to impose the desired (conservative) ending; Imray's treacherous servant pays the price for his actions and Morrowbie Jukes is rescued. Furthermore, the incidents themselves are isolated, framed and hemmed in by the continued operation of an imperial order projected by the narrator beyond the boundaries of the text; the bad servant is only one among a number of faithful servants, while Jukes's pit is an arena of suspension not obliteration, an anomaly, and the reader is always aware of imperial jurisdiction carrying on normally somewhere outside. However, those texts displaying allegorical potential are not reducible to the level of imperialist morality plays. They exhibit a disconcerting *life* of their own in that no imposed resolution is adequate to erase contradiction. Similarly, while 'The Mark of the Beast' may depict the salvation of Fleete from the wrath of the 'Gods and Devils of Asia', that source of subversive power which set in motion the train of retributive events is still at large in the empire, and the methods used to effect Fleete's rescue are morally ambiguous to say the least.

Of course, potential allegories like 'The Mark of the Beast' require a conscious act on the part of the reader to realize their potential and bring them into existence as allegories; just as the conservatism and reassuring dénouements of the first kind are the product of conscious suppressions and omissions on Kipling's part. One must take one's place as the implied or implicit reader sought by the text, but at the same time reject the role of complicit reader the author encourages: compliant in producing a meaning for the text through evasion and political manipulation. Indeed, one must, with Macherey, read the text 'against the grain of its intended meaning' (Macherey 1978, 230), not so much to reveal ideology, since its presence is unavoidable in Kipling's work, as to reveal ideological–literary anxiety. It is possible to claim that the supernatural texts effect a more drastic exposure of self-contradictions within the discourse both in the non-linguistic methods of communication they choose, and by the challenge they pose to those easy binarisms which are the basis of racial–imperial hierarchies. The supernatural introduces a dangerous ambiguity into what is often held to be a simplistic master-slave relationship. One might say that it is a weapon of that ambivalence or hybridity recognised by Homi Bhabha which marks 'the disturbance of ... [English imperialism's] authoritative representations by ... uncanny forces ... the paranoid threat from the hybrid is finally uncontainable because it breaks down the symmetry and duality of self/other, inside/outside' (Bhabha 1994, 114, 116).

The difficulties of fulfilling the roles ostensibly decreed by that 'heaven-born/follower' dichotomy, explicitly stated by Kipling in some texts, reveal the colonial position as one fraught with dangers and characterized by struggle illustrated in the peculiar fluidity of power relations in supernatural texts. The supernatural itself forms a critique of those binarisms – subject/object, us/them, colonizer/colonized, English/Indian – through which imperial discourse seeks to perpetuate hegemony. In the horror stories, for example, those usually *acting*, the English, and those *acted upon*, the Indians, often change places. Once inversion is effected the rest of the tale is concerned with the attempt at redress and the reactivation of colonial power. The success of this endeavour is dependent on whether Kipling has reined in the text through gothic or 'given it its head' through the supernatural.

The radicalism of the supernatural is paradoxically revealed by the conservatism of a gothic text explicitly concerned with a practical demonstration and reinvocation of the master–slave dyad after its temporary violation. 'The Return of Imray' literally centres on a master–servant relationship and is designed to operate as an allegory of the loss of imperial power and the steps necessary to reassert it. The sudden disappearance of the civil servant Imray is a mystery. After a few months Strickland of the police – that transgressive figure whose hobby is gaining knowledge of India – rents Imray's bungalow.

When the narrator quarters himself upon his friend, he is witness to unaccountable and disconcerting events. Strickland's dog, Tietjens, refuses to sleep in the house with his master at night and bays at the moon; a strange visitor apparently calls to see the narrator but disappears before they meet; and the narrator has the impression that someone is calling him during a stormy night. The implication in all this is that Tietjens, as a dog, has access to an extra-sensory world not shared by the humans and has witnessed the manifestation of Imray's ghost. Despite the somewhat heavy-handed gothic touches of the voice in the storm and the spectral visitor who may have been a trick of the light, at this point the tale still stands neatly poised between gothic (conservative) and supernatural (radical) potentialities. However, the nature of the allegory, like the fate of the murderer, is sealed when Strickland, in pursuit of some snakes, discovers the body of Imray on the beam between the ceiling cloth and the roof. The rest of the narrative is concerned with the detection and punishment of the murderer and the reinvocation of the white man's power over the insubordinate native. Strickland's rationalism and relentless logic in pursuit of the murderer is invoked to underpin imperialist generalizations about the moral inferiority of Indians, as when Strickland remarks,

> 'If I call in all the servants they will stand fast in a crowd and lie like Aryans. What do you suggest?' 'Call 'em in one by one', I said. 'They'll run away and give the news to all their fellows,' said Strickland. 'We must segregate 'em!'. (1891, 271–2)

Thus one sees recommended a policy of divide and rule to gain knowledge and reinstate power, like that by which England seeks to control the wider empire in India.

Eventually, Imray's own servant, Bahadur Khan, admits to murdering his master because he believed that Imray had cast an evil eye upon his son, causing his death. Here is the centre of the allegory's horror: the body-servant's treachery recalls the vulnerable position of the sahib, and the very personal horror of the Mutiny, a recent and vivid memory for Kipling's Anglo-Indian contemporaries. The worst Anglo-Indian nightmare, the treacherous servant, is a metaphor for India in revolt. Nevertheless, over against this horror is revealed Strickland's capacity for solving the mystery, while Bahadur Khan's confession is a handing over of knowledge to the sahib and an acquiescence in the process of power. Furthermore, Bahadur Khan's quasi-British sense of honour is shown to be intact by his preference to make redress through suicide rather than go to the gallows. His vindication of Anglo-Indian codes of honour and fidelity, in the teeth of his own treachery confirms the social *status quo*, and is part of the process of reinstituting the original set of power relations. Rationalism's reply is shown to be more than a match for a controlled eruption of what might have been the supernatural. Indeed, the ostensibly supernatural events of the story merely serve to help the English detective by convincing him that there is a mystery for him to solve. The supernatural is therefore merely a function of Kipling's text: helping to confirm the superiority of the colonizer. At no time does the English *ghost* threaten to disturb the living Englishman's power, and once it has performed its role it disappears from the text never to return.

So too Kipling acts to thwart the potentially disquieting consequences of a richer and more fully developed gothic allegory, 'The Strange Ride of Morrowbie Jukes'. The full horror of the pit into which Jukes tumbles after his semi-delirious ride is established by the practical rather than imaginative character of Jukes's narrative. The detailed description of its geographical features and careful measurements reflect the civil engineer's cartographical first instincts; he deals with the mapping, planning and settling of land, a key part of the colonization process. However, that the deference and hierarchies subtending from normal colonial power relations are here, somehow, in a state of suspension, is suggested when Jukes's search of the river front which bounds one side of the pit, for a means of escape is, 'the signal for a bombardment from some insane native in a boat' (1895, 173), prefiguring Conrad's man-of-war shelling the bush in *Heart of Darkness*. However, here it is an example of anti-colonial, rather than colonial, aggression: roles are reversed with the colonizer at the mercy of the native, anticipating the allegory's nature.

That imperial race roles are disrupted here is made explicit when Jukes is confronted by the troglodytic inhabitants and reflects:

> I have been accustomed to a certain amount of civility from my inferiors, and on approaching the crowd naturally expected that there would be some recognition of my presence. As a matter of fact there was, but it was by no means what I had looked for. The ragged crowd actually laughed at me ...; some of them literally throwing themselves down on the ground in convulsions of unholy mirth. 'The Strange Ride of Morrowbie Jukes' (1895, 174)

Similarly, Gunga Dass, an ex-government servant of Jukes's acquaintance and now a resident of the pit, tells his former superior that he has stumbled upon a town where the dead 'who do not die' – those given up for dead because of catalepsy or a trance – are allowed to dwell by some unspecified authority. He utters a 'long low chuckle of derision – the laughter, be it understood, of a superior or at least of an equal' (1895, 178). Yet the real terror of the allegory is only brought into full relief when Jukes himself begins to recognize and acquiesce in the revised realities of his powerless state. He comments, 'being only a man [not a "heaven-born" now] ... I felt hungry and said as much to Gunga Dass, whom I had begun to regard as my natural protector' (1895, 179), after which Gunga Dass verbalizes the inverted master–slave disequilibrium now existing: he 'propounded the terms on which he would consent to "do" for me'. Jukes is forced to admit, 'Here was a sahib, a representative of the dominant race, helpless as a child and completely at the mercy of his native neighbours' (1895, 182). The political allegory is made explicit and Gunga Dass cites 'greatest good of greatest number' as the governing maxim, then glee-fully proclaims, 'We are now Republic'. Empire is suspended and what is set in its place is a kind of perverse Utilitarianism: a mockery of Western political systems.

However, at the height of its imaginative power, Kipling shies away from the revolutionary propensities of his narrative and 'The Strange Ride of Morrowbie Jukes' undergoes a kind of narrative breakdown. Morrowbie Jukes strikes Gunga Dass for refusing to tell him about the other sahib who had apparently fallen into the pit, whereupon, 'He stepped down from the platform at once and cringing and fawning and weeping and attempting to embrace my feet led me round to the burrow which he had indicated' (1895, 191). The incident suggests that native fear of and deference to the white man is inherent despite the contingencies of their present position. In order for Kipling to resolve the allegory satisfactorily and reactivate colonial power it must appear that the 'natural order' has simply been temporarily upset. In the same way Jukes decides not to ask Gunga Dass the whereabouts of the dead sahib's gun, 'knowing he would lie'; although this is a defamiliarizing narrative, Orientalist adages about native deceit are still in place, indeed their treachery is part of the horror. Likewise, when the sahib's escape route is discovered, Gunga Dass's eagerness to accompany Jukes back to 'terra firma' implies the native's realization of the over-riding benefits of imperial rule instead of the pit's communal anarchy. Armed with the sahib's notebook, the Englishman literally reclaims the land step by step: mapping the uncharted territory in a process of re-colonization. While it is suggested that the cartographer and the communicator – Dass is a former telegraph-master who deciphers the sahib's notes – need each other to effect escape, it requires an Englishman among all these natives to achieve it. Additionally, the white man must always be on guard for the black's treachery; as is demonstrated when Gunga Dass assaults Jukes leaving him senseless on the ground yards from freedom. Yet even this predicament can be salvaged by Kipling the eternal optimist; Jukes is rescued by the faithful servant figure of Dunnoo the dog-boy, who certainly is this man's best friend.

Kipling's idealized India comes to the rescue – the one that is happy with British rule – and his conservative will-to-power resurfaces in the slick and unlikely resolution needed to reactivate colonial power. The tale begins as an allegory of white loss of status and privilege: the 'nightmare scenario' in which a dissolution of imperial power relations takes place. It ends as a tale of British pluck, white moral superiority and the fidelity of those natives who know what is good for them. The text raises the question of how one survives, as a sahib, in a land where hegemonic signs are turned upside down, and then shrinks from an honest answer. To appreciate the disturbing radical possibilities of the events narrated one need only imagine the difference which would be made to the tale as allegory if Jukes had failed to escape from his pit and, say, his diary had been posthumously discovered containing this narrative; in other words, if British power were left in a state of suspension and not reactivated. (The horror of 'The Man who would be King', for example, exists in just such an inability to reactivate imperial power.) But this narrative is never told. Indeed, Kipling prevents any chance of such a narrative ever being told at the outset when the narrator introduces Jukes's own account, discussing the teller in the present tense, informing the reader that, 'He never varies the tale in the telling, and grows very hot and indignant when he thinks of the disrespectful treatment he received' (1895, 169) and – surely a significant comment given Kipling's own adulterating project – that Jukes has 'touched it up in places and introduced Moral Reflections'. The narrator's introduction ensures we know that Jukes has escaped his ordeal. It consigns the tale to the level of an unpleasant dream. The narrative is thus effectively neutered, defused of any revolutionary inclinations, and this highly conservative tactic – policing the defamiliarizing inner-narrative – allows the imperial reader to enjoy the fright and sleep easily in his bed afterwards.

Supernatural tales, potential allegories, frustrate such narrative castration. In so doing they expose certain truths about the methods by which Kipling can manipulate those more plastic texts we have examined. In 'The Simple Adventures of a Memsahib', Sara Jeanette Duncan comments, 'in India we know only the necessities of speech, we do not really talk' (1909, 309). This is a revealing comment on the nature of communication, the redundancy of words, in a society in which so much is recognized by outward signs and received notions of 'good form'. However, one can apply the statement, with equal validity, to Kipling's supernatural narratives to register the discrepancy one perceives between the attempt to create what one might call a Pukka Narrative – by ordering and reclaiming events from the twilight of irrationality and confusion: forcing them to obey 'the necessities of speech' – and what this Ultimate Other would say if it was allowed to 'really talk'. In 'The Mark of the Beast' the attempt to discipline the delinquent narrative consists of a twofold manipulation of language: a conspiracy to misuse speech among the characters, and the manipulation of information by the narrator in an attempt to render events. Indeed, the tale is only completed at all through that multi-purpose will-to-power, this time on the part of the putative narrator and witness to the events. In order for Western cognitive systems to survive they must triumph over the dissolution of reason, implicit in the power of 'the Gods and Devils of Asia'; they must efface and outface it. To tell the story, even if as the last paragraph suggests it will not be believed, is to reintegrate irrational events into the rational, linear narrative valued by the West and to reclaim them as a fund of knowledge through which the West can frame, represent and govern the East. An East/West power struggle is directly posited in the opening paragraph:

> East of Suez, some hold, the direct control of Providence ceases; Man being there handed over the power of the Gods and Devils of Asia, and the Church of England Providence only exercising an occasional and modified supervision in the case of Englishmen. (1891, 240)

In this context Church of England Providence is as much a cultural symbol, a euphemism for Western power, as a literal, theological entity. A number of late-nineteenth-century imperialists were quick to attribute British imperial power to the dispensation of an omniscient Providence.[1] In the mouths of paternalists, Providence comes to represent that 'moral right' by which the British rule India, projected in third person terms to signify its objectivity, its naturalness. However, here the words 'modified supervision' call attention to the reduction in that power which 'oversees'. For all his knowledge of the native, the detective Strickland is confronted in this tale with phenomena beyond the boundaries of his experience. As a result he is only slightly less vulnerable than the newcomer Fleete of whom we lear: 'His knowledge of natives was of course limited and he complained of the difficulties of the language' (1891, 241). His lack of knowledge leaves him unprotected while language difficulties mean that he cannot read native signifiers, written, spoken or implicit. His drunken attack on the statue of Hanuman, the Monkey God, which provokes the wrath of the priests, is a result of his ignorance. Fleete's 'Mark of the B–beasht' parodies significations of divinity – the mark on Hanuman's forehead caused by his cigar-butt is a mockery of the Hindu caste mark – and turns it into a sign of the diabolic.

Hanuman has been 'defaced' and it is suitably ironic that vengeance should be initiated by the Silver Man, literally a faceless leper and thereby beyond Western description. By marking Fleete's chest, the Silver Man is able to cast some sort of spell on the Englishman which progressively reduces him to the level of a beast. He bolts his food like an ostrich, grovels about in the garden, Strickland's horses rear away from him in terror, and his own language becomes a bestial howl. In de-civilizing Fleete, this manifestation of native power burlesques British imperialism's much-vaunted 'civilizing mission'. Fleete's dehumanization constitutes a fall down that social Darwinian scale which characterizes nineteenth-century anthropological thought.[2] Such reversal defines him as now Other, something less than normal. It contains implicit value judgements about human worth based on race and culture. Such complication exemplifies this text's dialectical methods. A struggle, based on the double play of power – East over transgressive West and West over transgressive East – epitomizes 'The Mark of the Beast' and is, at times, written into its structure. (For this story to be written at all the West must triumph but, as will be seen, the victory is somewhat Pyrrhic). Fleete's body becomes at once the sovereign's body (attacked) and the marked body of the transgressing criminal. The Mark of the Beast is, for both cultures, the sign of an alien power and an act of war. For the native it is an attack on the dignity and divinity of the god Hanuman that is punishable by retribution on the criminal's body. For the English it is an attack on the body of a white sahib, who stands in lieu of the Viceroy who stands in lieu of the Queen: an indirect assault on the sovereign.

The Silver Man's offensive presents a problem to Strickland, who makes it his business to know the native. He says of the Silver Man, 'I think I should peculiarly like to lay my hands on him' (1891, 249), recalling the Christian method of identification with another before God and, in this context, Christ's healing of lepers. (Likewise, the invocation of Christ represents a petition to the Ultimate Authority in Christian hagiology. With his preferred rationalism removed as an option Strickland appeals to a higher authority, yet one still within his own culture.) Yet in another sense the phrase records the frustration of powerlessness and a desire to inflict physical violence: 'just wait till I lay my hands on him!', the exercise of quite another kind of power and what will ultimately be required here. Thus the problem, and its possible solutions are presented. The text then proceeds to enact a struggle of its own in language. Those ideas and images which gainsay norms and threaten the illusion of benevolence that forms the foundations of imperial discourse, must be reclaimed in some way, made presentable, and the unpalatable necessities of the reactivation of power must be hidden behind a cloak of 'stiff-upper-lip' reticence. This can only be achieved by a determined and multi-faceted manipulation of language. In a sense, the text is tortured, like the Silver Man, but not to confess anything, rather to enforce a conspiracy of silence about that which its narrator would not have heard.

Such a conspiracy originates in the English characters through fear. Although he is aware of what is taking place, Strickland at first refuses to communicate his knowledge – that kind of knowledge which bespeaks an absence of power – to the narrator: 'I can't tell you what I think now … because you would call me a madman' (1895, 248). In the same way the narrator falters in his diagnosis, 'I tried to say "Hydrophobia" but the words would not come, because I knew I was lying' (1895, 251). In the face of this sudden paralysis of Western language the narrator must discover new ways of uttering the unutterable. As T.E. Apter says of fantasy literature in general:

> figurative language becomes the only means of making literal assertions, for ordinary meanings fragment, expand, splinter, either because some new, unknown order prevails, or because the former order functions haphazardly or piecemeal. Thus the fantasist must piece together a new language. (Apter cited in Kemp 1988, 31)

The narrator begins this process by reducing the horrors of Fleete's degeneration to a list or table of symptoms, narrated in a shocked staccato, in an endeavour to retain control over events: 'Strickland dashed into Fleete's room. [/] I followed, [/]and we saw Fleete getting

out of the window.[/]He made beast noises in the back of his throat.[/]
He could not answer us when we shouted at him.[/]He spat' [Obliques
added for emphasis.] Yet, as the horror grows, both characters and narrator become more desperate in the search for linguistic control. Thus
when the protagonists summon Dumoise the doctor to examine Fleete
they tell him the patient has suffered dog-bites and, although Dumoise
knows this is untrue, he agrees to certify that Fleete's anticipated death
was caused by Hydrophobia. The doctor and detective, Kipling's
'authorities' and authors of Pukka Narratives, merely admit their lack
of knowledge and absence of power.

Here, as Dr Jekyll might have noted, is 'one of those affairs that
cannot be mended by talking', and Strickland appears to admit as
much when he recommends a course of action, rather than words: 'we
must trust in Providence and go out softly with polo-sticks into the
shrubbery at the front of the house' (1891, 254) where the Silver Man
now hides. As we know, Providence is currently in a state of flux so the
plan may or may not work. However, the battle must be enacted on a
physical, as well as metaphysical and narrative, level 'with all the tortures that might be needful'. Similarly, the narrator begins to admit the
inability of English to codify and represent events when he concedes,
'the scene was beyond description.' Yet here the admission is charged
with a political motive because, of course, what comes to be literally
beyond description, and any inscription in the text at all, are the
tortures the English inflict on the leper to force him to lift the spell.
After describing trussing the leper, the narrator's self-imposed task of
censorship begins: 'Several things happened ... but they cannot be put
down here' (1891, 255). Moreover, the narrator endeavours to justify
the violence the sahibs use in an image which betrays the operation of
physical repression beneath the veneer of benevolent supervision:
'I understood then how men and women and little children can
endure to see a witch burnt' (1891, 255). Yet just as he is about to
damage irreparably his ethic of benevolent rule, the narrator
remembers himself and breaks off:

> though the Silver Man had no face, you could see horrible feelings
> passing through the slab that took its place, exactly as waves of heat
> play across a red-hot iron-gun barrel for instance. ... This part is not
> to be printed. (1891, 256)

This lapse into silence constitutes the ultimate use of the author–
narrator's censorship. The principle of spectacle is to be denied the

civilian reader. The operation must be hidden because this attempt to reintroduce an unquestionable power that can once again rely on supervision and surveillance involves use of that ur-power, physical coercion, which allowed colonization in the first instance. The narrator shrinks from depicting the brutal reactivation of sovereignty as it is anathema to the ideal of the British–Indian relationship. Yet, at the same time, in the teasing allusion to the instrument of torture, the heated gun barrel, the writer encodes a kind of knowingness into the text. The suggestion is that a true knowledge of the exigencies required by Empire is the preserve of a Masonic few, the insiders, the imperial ruling caste. Thus a second implied reader is invoked, one who understands and approves of the force necessary to maintain control. This reader is a sympathetic contemporary of the author–narrator who can participate in the flirtation around violence in the way a post-colonial reader can recognize but not condone.

Almost shamefacedly the Englishmen release the leper. The West has re-established its sovereignty over the East, although less by rational means than by violence, and even then the source of potential power must be returned to its natural environment. The trauma involved in a revelation of the arbitrary yet dependent nature of British power is revealed by Strickland's hysteria and the narrator's comment that, 'we had disgraced ourselves as Englishmen forever' (1891, 258). Boundaries have been crossed, essential hierarchies violated. Fleete has been rescued, but at a price. The narrator concludes: 'no one will believe a rather unpleasant story and … it is well known to every right-minded man that the gods of the heathen are stone and brass, and any attempt to deal with them otherwise is justly condemned' (1891, 259). Clearly this is heavily ironic. Yet it is consistent with that narrative will-to-power by which he has expunged unacceptable aspects and through which he has been able to draw the text to a comfortable and reassuring close.

Yet the ending to this truly supernatural tale can never be as neat and all-embracing as in the gothic allegories. Western 'right-minded' knowledge has investigated, digested and tabulated 'the gods of the heathen'. The supernatural confounds this process since the phenomena it offers are beyond words: thereby interrupting the power-knowledge taxonomical current. To believe this story is to surrender power through knowledge. Belief is 'justly condemned' on rational grounds because 'stone' and 'brass' things do not behave in this way – and because affording belief means also affording a subversive power to the 'gods of the heathen'. It is precisely this territory of cognitive and political anxiety that 'The Mark of the Beast' plays upon. The uneasy peace of the ending is unable to disguise the fact that the narrative framework cannot contain the horror of events, just as imperial discourse cannot support what has happened to Fleete and, more to the point, what must be done to reclaim him. The attempt to normalize events through language, to reclaim them in speech, is doomed, owing to the metamorphic nature of the attack, which operates on Fleete's body, bypassing and subverting the colonizer's language, as well as functioning beyond the jurisdiction of 'the known'. Like Mr Hyde's irrational violence, this Other power communicates by 'the mark' not 'the sign'. Indeed, the strong central images of the mark and the faceless Silver Man work to counteract the reclaiming narrative drive of the English narrator. In so doing they work in the way suggested by Clare Hanson, who correctly identifies a tension between image and narrative as the operative force in Kipling's stories:

> the image (even the image in words) negates language with all its differences and deferrals ... Language, or narrative, cannot attain such fullness of expression ... it is by its very nature un-full, partial, analytic, concerned with endlessly ... multiplying logical and causal relations. (Hanson 1984, 96)

Moreover, these large central images contribute to a critique of the ideology the tales apparently convey. For example, the image of the powerful yet dehumanized Silver Man questions the Englishmen's sovereignty over nature and the Other implicit in the very definition of empire by the *OED* as 'supreme and extensive dominion; absolute control'. The uncertain resolution of several tales illustrates the position of Kipling's texts between historicist certitude and nightmare image; a position which owes as much to Macherey's 'unconscious' of the text, 'the play of history beyond its edges', as to Orientalist clichés about the terrifying Indian climate and topography, or to Kipling's own unconscious. The symbolic force of an image like the Silver Man is considerable in range and implication. In a sense the Silver Man connotes history, and those otherwise excluded historical processes – Russian ambitions and embryonic nationalism for example – that trouble the text's unconscious. In this way, almost by accident, Kipling confronts an ideological utterance with a fictional utterance: ideological anxiety appears through the fissures which constitute formal aspects of a fictional text designed to demonstrate British ingenuity and support 'vulgar' imperial ideology.

The intrusiveness of ideology is always accompanied in Kipling by uncertainty. Such uncertainty frustrates the writing, by characters, narrator and author, of Pukka Narratives. A virtuous Aristotelian narrative of beginning, middle and end, is something the stories strive for but never achieve. Against the confident text there exists a sub-text which, despite the author's best endeavours, does not 'understand'. The text's double project is to 'speak India', and to acknowledge and contain the contradictions, deviations and disobedience which appear when this act of imaginative colonization is undertaken. The strained peace which Kipling imposes when his problems prove insoluble forms an infinite resource of deferral: he avoids directly facing his anxieties but, at the same time, his texts are unable to escape from them.

In avoiding the conclusion towards which his narratives tend, Kipling transfers the burden of resolution and interpretation to the reader in a way that anticipates Modernist poetics.[3] It is in this transfer that one may identify the distinguishing feature of potential, rather than realized, allegories. Potential allegories are 'do-it-yourself' allegories: the reader must make some sense out of them as Kipling cannot. They form areas where anxiety can no longer hide behind the regular structures of control. Potential allegories have a special, ongoing life as what they say, or more often what they do not say, changes in implication with succeeding generations of readers. While this may be true of all texts to a certain extent, the point is that the reader's willingness to empathize with the offered narrative position alters irretrievably with Independence. After 1947 the British imperial world-view begins to crumble and that very different creature the postcolonial reader emerges from the rubble with a different set of political priorities. He brings to bear special historical knowledge which would have been unavailable to a contemporary of Kipling. The hindsight offered by a late-twentieth-century perspective encompasses nothing less than the end of the empire Kipling presents. The post-imperial reader supplies that completion the author declines to furnish, in the light of decolonization. In short, the reader recognizes in certain strategies of evasion – those textual hesitations and omissions – seeds of doubt about the imperial project, its future and how to write it. Reticence characterizes the imperial narrative but the modern reader can read it against the grain so as to reveal it for the subterfuge it really is. From a crisis of grammar emerges a crisis of reading which the reader is able to resolve. As she does so the text changes from vehicle for conservatism into untameable source of power for the Other. Kipling's supernatural tales no longer tell the story he originally wrote.

Notes

1. These include the Earl of Meath (cited in John M. MacKenzie 1984, 232) and the Viceroy, Lord Dufferin (cited in Parry 1972, 20). Rosemary Jackson comments that fantasies locate good and evil 'outside the merely human. ... It is a displacement of human responsibility on the level of destiny: human action is seen as operating under the controlling influence of Providence, whether for good or evil' (1988, 53).
2. As Jackson writes: 'recidivism and regression to bestial levels are common post-Darwinian fantasies' (1988, 116). One can see another example of this popular sub-genre which also features the fragementation of language, in Wells's *The Island of Doctor Moreau.*
3. David Lodge exposes the anti-teleological nature of Kipling's work (Mallet 1989, 35–6).

12

Archaeology and Gothic Desire: Vitality Beyond the Grave in H. Rider Haggard's Ancient Egypt

Richard Pearson

H. Rider Haggard's fiction has not often been connected with forms of the gothic in Victorian culture, and yet it contains many of the regular motifs of the gothic tradition. Indeed, in his book on the gothic, Devendra P. Varma contends that Haggard's literary style was influenced by that of Beckford in *Vathek* (1987, 133). At a purely mechanistic level, Haggard's best known works deploy typical tropes of gothic fiction to create dramatic situations of terror: the sealed tomb and labyrinth of *King Solomon's Mines* (1885), the death pit of *She* (1886), the eerie bat-infested pyramid tomb of *Cleopatra* (1889), the torture dungeon of *The World's Desire* (1890). In the most derivative example, Thomas Wingfield, the hero of *Montezuma's Daughter* (1893), watches helplessly as Spanish priests bury alive in a dungeon wall a nun and her illegitimate baby (Haggard 1908, 66–7).[1] In addition, powerful and menacing figures who control and manipulate other characters by the exertion of dark preternatural or supernatural forces are central in many texts: the witch-like Gagool; Ayesha (and her priest); Harmachis, high priest of Isis in *Cleopatra*, and Cleopatra herself; Meriamun, the Pharaoh's queen in *The World's Desire*; Swanhild in *Eric Brighteyes* (1891). Add to these a stock of amulets, powders and poisons, resurrected corpses, dangerous shrines, murdering priests, curses and hauntings, Faustian pacts, ghostly temples, scenes of bondage and seduction, phantom ships and prophesies of doom, and the stories become reflections of a gothic sensibility. Good battles evil every page of the way, and the novels move unerringly towards their preordained but complicated resolutions, uneasily compromised by the complex set of cultural influences which produced them.

It is not the intention of this chapter to explore the 'gothickness' of Haggard's fiction. Rather, I wish to contend that Haggard was engaged on a project to restructure the gothic around the new discipline of archaeology (and, less interesting to me here, anthropology) being fashioned in the excavations in Egypt and elsewhere at the time. Moreover, Haggard's texts emphasize a linking of sexual desire and death, a gothic desire (Bristow 1997, 117), which is implicated in the processes of exhumation and 'resurrection' characteristic of late-Victorian archaeology. This, in turn, is a precursor of the Freudian 'death-drive'. Wherever archaeology features in Haggard's fiction, sexual desire and orgasmic death are never far off. Indeed, the archaeological site – the tomb or the temple – is invoked in his romances as a focalizing point for the intersection of physical desire, morbidity, and the displacement of ideal love into a spiritual realm beyond life. Archaeology releases forces of desire which the narrative seeks to re-contain; heroic love, for Haggard, involves a doomed perversity which condemns the hero to endless dissatisfaction and deferral of desire in the separation of death. If one wishes to read this symbolically, it might be suggested that Haggard viewed archaeology as ultimately dis-satisfying. The romantic desire to uncover the past only results in the replaying of eternal tragedies, it cannot intervene to break the inevitable cycle. Moreover, the sensibility which drove his contemporaries (and Haggard himself) to excavate and sift the debris of the past is, to Haggard, a manifestation of the intermingled forces of civilized culture and primitive instinct which characterizes his understanding of the human mind.

I shall focus my discussion on Haggard's Egyptian romances, *Cleopatra* (1889) and *The World's Desire* (1890), but would suggest that many of the series of books from *King Solomon's Mines* (1885) to *Montezuma's Daughter* (1893) partake of this fascination with the *un*dead of antiquity. Haggard himself recognized this series of texts to be his best work (1926 II, 12). Certainly, they are the most closely associated with the cultural popularity of archaeology, and at very least one might argue for Haggard's participation in the spread of public interest in this discipline.

Archaeology had progressed through the eighteenth and nineteenth centuries, away from its amateur aristocratic origins and towards a greater middle-class professionalism.[2] By the 1880s, the audience for archaeology was also changing. Discoveries in Egypt, in particular, were opening up the ancient world to a mass market of readers in

England and France keen to partake of the dramatic stories, both of discovery and of history, unfolding. The tourist industry had advanced on Egypt from the 1840s when Thomas Cook ran Nile river cruises. By the 1880s, Cook was investing in hospitals and hotels in Thebes and the Valley of the Kings (Romer 1981, 125). Interest was fuelled by Sir Gaston Masparo and Emile Brugsch Bey's discovery, in 1881, of a cache of mummified kings in the tomb of the Pinejem family. This tomb, surrounded by the romantic story of its discovery and robbery by the native Abd er Rassul family, and their subsequent torture and eventual succumbing to reveal its whereabouts, proved to contain the bodies of several key figures from the Nineteenth Dynasty, including Seti I and his son, Rameses II, the latter being the supposed pharaoh of Exodus and the Israelites' departure from Egypt. The English press went wild with the discoveries; the most informed report of the time was probably that by Amelia Edwards, full of exquisite line drawings, in the *Illustrated London News*, 4 February 1882. Egypt was hardly out of the newspapers that year, since the discoveries coincided with the British naval shelling of Alexandria and a British Expeditionary force's success in taking Cairo from armed Nationalist insurrectionists (Romer 1981, 155). Interest in Egyptology continued to grow throughout the 1880s. In June 1886, Masparo's unwrapping of several of the cache mummies was turned into a media and tourist event in Cairo. The unwrapping of Rameses II was the highlight of the show. In the English magazines, scholarly papers by popular writers began to appear. *Blackwood's Magazine*, for instance, published the work of Haggard's great friend (and collaborator on *The World's Desire*), Andrew Lang's 'Egyptian Divine Myths' in September 1886. In May 1887, *The Century Magazine* published a double feature of an account of the discovery of the Rameses II cache, 'Finding Pharaoh' by Edward Wilson (which included interviews with Brugsch Bey and Masparo), and an analysis of racial features in the mummies of the Dynasty in 'Pharaoh the Oppressor, and his Daughter'. Books were appearing, too, such as Samuel Manning's *The Land of the Pharaohs* (1887). While one of Haggard's acquaintances, who figures in his autobiography, Ernest A. Wallis Budge, brought out *The Mummy: Chapters on Egyptian Funereal Archaeology* in 1893.[3]

It is against this background that Haggard, in January 1887, undertook his own tour of Egypt. This included a trip to Boulak Museum, where Brugsch recounted to him the story of the finding of the 1881 cache and showed him the royal mummies, and to the pyramids at Giza, as well as a torchlight descent into the tomb of Seti I at the

Theban Valley of the Kings, and a near burial in a cave-tomb at Aswan (*Days of My Life*, I, 257–61). Haggard returned from Egypt to begin writing *Cleopatra* in May 1887 (the same month as Wilson's article appeared), and the novel was serialized in, of all places, the newspaper most keen to depict (literally) the sensational discoveries, the *Illustrated London News*, in 1889. When it did come out it was alongside accounts of British forces fighting in Egypt (against the Sudanese) and one can observe in *Cleopatra* a narrative dealing with the rise of Egyptian nationalism, since Harmachis, the central figure, intends to rid Egypt of the Greek yoke, represented by Cleopatra and the Ptolemaic line. In 1889, a few months before the serialization of *Cleopatra* in the *Illustrated London News*, the newspaper printed line drawings of a new exhibition of Egyptian artefacts from the area of the Labyrinth uncovered by Flinders Petrie in the spring of that year, and displayed in the Egyptian Hall in Piccadilly. Preparing the reader for exotic discoveries to come, the journalist commented, 'the gilded mummy cases with their painted portraiture ... are quite a revelation' ('JFR' 1888, 718). As if to emphasize a continuity in his work, Haggard set his next historical romance, *The World's Desire*, written in 1889 and serialized in the *New Review* in 1890, against the departure of the Israelites from Egypt (in a sense, although very marginal to the story-line, another narrative of national liberation), at approximately the time of Rameses II just unwrapped. The references are cryptic and oblique, however, and Haggard's hen-pecked pharaoh, Meneptah, of that text doesn't much remind one of Rameses the Great (and, indeed, it would seem that Haggard used the name of one of Rameses II's sons, Meriamun, as the name for his Queen).[4]

In a recent essay on *She* and archaeology, Shawn Malley argues that archaeology is essentially hermeneutic (1997, 275–97). It deals with a search for origins, and constructs an evolutionary sequence which establishes material continuity to the development of civilization. For him, this is also the pattern of *She*. Malley associates Haggard with the anthropology of his friend Andrew Lang; his line is a familiar one. As Rebecca Stott notes, while suggesting an anthropological reading of Haggard,

> The anthropologists were to tailor and adapt evolutionary theory to a more accessible and less troubling shape for the general public.

Anthropology both played to (and played out) the widespread alarms caused by the 'discovery' of the common ancestor of man and the ape and alleviated such fears by confirming at every point the evolutionary superiority of the white races. (1992, 10)

Supporting this reasoning, there is clearly present an Imperial dynamic in many of Haggard's texts: in *Cleopatra*, for instance, there is an interesting correlation between current Egyptian history and exploration and the novel's events – of conquest, of the new order replacing the old, and, in the modern day opening scene of the tomb descent, a sense of the white having superceded these ancient civilizations. In *The Illustrated London News* during the serialization of the novel, there were reports on the border wars in Egypt, led by Kitchener and the British, and, on 23 March 1889 (*ILN*, 372), a drawing of Scottish troops sitting at ease on the Sphinx (Figure 12.1).

However, archaeology does not quite support the same kind of world-view as anthropology. Archaeology is about desire: and Egyptian archaeology more so than any other. Egypt is the East; to many it is erotic, shameless, liberating, sexually threatening, fascinating. It was

12.1　An illustration, published in the *Illustrated London News* of 23 March 1889, of the King's Own Scottish Borderers sitting at ease on the Sphinx, in their bicentennial year.

more alien to the Victorians than Greek or Roman civilization. The archaeology of Egypt was more often than not associated with romance and excitement, with erotic desire – and also with death. John Barrell cites William Prime's 1857 account of his amateur archaeological experiences in Egypt to suggest the potency of Egypt to invoke Western male fantasies. Prime imagines a tomb-robbery and 'rape' of a female mummified corpse:

> What fingers tore the coverings from her delicate arms! What rude hands were around her neck, that was once white and beautiful! What sacrilegious wretches wrested the jeweled amulet from its holy place between those breasts, once white and heaving full of love and life, and bared her limbs to the winds, and cast them out on the desert sand! (Barrell 1991, 111)[5]

Such a sexualizing of the act of archaeological resurrection finds its counterpart in Haggard's texts, as indeed in other texts of late Victorian literature.[6] Prime's account is perhaps unusual, but even the general newspaper and magazine writing on Egyptian discoveries participate in the presentation of such archaeology as a romantic narrative of personal relationships. Edward Wilson writing of the finding of the cache of royal mummies in 1881, in the *Century Magazine*, May 1887, considers the 'story' as 'more romantic than any told in Egypt since Isis gathered the scattered remains of Osiris' (a story of lost desire referred to at the beginning of *Cleopatra*, *ILN*, 5 Jan. 1888, 11); he continues, '[n]ot until June last was this most royal mummy released from its bandages. That event is my plea for telling now what I know of the romantic finding and the place thereof' (Wilson 1887, 4, 5). In the same edition, there are also references to Hathor, 'the Egyptian Venus', a figure used centrally by Haggard in *The World's Desire*, and a citation of Amelia Edwards, who described the atmosphere of an exhumation thus: 'there is wafted to us a breath from the shores of old romance. We feel that love once passed this way, and that the ground is still hallowed where he trod' (Anon. 1887, 11–27).[7] It is this association of love, romance, eroticism, sensationalism and death, which made writing on Egypt so potent. As the reporter noted in an account of Flinders Petrie's exhibition of Egyptian funerary objects in Piccadilly in 1888, 'the Egyptians in all ages did their best to make death beautiful' (*Illustrated London News*, 30 June 1888, 718).

Egyptian archaeology had a particular place in Victorian England. It gathered around it stories of love, death, mystery, passions and dark forces, all of which became concentrated in the spectacular events such as the opening of a new tomb or the unwrapping of a mummy. Certainly, as archaeology historians have noted, archaeologists of the late Victorian period became obsessed with the uncovering of tombs to the detriment of other archaeological details present. Sexuality was attracted to Egyptology. Witness a comparison of the illustrations of *Cleopatra* in the *Illustrated London News* (2 March 1889) with an advertisement for soap (ILN, 9 March1889, 314) (Figure 12.2).[8]

Rather than read Haggard as using archaeology to support an imperial project to assert Victorian superiority, I want instead to read Haggard's fiction alongside a Foucauldian comment from *The History of Sexuality*:

> Rather than the uniform concern to hide sex, rather than a general prudishness of language, what distinguishes these last three centuries is the variety, the wide dispersion of devices that were invented for speaking about it, for having it spoken about, for inducing it to speak of itself, for listening, recording, transcribing, and redistributing what is said about it: around sex, a whole network of varying, specific, and coercive transpositions into discourse. Rather than a massive censorship, beginning with the verbal properties imposed by the Age of Reason, what was involved was a regulated and polymorphous incitement to discourse. (Foucault 1978, cited in Bristow 1997, 173–4)

Discussing sexuality and Haggard is nothing new. Feminist critics in particular have produced readings of his works which suggest, for instance, a conflation of imperial and sexual desire in the subjection of the Woman's/Africa's body. Sandra Gilbert, 'Rider Haggard's Heart of Darkness', makes this point clearly in her analysis of *She* (Gilbert 1996, 39–46). The column of fire which creates and then destroys Ayesha, 'this perpetually erect symbol of masculinity is not just a Freudian penis but a Lacanian phallus, a fiery signifier whose eternal thundering return bespeaks the inexorability of the patriarchal Law She has violated in Her Satanically overreaching ambition' (Gilbert 1996, 43). She adds that Haggard's *She* fits in with a tradition emerging around Salome, Lilith, Dracula, and Lawrence's *The Woman who Rode Away*, representing the sacrifice of the powerful female: 'In all these works, a man or group of men must achieve or at least bear witness to a ceremonial assertion of phallic authority that will free all men from the unmanning enslavement of Her land' (Gilbert 1996, 43). Rebecca Stott sets Africa and

12.2a   An R.C. Woodville drawing, published in the *Illustrated London News* of 2 March 1889 and inspired by H. Rider Haggard's *Cleopatra*, depicting Charmion with Cleopatra's chaplet.

Woman together too, pointing to the readings of the mountains of Sheba's Breasts in *King Solomon's Mines*, which lead down towards the mine-as-vagina and treasure–cave-as-womb. Stott also suggests how Ayesha's death is a moment of sexual ecstasy, 'the final sex/death

12.2b   A contemporary illustration, published in the *Illustrated London News* of
9 March 1889, for Pears Soap.

equation of the book' which completes the Cathartic revenge of man to
expel the overpowerful woman (Stott 1992, 123).

Such readings of Haggard are misleading, however. They ignore the
foregrounded and predicated central narrative drive, the death drive. It
is too simplistic to select novels where a female character dies at the
end and suggest that this is significant. Although Stott lists Beatrice
(suicide), Cleopatra, and Ayesha as examples, she ignores the deaths of
Odysseus (*The World's Desire*), Harmachis (who is the real centre of
Cleopatra), or Eric Brighteyes, all from the same period and some of the
same texts. Indeed, her reading of *She* ignores the detail that the death
of She Who Must Be Obeyed condemns the male hero, Leo, to an
eternal living death, an eternal loss of desire, a position which equates
him with Helen of Troy in *The World's Desire*. Indeed, the real narrative
here indicates that, as in Haggard's other texts of the period, the
moment of orgasmic fulfillment, of symbolic sexual union, becomes a
moment of frustration and separation, of lack, and of the defeat of
desire. It is the desire to transgress, to evoke and satisfy a gothic perversity of desire, which results in the destructiveness of desire, and the
separation in death suggested by these texts. And, most importantly, it
is the *inevitability* of this within male/female relations which attracts
and fascinates Haggard.

Consider for a moment Haggard's 1887 article, 'About Fiction', published while he was in Egypt, and which created a literary storm to
which he returned in April of that year (Haggard 1887, 172–80).
Writing on cultural difference, and attempting to unite the primitive
and the civilized in the nature of all mankind, Haggard suggests of
sexual love that 'those who are aquainted with the habits and ways of
thought of savage races will know that it flourishes as strongly in the
barbarian as in the cultured breast. In short, it is like the passions, an
innate quality of mankind. In modern England this love is not by any
means dying out ...' (Haggard 1887, 172). This is a strange article
which attacks modern Zola-esque writing as exposing the sexually
degrading, a conventional view of the day. And yet it also makes clear
that Haggard's own preoccupations of this time are with sexuality and
desire. 'Society', he says, 'has made a rule that for the benefit of the
whole community individuals must keep their passions within certain
fixed limits, and our social system is so arranged that any transgression
of this rule produces mischief of one sort or another, if not actual ruin,
to the transgressor' (Haggard 1887, 176). However, he points out the
tensions of such codification: 'human nature is continually fretting
against these artificial bounds' (Haggard 187, 176). What is wrong with
current literature, Haggard declares, is that it cannot see the heroic in
humanity, but only the base. For him, this struggle is an ancient and
heroic one: 'Doubtless under the surface human nature is the same
today as it was in the time of Rameses' (invoking the Pharaoh whose
body had recently been unwrapped; Haggard 1887, 179). Haggard's
greatest worry is the most illuminating part of the article – the power
of the author to influence behaviour. 'Sexual passion', he states, 'is the
most powerful lever with which to stir the mind of man, for it lies at
the root of all things human; and it is impossible to overestimate the
damage that could be worked by a single English or American writer of
genius, if he grasped it with a will' (Haggard 1887, 176–7). Sexual
passion, transgression, artificial bounds – savage passion in civilized
humanity – and the time of Rameses – these are all preoccupations of
Haggard's fiction during this fertile period. Such transgression cannot
be accommodated within the constraints of modern society, but
within the site or the relic of the archaeological past ('the time of
Rameses') such things can happen.

'Sexual passion is the most powerful lever' – the savage is within the
civilized; for Haggard, humankind battles against a social transgression
which is difficult for his complex psychology to evade. As Haggard's
friend (and co-author of *The World's Desire*) Andrew Lang nicely puts

it, 'The advantage of our mixed condition, civilized at top with the old barbarian under our clothes, is just this, that we can enjoy all sorts of things' (Lang 1887, 690). Haggard's texts are about masculinity, as feminist critics have suggested. But they are not chauvinistic and uncritical in their portraits. True, in some ways they are akin to what Barthes says of pornography, or 'books of Desire': 'So-called "erotic" books ... *represent* not so much the erotic scene as the expectation of it, the preparation for it, its ascent; that is what makes them 'exciting'; and when the scene occurs, naturally there is disappointment, deflation' (1975, 58). The narrative trajectory of Haggard's romances is usually towards this fulfillment of the male desire, towards orgasm and the preparation for the possession of desire. And yet the narrative always in the end thwarts this desire and leaves the male protagonist in a state of unsatisfied frustration and prolonged repetition of desire.[9]

Secondly, the site of sexual exchange in Haggard is frequently the site of archaeology. King Solomon's Mine, beneath Sheba's breasts, is a treasure reliquary and labyrinth, reused as a burial chamber by the recent local tribes, but which has the imprint of a lost Egyptian heritage. This early novel, written prior to Haggard's trip to Egypt, plays out briefly the pattern of the later stories when the relationship between Foulata the native girl and Good the Englishman comes to an end with her death in the treasure chamber-tomb. Their transgressive love, breaking racial codes, is ended at the site of the archaeological treasure the group searched for. In *She*, Ayesha too is of Egyptian origins and is tormented by the thought that Kallikrates and the Egyptian woman who murdered him might be together in death. Archaeological sites abound; the chamber where Holly and Job eat 'had served as a refectory, and also, probably, as an embalming-room' (Haggard 1911, 133–5). The chamber of the flame of eternal youth has 'the appearance of a tomb', the mummified corpse of Kallikrates lies within, and the walls reveal 'scroll and detail' of ornamentation (1911, 160–1). The chamber is clearly based on Haggard's knowledge and experience of archaeological sites. Love and death merge in this place, but they will again be parted in the moment of sexual ecstasy described by Rebecca Stott.

Haggard's engagement with archaeology, then, enabled him to depict sexuality as an intimate part of the structures of meaning surrounding the grave. He was able to write sexual desire into his texts because of the charged eroticism of the terms of reference within the archaeological enterprise. As John Barrell comments, much Western writing on Egypt repeats a series of conventions:

the expression of simultaneous desire and disgust for the Arab woman; the habit of personifying the East ... as a woman who is to be seen unveiled if the true East, or the true Egypt, is to be dis- covered; the representation of the landscape of Egypt, especially, as a place of death. (Barrell 1991, 106)

Haggard's fiction moves a step further than Lang's comment in 'Realism and Romance' that 'not for nothing did Nature leave us all savages under our white skins' (Lang 1887, 689). Lang rejects the writing out of primitive passions in man by scientific anthropologists, just as Haggard insists on representing the violent sexual energies which dominate civilized and heroic behaviour in the pasts and pre- sents of his novels.

Cleopatra (1889) is a novel which foregrounds these connections between desire, sexuality, the grave, the death drive, resurrection, vital- ity in death, and the terror of defeat and separation. Haggard is explor- ing what becomes later for Freud a central tenet in his understanding of human behaviour: 'The pleasure principle seems actually to serve the death instincts' as he says in *Beyond the Pleasure Principle* (Freud 1961, 57). However, in Haggard's work, death as a form of perverse fulfillment (a sexual 'little death') is denied.

Harmachis is the centre of *Cleopatra* (his name means 'Sphinx'). The son of an Egyptian priest of royal lineage, he is brought up as a devotee of Isis in the belief that his physical purity and male virginity will ensure the success of his aim to regain the throne of Egypt from the Greek Ptolemies, an interesting reversal of Victorian genderization. Becoming a favourite of the Queen, he has opportunity to slay her with a dagger (a phallic signifier, the handle of which is a gold sphinx), but his desire is also his impotency, and his love of Cleopatra prevents the fulfillment of his goal and he betrays his cause for his desire of the woman. Ironically, he is simultaneously betrayed by the maid, Charmion, who loves him with a similar passion. Cleopatra uses her power over Harmachis to force him into an alliance with her, which he accepts, thinking to be her husband. When she begins to ensnare Mark Antony, and scorn Harmachis, he flees. Living in the Valley of the Kings in Rameses III's tomb, he becomes a man of wisdom, and even- tually (in disguise) comes to advise Cleopatra, and his mystical voice urges her to flee the sea battle of Actium. Harmachis' narrative becomes one of revenge, but, like his desire, it is also doomed to failure. Although Haggard posits him as responsible for Cleopatra's downfall, Harmachis, too, is unable to escape from the fate of unrequited desire that awaits him. 'Free we are to act for good or evil', he tells Charmion, 'and yet methinks there is a Fate above our fate, that, blowing from some strange shore, compels our little sails of purpose, set them as we will, and drives us to destruction' (*ILN*, 29 June 1888, 816). This fatalism is a repeated motif in Haggard's novels of this period.

The opening of the text reproduces our significant moment of modern archaeology, referred to already – Brugsch's descent into the tomb of the royal mummies in 1881 (*ILN*, 5 Jan. 1889, 12) (Figure 12.3). Here, the unknown narrator descends into a tomb in Libya, 'the supposed burial place of the holy Osiris' (*ILN*, 5 Jan. 1889, 11), and discovers a coffin without ornamentation or name. Inside is a mummy; 'this mummy lay upon its side, and, the wrappings notwithstanding, its knees were slightly bent. More than that indeed, the gold mask, which, after the fashion of the Ptolemaic period, had been set upon the face, had worked down, and was literally pounded up beneath the hooded head' (*ILN*, 5 Jan. 1888, 11).

The narrator arrives at the horrific conclusion: 'the mummy before us had moved with violence *since it was put in the coffin*' (ILN, 5 Jan. 1888, 11). Harmachis (who we eventually realize is the mummy) had been buried alive by his priests for failing to remain pure to Isis. The significance of this find, then, is not a revelation of history, but of the mind of man. The tomb in fact reveals the perversity of a buried desire – the struggle of Harmachis in death ineffectually to subdue the haunting image of Cleopatra. Set alongside the 'married' couple of a Pharaoh and Queen, a normative group, the heroic desire is seen as the product of a perverse dynamic. For Harmachis, as for Cleopatra, there is no rest and no fulfillment, no symbolic satisfaction, in death. The tomb reveals the conflicts of desire still being fought out in death. Death is not the (sexual) climax expected.

As in the relationship between Ayesha and Kallikrates, Harmachis is cursed by eternal separation from his desire, a never-resolved desire for Cleopatra. This unremovable memory, a haunting in death, is placed upon Harmachis by Cleopatra herself, aware of her powers of fascination. Having taken the poison prepared for her by Harmachis (she is not killed by an asp, which was a symbolic death giving her immortality in dying for Egypt) whom she believes a physician, and then having found out the truth of his revenge, Cleopatra exposes her breasts to Harmachis, declaring: 'Now, put away their memory if thou canst! I read it in thine eyes – that mayst thou not! No torture which I bear can, in its sum draw nigh to the rage of that deep soul of thine, rent

12.3   An R.C. Woodville drawing, published in the *Illustrated London News* of 5 January 1889, showing the narrator of the Haggard story descending into the Libyan tomb.

with longings never, never to be reached! ... I spit upon thee ... and, dying, doom thee to the torment of thy deathless love!' (*ILN*, 22 June 1888, 788).[10] The archaeological tomb, then, has become the site of Harmachis' torment, but his is only a more startling fate to that which attends the other characters. Charmion is his female double: 'She has brain and fire and she loves our cause; but I pray that the cause come not face to face with her desires, for what her heart is set on that will she do, at any cost she will do it' (*ILN*, 16 Feb. 1888, 201). Cleopatra, also, is cursed by the spirit of the pharaoh whose pyramid tomb she 'excavated' and robbed, and is doomed to a Hellish separation from Antony.

Like most of Haggard's fiction, the narrative drive is predicted early in the story; central to the narrative dynamics is the inevitability of the death drive, the driving to destruction of the hero/ine by a fatal sexual desire. Harmachis knows his fate very early in the text, and states it in sexual terms: 'Alas! the seed that I had been doomed to sow was the seed of death!' (*ILN*, 2 March 1888, 268). But the text also establishes a gender reversal – the 'Fall' of Harmachis in the subheadings implies his sexual impurity, and his defeat by Cleopatra shows her to be his master – 'For she had conquered me, she had robbed me of my honour, and steeped me to the lips in shame, and I, poor fallen, blinded wretch, I kissed the rod that smote me, and was her very slave' (*ILN*, 30 March 1888, 392). Harmachis is a 'Fallen Man'; the sexual taint resides in both Harmachis and Cleopatra. As Haggard's essay 'About Fiction' had suggested, all are driven by such instincts. The inversion of Victorian gender ideology here serves to emphasize the potential for degeneration in both sexes, and the heroic fatalism of this force.

Cleopatra's fall is identified with another archaeological site – the pyramid (*ILN*, 13 April 1889, 465) [Figure 12.4]. Cleopatra and Harmachis enter the tomb (called *Her*) to rob its pharaoh of his treasure. The passage is a central moment in defining the perversion of desire within Cleopatra. Yet it also creates an identification between Cleopatra and Harmachis, both of whom will betray their nation for their sexual desires, their duty for their lusts. The pyramid contains a secret cache of hidden treasure, known only to successive pharaohs, and cursed with a demand that none shall take the wealth except to save Egypt (or the Empire). Cleopatra robs the pyramid in order to support her own luxurious lifestyle, and to seduce Antony, dragging her lover Harmachis reluctantly into the plot. The robbery is the most overtly gothic scene in the text, with a giant bat flying out as a representation of the spirit of the entombed pharaoh (a bat which will be called up at Cleopatra's death to curse her to tortures beyond the grave), and provides the clearest illustration of the decadence of Cleopatra's heart. The scene is also filled with overt sexual symbolism. As Lucy Hughes-Hallet's reading of the 'vulvaic wound' illustration suggests (*ILN*, 13 April 1888, 464) (Figure 12.5), the male pharaoh (and, by implication, Harmachis) is symbolically raped by the female Queen as she thrusts her hand repeatedly into the body to grasp the jewels (Hughes-Hallett 1991, 305).

12.4 An R.C. Woodville drawing, published in the *Illustrated London News* of 13 April 1889, showing Cleopatra, watched by Harmachis, about to plunge a dagger into the dead breast of the pharoah.

Haggard's repetition of the action indicates his meaning here: 'Cleopatra plunged her hand into that dread breast. ... Again, again, and yet again, she plunged in her hand. ... Again and again she plunged her white hand into that dread breast, till at length all were

12.5   The decorative lettering at the start of Haggard's *Cleopatra* from the *Illustrated London News* of 13 April 1889 showing the hand of Cleopatra plunging into the breast of pharoah to steal the jewels.

found ... I piled the torn mummy cloths over him and on them laid the lid of the coffin' (*ILN*, 13 April 1888, 464). As elsewhere in Haggard's fiction (particularly in the Viking saga, *Eric Brighteyes*) the (sexual) feminization of the male is a strong theme. The rape of the body further echoes the earlier seduction of Harmachis, using again the symbolic dagger: '[Cleopatra] took the dagger, and with set teeth the Queen of this day plunged it into the dead breast of Pharaoh of three thousand years ago. And even as she did so there came a groaning sound from the opening to the shaft where we had left the eunuch!' (*ILN*, 13 April, 464). The presence of the castrated eunuch offers a suggestive link to the violence of this attack. Cleopatra's power is sexual and corrupt (as the illustrations imply).

Cleopatra plays with the understanding that sexuality and death are intimately connected. Freudian annihilation is predicted in the climax of love; as Harmachis says, 'the love of women is a torrent to wash in a flood of ruin across the fields of Hope, bursting in the barriers of design, and bringing to tumbled nothingness the tenement of man's purity and the temples of his faith' (*ILN*, 2 March 1888, 268). Harmachis' 'fulfillment' is in death – the killing of Cleopatra to gain the throne. This later is restructured around his sexually-based revenge at rejection, a kind of rape. The killing of Cleopatra becomes a sexual moment of jealous revenge, the spurned lover taking his satisfaction, a moment related to Cleopatra's seduction of Harmachis (symbolized by her appropriation of his dagger from within his clothing; *ILN*, 23 March 1888, 365–6) and her 'rape' of the body of the pharaoh, Menka-ra (in later editions, written as 'Menkau-ra'). Throughout, though, Harmachis knows that the real death will be his own, entwined 'hand in hand ... towards our common end' with Charmion (*ILN*, 2 March 1888, 268). The priests of Isis to whom Harmachis belongs hold up death as the ecstasy sought by all: 'Shall we then fear to pass pure-handed where Fulfillment is and memory is lost in its own source, and shadows die in the light which cast them' (*ILN*, 9 Feb. 1888, 171). Yet, driven by the 'sexual lever of passion', the hero cannot gain such a fulfillment or lose the memory of his desire. His fate is the fate of humanity. Haggard writes in *The World's Desire*, of Helen, who has 'that Beauty which men seek in all women, and never find, and of the eternal war for her sake between the women and the men, which is the great war of the world' (Haggard and Lang 1890, 287).

Cleopatra is also denied her desire beyond death. As the poison overtakes her and she cries, "Oh, I die! – come, Antony – and give me peace!" (*ILN*, 22 June 1888, 788), her longed for union with Antony (vouchsafed her in many versions of the narrative) is denied. The spirit of Menka-ra intervenes and those she has murdered or spoiled return to drag her to her Hell, a Hell created by her own perverse desire. The scene is an echo of that within the gothic pyramid.

> The casement burst asunder, and on flittering wings that great bat entered which last I had seen hanging to the eunuch's chin in the womb of the pyramid of *Her*. Thrice it circled round, once it hovered o'er dead Iras, then flew to where the dying woman stood. To her it flew, on her breast it settled, clinging to that emerald which was dragged from the dead heart of Menka-ra ... (*ILN*, 22 June 1888, 788)

The language returns the reader to that trans-sexual rape of Menka-ra, the violation of the womb-pyramid of Her (the female nomenclature is surely deliberate, as the name is changed to *Hir* in a brief reference in *The World's Desire*). Cleopatra's union in love-beyond-the-grave with Antony is not permitted in this complex world of sexual motivations and drives. All are torn apart by such 'levers'. Even Harmachis, in his moment of triumphant revenge, realizes the fate which awaits him: 'For though that thing we worship doth bring us ruin, and Love being more pitiless than Death, we in turn do pray all our sorrow back; yet we must worship on, yet stretch out our arms towards our lost Desire, and pour our heart's blood upon the shrine of our discrowned God' (*ILN*, 22 June 1888, 789). Meriamun, too, faces such a fate in *The World's Desire*, when she strips naked to forge a pact with the evil within herself represented by a snake, 'that which brought on thee the woe that is in division from the Heart's Desire, and the name thereof is Hell' (1890, 191).

Rider Haggard's text uses two central scenes associated with the current popular vogue for Egyptology in order to explore this gothic desire. Harmachis becomes the mummified corpse of the discovered archaeological tomb, and his symbolic 'unwrapping' through the parchment narrative found with his corpse reveals him to be the epitome of the victim of his own sexual drives: driven into actual death, entombed in a frenzy of inescapable desire, unable to block out his own hormones and the image of the sexual desirability of Cleopatra. Secondly, the symbolic rape which is the unwrapping of Menka-ra in the pyramid tomb creates a complicated inter-relationship between archaeology and sexual perversity. The description of the discovery of the mummy suggests an awkwardness which carries over into Haggard's present world of excited archaeological investigation. Like Harmachis, reopened to the world by the modern archaeologists at the beginning of the text, Menka-ra is violated by Cleopatra and Harmachis. Haggard's description of this event is clearly influenced by what he learned in the Cairo museum being shown the mummified remains of Rameses II by Brugsch Bey in 1887.

> Then together we mounted on the Sphinx, and with toil drew forth the body of the Divine Pharaoh, laying it on the ground. Now Cleopatra took my dagger, and with it cut loose the bandages which held the wrappings in their place, and the lotus-flowers that had been set in them by loving hands, three thousand years before, fell down upon the pavement. Then we searched and found the end of the outer bandage, which was fixed in at the hinder part of the neck. This we cut loose, for it was glued fast. This done, we began to unroll the wrappings of the holy corpse. Setting my shoulders against the sarcophagus, I sat upon the rocky floor, the body resting on my knees, and, as I turned it, Cleopatra unwound the cloths; and awesome was the task. ... At length all the bandages were unwound, and beneath we found a covering of the coarsest linen ... we laid the mummy down and ripped away the last covering with the knife. First we cleared Pharaoh's head, and now the face that no man had gazed on for three thousand years was open to our view ... and then, made bold with fear, [we] stripped the covering from the body. There at last it lay before us, stiff, yellow, and dread to see ...
> (*ILN*, 13 April 1888, 464)

These moments bring with them the sense that Haggard saw in modern archaeological tomb excavations a part of the primitive drive present in other aspects too of the civilized man. The tendency of his age was ambivalent; in his characterization of human nature, Haggard saw integrity and betrayal, beneficence and selfishness, good and evil, intertwined. What Jonathan Dollimore has called 'perverse desire' (1996, 26) in early twentieth-century fiction, is clearly present in Haggard's (and other 1890s) texts. '[D]esire', Dollimore contends, 'is simultaneously in the grip of regression and progression, both of which drive it deathwards ... a brilliant subject of an 'advanced' culture makes a fatal deviation from that culture's normative trajectory, embracing in the process what it defines itself over and/but also against' (Dollimore 1996, 98). Dollimore is talking about Kurtz in

Conrad's *Heart of Darkness* (1899), and about the primitive within the civilized – precisely those terms used by Lang and Haggard in their essays. For Dollimore, this perversion is part of an imperial trajectory: by taking the ideology of Empire to the extreme, Kurtz finds savagery; in essence, overcivilization leads back to the primitive and death. Cleopatra is a sexual version of this: decadent, sensual, erotic, surrounded by snake imagery (as are many female characters in Haggard, including Ayesha, Meriamun and Swanhild), she is power corrupted by perverse desire. In its transferring of gender roles between characters, the narrative shows how desire collapses identity, forcing the individual to occupy a defining position as its own otherness. The pursuit of sexual power and possession is driven by a desire which will only result in powerlessness and thralldom. This is what Freud, beginning his work in this period, later came to define as the death drive.

Haggard moved on in his fiction to explore the theme of desire in more detail in *The World's Desire*, a book co-authored with Andrew Lang, who was responsible only for the opening pages dealing with Odysseus' journey back to Ithaca.[11] This is a strange and fragmented book, moving from Odysseus' returning to Ithaca to find Penelope slain by plague, and the goddess Athene telling him to search for the World's Desire, Helen of Troy, in Egypt, to his adventures in Egypt in what appears to be the time of the Israelite exodus. The plot, however, is a simple one and similar to *Cleopatra*, *Eric Brighteyes* and others. Odysseus finds Helen, they fall in love, but the hero is seen by the Queen, the evil and magical Meriamun, who comes to desire him with a more bitter lust. Intending to escape with Helen, Odysseus is duped by Meriamun, who substitutes herself for Helen and sleeps with him. When they awaken, and Odysseus realizes he has been tricked (a scene used again in *Eric Brighteyes*), Meriamun accuses him of rape and has him bound and cast in a dungeon. Odysseus is subsequently released on the promise that he will fight the invading Greeks of his own nation and save Egypt, but, being slain by his own son in the battle, Odysseus is cremated on a funeral pyre. As his body burns, Meriamun throws herself on the flames and her snake girdle (symbol of an evil power to which she has devoted herself) wraps itself around the two of them and drags them down to Hades. The veiled Helen walks sadly away and wanders the earth waiting for Odysseus to return (an antique version of Ayesha).

In this story, Helen is the ideal of male desire (perhaps rather than the world's, although in Odysseus' heroic muscularity it is possible that Haggard intended his hero, too, to be an embodiment of the erotic male): 'there is but one thing that all men seek and are born to find at last, the heart of the Golden Helen, the World's Desire, that is peace and joy and rest' (1890, 205). As elsewhere, this desire is bound together with death, of course. Helen is 'the centre of all desire' and also 'the daily doom of men' (1890, 187). Such a role is enacted by her in the Temple of Hathor (the goddess equated to Venus by Egyptologists). The temples of the novel appear as another set of archaeological sites, symbolic of Woman and associated with their powers. Meriamun attends the Temple of Osiris, 'Lord of the Dead' (1890, 84), in Tanis. This has 'curtains that veil the sanctuary of the Holy Place ... no fire must enter there, save that which burns upon the altar of the dead' (1890, 80). The juxtaposition of fire and death symbolizes the kind of destructive sexual love offered by Meriamun. Helen's temple indicates the closeness of competing imagery between Helen and Meriamun. Where the statue of Osiris in Meriamun's temple is made of 'the black stone of Syene' (1890, 80), here it is the walls of the temple themselves (1890, 122). Helen's temple is arrived at via an 'avenue of sphinxes' (1890, 123), an image also associated with Meriamun, whose face on beholding the seduced Odysseus, 'was as cold as the face of the dead, and on it was a smile such as the carven sphinxes wear' (1890, 220). But Helen's temple is a temple of life, despite the destruction it causes: '[Hathor] wore a cow's head, and here the face of a woman, but she always bore in her hand the lotus-headed staff and the holy token of life ...' (1890, 122).

The Siren-like singing of Helen draws men to enter her Temple, and as they seek to penetrate into the inner sanctuary-chamber, in erotic madness, they are slain by invisible swords protecting the gateway to her physical self. She is 'Beauty's self – the innocent Spirit of Love sent on the earth by the undying Gods to be the doom and the delight of men; to draw them through the ways of strife to the Unknown end ... to the peace beyond the strife, to *the goal beyond the grave*' (1890, 156, my emphasis). Yet it is the physicality of her presence which maddens the Egyptian men and destroys normative Egyptian relationships. The ordinary women wail in anguish as Helen's beauty leads the men of the city to their deaths. Odysseus, the hero, conquers the temple (like an ancient Lancelot) and wins her love.

However, on the surface, Helen's destruction of men is unwitting and innocent, the consequence of their flawed natures and not of her manipulation of their desires. Meriamun, on the other hand, is the all-consuming female desire that tempts and destroys the male-beloved. Her dungeons contain a symbolic Gothic cage in the shape of a woman

– the 'cage of Sekhet' – in which the imprisoned man is chained and burned alive ('the last torment by fire') (1890, 250). She it is who represents the destroyer: 'For thou [Meriamun] art she in whom all woes are gathered, in whom all love is fulfilled … evil shalt thou ever bring on him whom thou desirest' (1890, 193).

Death is the male's doom whichever way he turns in this novel – either lured to death by female beauty that has no concern for him, or seduced and destroyed by a willful and selfish female sexual gratification. The death drive is complete here. Desire and death are inseparable; male desire will always be consumed and never fulfilled except in such fulfillment as brings only misery and an 'undead' death, a life-in-death. Woman, as Helen, 'goes wandering, wandering, till Odysseus comes again' (1890, 223). As Odysseus dies, he hopes for a reunion with Helen in death – she offers, for him, the possibility of some future fulfillment of his desire beyond the grave. But Odysseus can only offer a cryptic and entangled answer, which, in its very ambivalence, suggests the perverse dynamics of the text: 'Yea … there or otherwise shall we meet again, and there and otherwise love and hate shall lose and win, and die to arise again. But not yet is the struggle ended that began in other worlds than this, and shall endure till evil is lost in good, and darkness swallowed up in light' (1890, 313). The entwining snake of Meriamun completes Odysseus' misery by destroying the reunion he hopes for beyond the grave; as in *She* or *Cleopatra*, death brings only unfulfilment and despair.

Fire imagery is present throughout this text as a symbol of all-consuming and destructive passion. Fire destroys Hathor's temple, and in fire Meriamun destroys Odysseus and herself in a consuming passion. The real physical force of fire however is the manifestation of consuming and self-destructive desire. Even at the beginning of the book, the loss of love – the death of Odysseus' wife, Penelope – is connected with fire: Odysseus finds only the charred remains of his wife and people, 'the charred black bones of the dead … the ashes of men and women … consumed on one funeral fire' (1890, 7). Odysseus' discovery of his dead wife is a grotesque parody of the archaeological find. Odysseus catches sight of a glittering bracelet amongst the ashes:

> it was the bone of a fore-arm, and that which glittered on it was a half-molten ring of gold. …At the sight of the armlet the Wanderer fell on the earth, grovelling among the ashes of the pyre, for he knew the gold ring which he had brought from Ephyre long ago, for a gift to his wife Penelope. This was the bracelet of the bride of his

youth, and here, a mockery and a terror, were those kind arms in which he had lain ... he gathered dust and cast it upon his head till the dark locks were defiled with the ashes of his dearest, and he longed to die. (1890, 8)

Odysseus is like a dead man, 'all his voyaging was ended here, and all his wars were vain' (1890, 9). But it is in this moment of spiritual death that he is blessed (or cursed) with the reawakening of desire. He is visited by a vision of Athene who determines to claim the warrior to a more potent desire: '[t]hou that hast never loved as I would have men love' (1890, 17). The Goddess scorns Odysseus' love of Penelope: 'thou didst love her with a loyal heart, but never with a heart of fire' (1890, 17).[12] It is this consuming and destructive passion that Athene inspires in Odysseus through a glimpse of the beauty of Helen, the World's Desire. It is this opening revelation of heroic desire which dooms Odysseus to his perverse sexual death.

Although this romance has less of the overt archaeological framing of *Cleopatra*, nevertheless, it employs a similar movement from archaeological site to the consuming life-in-death of an unfulfilled desire, a gothic desire which blends death and love in one. Again, it is the cyclical nature of the narrative which remains potent. Odysseus, like Penelope, is consumed in a funeral pyre, leaving Helen to assume the role of forsaken and dissatisfied wanderer. The great cycles of human passion, destructive, and never ending, never reaching consummation, continue forever, over-laying the small local histories which archaeology reveals. Haggard signifies this in *Beatrice*, published in 1890, the same year as *The World's Desire*; the Roman ring which cemented the love of Beatrice and Geoffrey returns with him to the grave,

it should never leave his hand in life, and that after death it should be buried on him. And so it will be, perhaps to be dug up again thousands of years hence, and once more to play a part in the romance of unborn ages. (1917, 297)

This relic is inscribed in Latin, 'Ave atque vale' – 'Greeting and farewell' – a suitable cyclical motto.

Desire in Haggard's fiction, then, is a 'gothic desire', a term used by Joseph Bristow to incorporate 'the potency of deathly desire' and the 'deathliness of sex' (Bristow 1997, 30). Using the culture of ancient Egypt, with its beliefs in life beyond death, he creates a significant intervention in the debates about sexuality current in the fin-de-siècle. For psychoanalysis, death may be the 'little death' of orgasm, the culmination of the narrative drive towards fulfillment of sexual gratification and desire. As Freud describes: 'We have all experienced how the greatest pleasure attainable by us, that of the sexual act, is associated with a momentary extinction of a highly intensified excitement' (Freud 1961, 56) and the sexual instincts 'prepare the excitation for its final elimination in the pleasure of discharge' (Freud 1961, 56). But death is not an ending for Haggard's characters. It is not rest either. The 'little death' of the narrative climax links the male protagonist not with a satisfying procreative sex, but with a perverse destructive sex, which arrives as the inevitable fulfillment of his inner drives. Haggard's narratives plot the sexual destruction of the male, but this destruction is always desired. The protagonist cannot avoid his fate; as Eric Brighteyes says, having awakened in bed with the woman he hates: 'I am an unlucky man who always chooses the wrong road' (1963, 228). In death, the protagonist is tormented by simultaneous recognition of the impotent nature of 'normal' desire and the recognition that eternity will be an insufferable ever-presence of perverse or gothic desire. Odysseus is dragged into Hell by Meriamun; Harmachis is (apparently) 'mummified' (or, at least, bandaged as a mummy) and buried alive with the image of Cleopatra tormenting his mind.

Sex/death is the fulfillment of expectation and fate set out in the text, it is prepared for throughout. But for Haggard's characters the arrival at this point is endless unfulfilment of sex/death. The unquiet grave brings us back, as readers, to the usurpation of archaeology as a site of sexual rather than scientific discourse. As the opening of the tomb at the beginning of *Cleopatra* suggests, archaeology is about resurrection. It defeats endings. Although a part of the processes himself, Haggard was to worry in his autobiography about this, echoing the symbolic structures of his fiction: 'It does indeed seem wrong that people with whom it was the first article of religion that their mortal remains should lie undisturbed until the Day of Resurrection should be haled forth, stripped and broken up, or sold to museums and tourists ...'. (1890 II, 158). In his late Victorian study of sexualities, of the perverse dynamics of death/desire, Haggard encoded that very haling forth. He describes the death which is no death; the desire which cannot be fulfilled but which requires the one who desires to return again and again, to come again, and re-enact for other times the failure of fulfillment. The terror of Haggard's fiction is actually the terror

of the male never quite dying, always never achieving in death the ultimate satisfaction of closure, of final consuming death. Death is never
death; vitality is never quite extinguished, but never quite fulfilled either.
The archaeological tomb is no tomb, only a site of further discourse, of
resurrection. For that reason, in Haggard's fiction, it becomes a potent site
for the conflicts of modern sexual desire.

Notes

1 There is no standard edition of Haggard's writings. I have therefore used,
   where possible, the Longmans Silver Library edition for many of the briefly
   referred-to texts. For the main texts, I have used the serial version of
   Cleopatra (5 January–29 June, 1889), and the first edition of *The World's
   Desire* (1890).
2 There are many sources for the history of Egyptian archaeology through the
   nineteenth century, but most details can be found in Rohl (1995) and
   Romer (1981).
3 Other contemporary books and pamphlets include important works by
   W.M. Finders Petrie, Gaston Masparo, and E. Naville. Earlier books by
   Sir John Gardner Wilkinson, Richard Lepsius, Giovanni Belzoni, and
   Auguste Mariette, among others, were also popular and probably available
   to Haggard.
4 As Budge indicates (1893, 91) Meneptah I reigned after Rameses II. Rohl
   cites him as 'Merenptah' with dates of 1213–1203 in the conventional
   chronology (1995, 20). Haggard might have been speculating on a new
   dating for the Exodus events or reflecting a current view.
5 Prime also refers to 'resurrectionists' (archaeologists) as robbers supplying
   tourists with relics (cited in Barrell 1991, 111).
6 See, for example, Marie Corelli's *The Sorrows of Satan* (1996) or Richard
   Marsh, *The Beetle* (1994), both of which draw their gothic inspiration from
   Ancient Egypt.
7 For a discussion of Amelia Edwards' romantic attitudes towards archaeology, see Billie Melman (1995, 254–9).
8 This advertisement appeared in the *Illustrated London News*, 9 March 1889.
   Lillie Langtry became the first woman to endorse a commercial product
   when she signed a contract with Pears in 1882. From 28 April 1890, she
   played the part of Cleopatra in a performance of Shakespeare's *Antony and
   Cleopatra*, produced by herself at the Prince's Theatre, undoubtedly building
   on the popularity of Haggard's novel. See accounts and photographs in
   Brough (1975, photo between 256–7) and Gerson (1972, 89, 151–2 and
   photo opp. 129). I am indebted to Dr Claire Cochrane for pointing out
   Langtry's performance.
9 For an argument that serial fiction mirrors the female sexual arousal and
   climax, see Hughes and Lund (1995, 143–64). I would contend, however,
   that Haggard's serial more closely symbolizes male desire seen as a repetition of sexual climax resulting in self-annihilation.

10 The female breasts as both a symbol of nurture and of temptation seems indicated in the imagery of *King Solomon's Mine*, too; in *The World's Desire*, Meriamun's stone snake bites her breast and then wraps itself around her as a girdle, naming itself as her 'sin' (190–1).

11 For biography and criticism of Haggard (both emphasizing an Imperial view of the author) see Pocock (1993) and Katz (1987).

12 Meriamun is part of this theme of familial relationships. She is the corrupt wife and mother – 'Pharaoh's wife, but never Pharaoh's love (1890, 182), and is the half sister of the Pharaoh. She uses the dead body of her son as a shield against an armed group come to seek revenge for the (Biblical) deaths of the first born (1890, 111).

Bibliography

Allen, Grant. 'Woman's Intuition'. *The Forum* IX (1890): 334.

Andrews, Malcolm. *Dickens and the Grown-Up Child*. Basingstoke: Macmillan, 1994.

Andriano, Joseph. *Our Ladies of Darkness: Feminine Daemonology in Male Gothic Fiction*. University Park, PA: Pennsylvania State University Press, 1993.

Anon. 'Pharaoh the Oppressor, and his Daughter, in the light of their Monuments'. *The Century Magazine* 34 (May, 1887): 11–27.

Anon. *Beowulf and the Fight at Finnsburgh*. Ed. F.R. Klaeber. Lexington: Heath and Company, 1950.

Anon. *The Lancet* (May 24 1890): 1133.

Apter, Emily. *Feminizing the Fetish: Psychoanalysis and Narrative Obsession in Turn-of-the-Century France*. Ithaca: Cornell University Press, 1991.

Arata, Stephen. *Fictions of Loss in the Victorian fin de siècle*. Cambridge: Cambridge University Press, 1996.

Armstrong, Isobel, and Joseph Bristow, eds. *Nineteenth-Century Women Poets: an Oxford Anthology*. Oxford: Clarendon Press, 1996.

Armstrong, Isobel. *Victorian Poetry: Poetry, Poetics, and Politics*. London: Routledge, 1993.

Arnold, Matthew. *Culture and Anarchy*. Ed. Samuel Lipman. New Haven: Yale University Press, 1994.

Arnold, Matthew. *Selected Criticism of Matthew Arnold*. Ed. Christopher Ricks. New York: Signet, 1972.

Arnold, Matthew. *Selected Prose*. Ed. P.J. Keating. Harmondsworth: Penguin, 1970.

Auerbach, Nina. *Our Vampires, Ourselves*. Chicago: University of Chicago Press, 1995.

Baldick, Chris. *In Frankenstein's Shadow: Myth, Monstrosity, and Nineteenth-Century Writing*. Oxford: Clarendon Press, 1987.

Barney, Stephen A. *Word–Hoard*. New Haven: Yale University Press, 1977.

Barrell, John. 'Death on the Nile: Fantasy and the Literature of Tourism, 1840–1860'. *Essays in Criticism*. 41 (April, 1991): 97–127.

Barrett Browning, Elizabeth. *The Poetical Works*. London: Smith, Elder, & Co., 1898.

Barthes, Roland. *Camera Lucida*. London: Vintage, 1993.

Barthes, Roland. *The Pleasure of the Text*. Trans. Richard Miller. New York: Noonday Press, 1975.

Batchen, Geoffrey. *Burning with Desire: the Conception of Photography*. Cambridge: MIT Press, 1997.

Baudrillard, Jean. *For a Critique of the Political Economy of the Sign*. Trans. Charles Levin. St Louis: Telos Press, 1981.

Beckson, Karl. *The Oscar Wilde Encyclopedia*. New York: AMS, 1998.

Bennett, Paula Bernat, ed. *Nineteenth-Century American Women Poets: an Anthology*. Oxford: Blackwell, 1998.

Berry, Philippa. 'The Burning Glass: Paradoxes of Feminist Revelation in *Speculum*'. In Carolyn Burke, Naomi Schor and Margaret Whitford, eds. *Engaging with Irigaray: Feminist Philosophy and Modern European Thought*. New York: Columbia University Press, 1994. 229–47.

Bhabha, Homi K. *The Location of Culture*. London: Routledge, 1994.

Binet, Alfred, and Charles Féré. *Animal Magnetism*. London: Kegan Paul, 1891.

Blake, William. *Blake: the Complete Poems*. Ed. W.H. Stevenson, 2nd edn. London: Longman, 1989.

Bloom, Harold. *The Anxiety of Influence*. Oxford: Oxford University Press, 1973.

Boos, Florence Saunders. *The Poetry of Dante G. Rossetti: a Critical Reading and Source Study*. The Hague: Mouton and Co., 1976.

Booth, Wayne C. *The Company We Keep: an Ethics of Fiction*. Berkeley: University of California Press, 1988.

Boothby, Guy. *A Bid for Fortune, or, Dr Nikola's Vendetta*. London: n.p. 1895.

Borch-Jacobsen, Mikkel. *The Emotional Tie: Psychoanalysis, Mimesis and Affect*. Trans. Douglas Brick *et al*. Stanford: Stanford University Press, 1993.

Botting, Fred. *Gothic*. London: Routledge, 1996.

Braddon, M.E. *Aurora Floyd*. Ed. and int. P.D. Edwards. Oxford: Oxford University Press, 1996.

Brake, Laurel. *Subjugated Knowledges: Journalism, Gender and Literature in the Nineteenth Century*. Basingstoke: Macmillan, 1994.

Brannigan, John, Ruth Robbins and Julian Wolfreys, eds. *Applying: To Derrida*. London: Macmillan, 1996.

Bridges, Robert. *Collected Essays*. London: Oxford University Press, 1931.

Bristow, Joseph. *Sexuality*. London: Routledge, 1997.

Bronfen, Elisabeth. *Over Her Dead Body*. Manchester: Manchester University Press, 1992.

Brough, James. *The Prince and the Lilly: The Story of Edward VII and Lillie Langtry*. London: Hodder and Stoughton, 1975.

Brown, Charles Brockden. *Edgar Huntley, or the Memoirs of a Sleepwalker* (1799). Bowling Green: Kent State University Press, 1984.

Browne, Nelson. *Sheridan Le Fanu*. London: A. Barker, 1951.

Browning, Elizabeth Barrett. *The Poetical Works*. London: Smith, Elder, & Co., 1898.

Bruhm, Steven. *Gothic Bodies: the Politics of Pain in Romantic Fiction*. Philadelphia: University of Pennsylvania Press, 1994.

Buchan, John. *Three Hostages*. Oxford: Oxford University Press, 1995.

Buchanan, Robert. 'The Fleshly School of Poetry: Mr. D.G. Rossetti'. *Contemporary Review* 18 (1871): 334–50.

Buckler, William. '*The Picture of Dorian Gray*: an Essay in Aesthetic Exploration'. *Victorians Institute Journal* 18 (1990): 135–74.

Budge, Ernest A. Wallis. *The Mummy: Chapters on Egyptian Funereal Archaeology*. London: n.p., 1893.

Bulwer Lytton, Edward. *A Strange Story: an Alchemical Novel*. (1861–62) London: George Routledge and Sons, 1888.

Bürger, Gottfried August. *Bürger's Gedichte*. Leipzig: Bibliographisches Institut, 1932.

Burne-Jones, Georgina. *Memorials*. London: n.p., 1904.

Burrow, J.W. *A Liberal Descent: Victorian Historians and the English Past*. Cambridge: Cambridge University Press, 1981.

Butler, E.M. *Sheridan: a Ghost Story*. London: n.p., 1931.

Calloway, Stephen. *Aubrey Beardsley*. London: V & A Publications, 1998.

Carroll, Lewis. *The Letters of Lewis Carroll*. Two Volumes. Ed. Morton N. Cohen. Basingstoke: Macmillan, 1979.

Castle, Terry. 'Phantasmagoria: Spectral Technology and the Metaphorics of Modern Reverie'. *Critical Inquiry* 15 (Autumn 1988): 26–61.

Castle, Terry. 'The Spectralization of the Other in *The Mysteries of Udolpho*'. In Felicity Nussbaum and Laura Brown, eds. *The New Eighteenth Century*. London: Methuen, 1987. 231–53.

Castle, Terry. *The Apparitional Lesbian: Female Homosexuality and Modern Culture*. New York: Columbia University Press, 1993.

Chandler, Alice. *A Dream of Order: the Medieval Ideal in Nineteenth-Century English Literature*. Lincoln: University of Nebraska Press, 1970.

Chapman, Alison, 'Phantasies of Matriarchy in Victorian Children's Literature by Non-Canonical Women Writers'. In Nicola Diane Thompson, ed. *Victorian Women Novelists and the Woman Question*. Cambridge: Cambridge University Press, 1999.

Chapman, Alison. 'Mesmerism and Agency in the Courtship of Elizabeth Barrett and Robert Browning'. In *Victorian Literature and Culture* (1998): 303–19.

Charcot. J-M, and Gilles de la Tourette. 'Hypnotism in the Hysterical'. In Daniel Hack Tuke, ed. *A Dictionary of Psychological Medicine*. 2 Vols. London: J & A Churchill, 1892.

Clark, Sir Andrew. Unnamed article in *The Lancet* (May 31, 1890): 1202.

Clery, E.J. *The Rise of Supernatural Fiction, 1762–1800*. Cambridge: Cambridge University Press, 1995.

Coleridge, Mary Elizabeth. *Poems by Mary E. Coleridge*. 4th edn. Ed. Henry Newbolt. London: Elkin Mathews, 1908.

Coleridge, Mary Elizabeth. *The Collected Poems of Mary Coleridge*. Ed. Teresa Whistler. London: Rupert Hart-Davis, 1954.

Coleridge, Mary Elizabeth. *The Lady on the Drawingroom Floor*. London: Edward Arnold, 1906.

Coleridge, Mary Elizabeth. *The Shadow on the Wall: a Romance*. London: Edward Arnold, 1904.

Corelli, Marie. *The Sorrows of Satan, or the Strange Experience of One Geoffrey Tempest, Millionaire: a Romance*. Oxford: Oxford University Press, 1996.

Cox, Julian. *Julia Margaret Cameron*. Malibu: The J. Paul Getty Museum, 1996.

Crabtree, Adam. *From Mesmer to Freud*. New Haven: Yale University Press, 1993.

Davie, Donald. *Purity of Diction in English Verse*. Routledge: London, 1969.

de Broglie, Gabriel. *Madame de Genlis*. Paris: Perrin, 1985.

De Man, Paul. 'Shelley Disfigured'. In Harold Bloom *et al. Deconstruction and Criticism*. New York: Continuum, 1979. 39–74.

Derrida, Jacques. ' "*As if* I were Dead": an Interview with Jacques Derrida'. In John Brannigan, Ruth Robbins and Julian Wolfreys. *Applying: to Derrida*. Basingstoke: Macmillan, 1996, 212–26.

Diamond, Cora. *The Realistic Spirit: Wittgenstein, Philosophy, and the Mind*. Cambridge: MIT, 1991.

Dickens, Charles. 'A Christmas Carol'. In *Christmas Books*. Ed. Ruth Glancy. Oxford: Oxford University Press, 1988. 1–90.

Dickens, Charles. *Bleak House*. Eds George Ford and Sylvere Monod. New York: W.W. Norton & Company, 1977.

Dickens, Charles. *Great Expectations*. Ed. Margaret Cardwell. Int. Kate Flint. Oxford: Oxford University Press, 1994.

Dickens, Charles. *Martin Chuzzlewit*. Ed. P.N. Furbank. London: Penguin, 1986.

Dickens, Charles. *Nicholas Nickleby*. Ed. Michael Slater. Harmondsworth: Penguin, 1986.

Dickens, Charles. *Our Mutual Friend*. Ed. Adrian Poole. London: Penguin, 1997.

Dickens, Charles. *Our Mutual Friend*. Ed. Michael Costell. Oxford: Oxford University Press, 1989.

Dickens, Charles. *The Pickwick Papers*. Ed. James Kinsley. Oxford: Oxford University Press, 1988.

Dickens, Charles. *The Uncommercial Traveller and Reprinted Pieces*. Int. Leslie C. Staples. Oxford: Oxford University Press, 1987.

Dodier, Virginia. 'Clementina, Viscountess Hawarden: *Studies from Life*'. In Mike Weaver, ed. *British Photography in the Nineteenth-Century: the Fine Art Tradition*. Cambridge: Cambridge University Press, 1989. 141–50.

Dollimore, Jonathan. 'Perversion, Degeneration, and the Death Drive'. In Andrew H. Miller and James Eli Adams, eds. *Sexualities in Victorian Britain*. Bloomington: Indiana University Press, 1996. 96–117.

Doyle, Arthur Conan. 'John Barrington Cowles: The Story of a Medical Student'. In George Redway, ed. *Dreamland and Ghostland: an original collection of tales and warnings from the borderland of substance and shadow; embracing remarkable dreams, presentiments, and coincidences; records of singular personal experience by various writers; startling stories from individual and family history; mysterious incidents from the lips of living narrators; and some psychological studies, grave and gay*. 3 Vols. London: G. Redway, 1888. III, 260–302.

Doyle, Arthur Conan. 'The Parasite'. In *The Horror of Heights and Other Tales of Suspense*. San Francisco: Chronicle Books, 1992. 55–91.

Duncan, Sarah Jeanette. *The Simple Adventures of a Memsahib*. London: n.p., 1909.

Eco, Umberto. *Art and Beauty in the Middle Ages*. Trans. Hugh Bredin. New Haven: Yale University Press, 1986.

Edmundson, Mark. *Nightmare on Main Street: Angels, Sadomasochism, and the Culture of Gothic*. Cambridge, MA: Harvard University Press, 1997.

Ellmann, Richard. *Oscar Wilde*. New York: Vintage, 1988.

Ellmann, Richard. *James Joyce*. Revised edition. Oxford: Oxford University Press, 1983.

Felman, Shoshana. *Literature and Psychoanalysis: the Question of Reading: Otherwise*. Baltimore: Johns Hopkins University Press, 1982.

Foucault, Michel. 'A Preface to Transgression'. In *Language, Counter-Memory, Practice: Selected Essays and Interviews*. Ed. Donald F. Bouchard. Oxford: Blackwell, 1977. 29–52.

Foucault, Michel. *Discipline and Punish: the Birth of the Prison*. Trans. Allan Sheridan. Harmondsworth: Penguin, 1977.

Foucault, Michel. *Madness and Civilization: a History of Insanity in the Age of Reason*. Trans. Richard Howard. London: Tavistock, 1971.

Foucault, Michel. *The Foucault Reader*. Ed. Paul Rabinow. Harmondsworth: Penguin, 1984.

Foucault, Michel. *The History of Sexuality, Volume I: An Introduction*. Trans. Robert Hurley. New York: Random House, 1978.

Freud, Sigmund. 'Femininity'. In *The Essentials of Psychoanalysis*. Harmondsworth: Penguin, 1986. 412–32.

Freud, Sigmund. 'On the Uncanny'. In *The Standard Edition of the Works of Sigmund Freud*. Vol. 17. Ed. and Trans. James Strachey. London: Hogarth Press and the Institute for Psychoanalysis, 1953–1974. 233–8.

Freud, Sigmund. 'The Uncanny'. In *Art and Literature*. Penguin Freud Library Vol. 14. Harmondsworth: Penguin, 1990. 339–76.

Freud, Sigmund. *Beyond the Pleasure Principle*. Trans. James Strachey. London: Hogarth Press, 1961.

Freud, Sigmund. *On Sexuality*. Harmondsworth: Penguin, 1991.

Gairdner, J. 'Untitled Letter'. *The Lancet*. (August 9, 1890): 308.

Gardner, Burdett. *The Lesbian Imagination (Victorian Style): a Psychological and Critical Study of 'Vernon Lee'*. New York: Garland, 1987.

Gauld, Alan. *A History of Hypnotism*. Cambridge: Cambridge University Press, 1992.

Gelder, Ken. *Reading the Vampire*. London: Routledge, 1994.

Gernsheim, Helmut. *Julia Margaret Cameron. Her Life and Photographic Work*. London: The Fountain Press, 1948.

Gerson, Noel. *Lillie Langtry: a Biography*. London: Robert Hale, 1972.

Gil, José. *Metamorphoses of the Body*. Trans. Stephen Muecke. Minneapolis: University of Minnesota Press, 1998.

Gilbert, R.A. *Revelations of the Golden Dawn: the Rise and Fall of a Magical Order*. London: Quantum, 1997.

Gilbert, Sandra, and Susan Gubar. *The Madwoman in the Attic: the Woman Writer and the Nineteenth-Century Literary Imagination*. New Haven: Yale University Press, 1979.

Gilbert, Sandra. 'Rider Haggard's Heart of Darkness'. In Lyn Pykett, ed. *Reading Fin–de–Siècle Fictions*. London: Longman, 1996. 39–46.

Gillespie, Michael Patrick. 'Ethics and Aesthetics in *The Picture of Dorian Gray*'. *Rediscovering Oscar Wilde*. Ed. C. George Sandulescu. Gerrards Cross: Colin Smythe, 1994. 137–55.

Gillespie, Michael Patrick. *Oscar Wilde and the Poetics of Ambiguity*. Gainesville: University Press of Florida, 1996.

Girouard, Mark. *The Return to Camelot: Chivalry and the English Gentleman*. New Haven, Yale University Press, 1981.

Glover, David. *Vampires, Mummies, and Liberals: Bram Stoker and the Politics of Popular Fiction*. Durham: Duke University Press, 1996.

Gogarty, Oliver St. John. *As I was Going down Sackville Street*. London: n.p., 1937.

Greenslade, William. *Degeneration, Culture, and the Novel, 1880–1940*. Cambridge: Cambridge University Press, 1994.

Griffiths, Trevor. *Comedians* London: Faber and Faber, 1979.

Grosz, Elizabeth. *Jacques Lacan: a Feminist Introduction*. London: Routledge, 1990.

Gurney, Edmund, F.W.H. Myers, and Frank Podmore. *Phantasms of the Living*. 2 Volumes. London: Trubner, 1886.

Haggard, H. Rider, and Andrew Lang. *The World's Desire*. London: Longmans, 1890.

Haggard, H. Rider. 'About Fiction'. *Contemporary Review* 51 (February, 1887): 172–80.

Haggard, H. Rider. *Beatrice: a Novel*. London: Longmans Silver Library, 1917.

Haggard, H. Rider. *Cleopatra*. Serial version published in *Illustrated London News* 94: 5 January–29 June, 1889.

Haggard, H. Rider. *Eric Brighteyes*. London: Macdonald, 1963.

Haggard, H. Rider. *Montezuma's Daughter*. London: Longmans Silver Library, 1908.

Haggard, H. Rider. *She: a History of Adventure*. London: Longmans Silver Library, 1911.

Haggard, H. Rider. *The Days of My Life: an Autobiography*. Two Volumes. Ed. C.J. Longman. London: Longmans, 1890.

Halberstam, Judith. *Skin Shows: Gothic Horror and the Technology of Monsters*. Durham: Duke University Press, 1995.

Hanson, Clare. *Short Stories and Short Fiction 1880–1980*. Basingstoke: Macmillan, 1984.

Hardy, Florence Emily. *The Life of Thomas Hardy 1840–1928*. Basingstoke: Macmillan, 1975.

Harpham, Geoffrey Galt. 'Ethics'. *Critical Terms for Literary Study*. Eds Frank Lentricchia and Thomas McLaughlin. 2nd edn. Chicago: University of Chicago Press, 1995. 387–405.

Harrington, Anne. 'Hysteria, Hypnosis, and the Lure of the Invisible: the Rise of Neo–Mesmerism in Fin–de–Siècle French Psychiatry'. In W.F. Bynum *et al.*, eds. *The Anatomy of Madness: Essays in the History of Psychiatry*. 3 Vols. London: Tavistock, 1988. III, 226–46.

Harris, Ruth. 'Murder under Hypnosis in the Case of Gabrielle Bompard: Psychiatry in the Court–Room in Belle Epoque Paris'. In W.F. Bynum *et al.*, eds. *The Anatomy of Madness: Essays in the History of Psychiatry*. 3 Vols. London: Tavistock, 1988. II, 197–241.

Hart, Ernest. 'Review of *Trilby*'. *British Medical Journal* (16 November 1895). Rpt in *Hypnotism, Mesmerism and the New Witchcraft* (1896) New York: Da Capo Press Reprint Series, 1982. 210.

Hart, Ernest. 'Schools and Doctrines of Hypnotism'. *British Medical Journal*. March 25 1891): 723.

Hart, Ernest. *British Medical Journal* (May 31 1890): 1264.

Hart, Ernest. *Hypnotism, Mesmerism and the New Witchcraft* (1896) New York: Da Capo Press Reprint Series, 1982.

Hawthorne, Nathaniel. *The House of the Seven Gables* Harmondsworth: Penguin, 1986.

Henderson, Philip. *William Morris: His Life, Work and Friends*. New York: McGraw-Hill, 1967.

Heron, Liz, and Val Williams, eds. *Illuminations: Women Writing on Photography from the 1850s to the Present*. London: I.B. Taurus, 1996.

Hogg, James. *Private Memoirs and Confessions of a Justified Sinner*. Oxford: Oxford University Press, 1995.

Holland, J. Gill. 'Hawthorne and Photography: *The House of the Seven Gables*'. *Nathaniel Hawthorne Journal* 8 (1978): 1–10.

Hopkins, Gerard Manley. 'Letter'. Notes by Fr. A. Thomas, S.J. *The Dublin Review*. 505 (Autumn 1965): 289–92.

Hopkins, Gerard Manley. *Further Letters of Gerard Manley Hopkins*. Ed. C.C. Abbott. London: Oxford University Press, 1938.

Hopkins, Gerard Manley. *The Correspondence of Gerard Manley Hopkins and Richard Watson Dixon.* Ed. C. C. Abbott. London: Oxford University Press, 1935b.

Hopkins, Gerard Manley. *The Letters of Gerard Manley Hopkins to Robert Bridges.* Ed. C. C. Abbott. London: Oxford University Press, 1935a.

Hopkins, Gerard Manley. *The Poem and Prose of Gerard Manley Hopkins.* London: Penguin, 1985.

Hopkins, Gerard Manley. *The Poetical Works of Gerard Manley Hopkins.* Ed. Norman H. MacKenzie. Oxford: Clarendon Press, 1990.

Hopkins, Gerard Manley. *The Sermons and Devotional Writings of Gerard Manley Hopkins.* Ed. Christopher Devlin, S.J. London: Oxford University Press, 1959.

Hopkinson, Amanda. *Julia Margaret Cameron.* London: Virago, 1986.

House, Humphrey, and Graham Storey, eds. *The Journals and Papers of Gerard Manley Hopkins.* London: Oxford University Press, 1959.

Howard, Jacqueline. *Reading Gothic Fiction: a Bakhtinian Approach.* Oxford: Clarendon Press, 1994.

Howells, Coral Ann. *Love, Mystery, and Misery: Feeling in Gothic Fiction.* London: Athlone Press, 1995.

Hughes, Linda K., and Michael Lund. 'Textual/Sexual Pleasure and Serial Publication'. In John O. Jordan and Robert L. Patten, eds. *Literature in the Marketplace: Nineteenth-Century British Publishing and Reading Practices.* Cambridge: Cambridge University Press, 1995. 134–64.

Hughes-Hallet, Lucy. *Cleopatra: Histories, Dreams, and Distortions.* London: Vintage, 1991.

Hurley, Kelly. *The Gothic Body: Sexuality, Materialism, and Degeneration at the Fin de Siècle.* Cambridge: Cambridge University Press, 1996.

Irigaray, Luce. *An Ethics of Sexual Difference.* Trans. Carolyn Burke and Gillian C. Gill. London: Athlone Press, 1993.

Irigaray, Luce. *Speculum of the Other Woman.* Trans. Gillian C. Gill. Ithaca: Cornell University Press, 1984.

'JFR'. 'Mr. Flinders Petrie's Discoveries in Egypt'. *Illustrated London News* 30 June, 1888. 718.

Jackson, Rosemary. *Fantasy: the Literature of Subversion.* London: Routledge, 1988.

Jacob, Joseph. *Old French Romances done into English by William Morris* (1896). Freeport Books for Libraries Press, 1970.

Johnson, Barbara. *The Critical Difference: Essays in the Contemporary Rhetoric of Reading.* Baltimore: Johns Hopkins University Press, 1980.

Katz, Wendy. *Rider Haggard and the Fiction of Empire: a Critical Study of British Imperial Fiction.* Cambridge: Cambridge University Press, 1987.

Kemp, Sandra. *Kipling's Hidden Narratives.* Oxford: Blackwell, 1988.

Kenner, Hugh. *The Pound Era.* Berkeley: University of California Press, 1971.

Kilgour, Maggie. *The Rise of the Gothic Novel.* London: Routledge, 1995.

Kincaid, James R. *Annoying the Victorians.* New York: Routledge, 1995.

Kincaid, James R. *Child-Loving: the Erotic Child and Victorian Culture.* New York: Routledge, 1992.

Kincaid, James R. *Erotic Innocence: the Culture of Child Molesting.* Durham: Duke University Press, 1998.

Kipling, Rudyard. *Life's Handicap.* London: Macmillan, 1891.

Kipling, Rudyard. *Wee Willie Winkie and Other Stories*. London: Macmillan, 1895.

Kittler, Friedrich. 'Dracula's Legacy'. *Stanford Humanities Review* 1 (1989): 143–74.

Kittler, Friedrich. *Discourse Networks 1800/1900*. Trans. Michael Metteer. Stanford: Stanford University Press, 1990.

Krauss, Rosalind. 'Tracing Nadar'. In Heron and Williams, eds, 37–49.

Kristeva, Julia. *Powers of Horror: an Essay on Abjection*. Trans. Leon S. Roudiez. New York: Columbia University Press, 1982.

Lang, Andrew. 'Realism and Romance'. *Contemporary Review* 52 (November, 1887): 683–93.

Lawrence, Jean. *Hypnosis, Will, and Memory: a Psycho–Legal History*. New York: Guilford Press, 1988.

Lawson, Julie. *Woman in White: Photographs by Clementina Lady Hawarden*. Edinburgh: Scottish National Portrait Gallery, 1997.

Le Fanu, Sheridan. *The Rose and the Key*. Int. Julian Cowley. Stroud: Allan Sutton, 1994.

Le Fanu, Sheridan. *Uncle Silas*. Ed. W.J. McCormack. Oxford: Oxford University Press, 1981.

Lee, Vernon. 'A Wicked Voice'. In *Hauntings: Fantastic Stories*. London: William Heinemann, 1890. Rpt. In *Supernatural Tales*. Ed. Irene Cooper–Willis. London: Peter Owen, 1987. 127–58.

Lee, Vernon. 'Amore Dure: Passages from the Diary of Spiridion Trepka'. In *Supernatural Tales*. Ed. Irene Cooper–Willis. London: Peter Owen, 1987. 86–126.

Lee, Vernon. 'The Phantom Lover: A Fantastic Story' ('Oke of Okehurst'). In *Hauntings: Fantastic Stories*. London: William Heinemann, 1890. 109–91.

Lee, Vernon. *Beauty and Ugliness and Other Studies in Psychological Aesthetics*. London: John Lane, 1912.

Leighton, Angela, and Margaret Reynolds, eds. *Victorian Women Poets: an Anthology*. Oxford: Blackwell, 1995.

Leighton, Angela. *Victorian Women Poets: Writing Against the Heart*. Hemel Hempstead: Harvester, 1992.

Lodge, David. 'Mrs Bathurst: Indeterminacy in Modern Narrative'. In Philip Mallet, ed. *Kipling Considered*. New York: St Martin's Press, 1989.

Lowndes, Marie Belloc. *The Lodger*. Oxford: Oxford University Press, 1996.

Lubbock, Percy, ed. *The Letters of Henry James*. London: n.p., 1920.

Luckhurst, Roger. '(Touching On) Tele-Technology'. In John Brannigan, Ruth Robbins and Julian Wolfreys, eds. Basingstoke: Macmillan, 1996. 171–83.

MacCarthy, Fiona. *William Morris: a Life for our Time*. London: Faber, 1994.

Macdonald, George. *Phantastes: A Faerie Romance for Men and Women*. London: Arthur C. Fifield, 1905.

Machen, Arthur. *The Three Impostors*. New York: Knopf, 1930.

Macherey, Pierre. *A Theory of Literary Production*. Trans. Geoffrey Wall. London: Routledge Kegan Paul, 1978.

Mackail, J.W. *The Life of William Morris*. New York: Longmans Green, 1932.

MacKenzie, John M. *Propaganda and Empire: the Manipulation of Public Opinion 1880–1960*. Manchester: Manchester University Press, 1984.

MacKenzie, Norman. *The Early Poetic Manuscripts and Note-books of Gerard Manley Hopkins in Facsimile*. New York: Garland, 1989.

Malchow, H.L. *Gothic Images of Race in Nineteenth-Century Britain*. Stanford: Stanford University Press, 1996.

Malley, Shawn. '"Time Hath No Power Against Identity": Historical Continuity and Archaeological Adventure in H. Rider Haggard's *She'*. *English Literature in Transition* 40 (1997): 275–97.

Marcus, Stephen. *The Other Victorians: a Study of Sexuality and Pornography in Mid-Nineteenth Century England*. London: Weidenfeld and Nicolson, 1964.

Marsh, Jan. *The Pre–Raphaelite Sisterhood*. New York: St Martin's Press, 1985.

Marsh, Richard. *The Beetle*. New York: G.P. Putnam's Sons, 1976.

Marsh, Richard. *Marvels and Mysteries*. London: Methuen, 1900.

Marsh, Richard. *The Beetle*. Int. William Baker. Stroud: Allan Sutton, 1994.

Martin, Robert Bernard. *Gerard Manley Hopkins: a Very Private Life*. London: Flamingo, 1992.

Maudsley, Henry. *Body and Will*. London: Kegan Paul, 1883.

Mavor, Carol. *Pleasures Taken: Performances of Sexuality and Loss in Victorian Photographs*. London: I.B. Taurus, 1996.

Mayer, David, ed. *Henry Irving and* The Bells*: Irving's Personal Script of the Play*. Manchester: Manchester University Press, 1980.

McCormack, W.J. *Dissolute Characters*. Manchester: Manchester University Press, 1993.

McCormack, W.J. *Sheridan Le Fanu and Victorian Ireland*. Dublin: Lilliput Press, 1991.

McGinn, Colin. *Ethics, Evil, and Fiction*. Oxford: Clarendon Press, 1997.

McGowran, Katherine. 'The Restless Wanderer: Mary E. Coleridge'. In Angela Leighton, ed. *Victorian Women Poets: a Critical Reader*. Oxford: Blackwell, 1996. 186–97.

Meade, L.T., and Clifford Halifax. 'The Adventures of a Man of Science VI'. *Strand Magazine* (July–December, 1902): n.p.

Meinhold, William. *Sidonia the Sorceress*. Trans. Francesca Speranza, Lady Wilde. London: Kelmscott Press, 1892.

Meinhold, William. *Sidonia the Sorceress*. Trans. Francesca Speranza, Lady Wilde. London: Reeves and Turner, 1894.

Melman, Billie. *Women's Orients: English Women and the Middle East, 1718–1918*. Ann Arbor: University of Michigan Press, 1995.

Mesmer, Anton. 'Dissertation on the Discovery of Animal Magnetism'. In Charles E. Goshen, ed. *Documentary History of Psychiatry: a Source-Book on Historical Principles*. London: Vision Press, 1967.

Meyer, Susan. *Imperialism at Home: Race and Victorian Women's Fiction*. Ithaca: Cornell, 1996.

Meynell, Alice. *The Poems of Alice Meynell: Complete Edition*. London: Burns Oates and Washbourne Ltd, 1923.

Miles, Robert. *Gothic Writing 1750–1820: a Genealogy*. London: Routledge, 1993.

Millard, Charles W. 'Julia Margaret Cameron and Tennyson's *Idylls of the King'*. *Harvard Library Bulletin*. XXI (1973): 187–201.

Miller, J. Hillis. *The Disappearance of God: Five Nineteenth–Century Writers*. New York: Shocken Books, 1965.

Miller, J. Hillis. *The Ethics of Reading: Kant, de Man, Elliot, Trollope, James, and Benjamin*. New York: Columbia University Press, 1987.

Miller, J. Hillis. *The Form of Victorian Fiction: Thackeray, Dickens, Trollope, George Eliot, Meredith, and Hardy*. South Bend: University of Notre Dame Press, 1968.

Mishra, Vijay. *The Gothic Sublime*. State University of New York Press, 1994.

Moore, John David. 'Coleridge and the "Modern Jacobinical Drama": *Osorio, Remorse*, and the Development of Coleridge's Critique of the Stage, 1797–1816'. *Bulletin of Research in the Humanities*. 85:4 (1982): 443–64.

Morris, William. *The Collected Works of William Morris, with Introductions by his Daughter May Morris*. New York: Russell and Russell, 1960.

Morris, William. *William Morris: Selected Writings and Designs*. Ed. Asa Briggs. London: Penguin, 1980.

Muddock, J.E. 'The Crime of the Rue Aber'. In *Stories Weird and Wonderful*. London: Chatto and Windus, 1889.

Mulvey, Laura. 'Visual Pleasure and Narrative Cinema'. *Screen*, 16:3 (Autumn 1975). Rpt. In *Visual and Other Pleasures*. Houndmills: Basingstoke, 1989. 14–28.

Murdoch, Iris. *The Sovereignty of Good*. 1970. London: Ark, 1985.

Myers, F.W.H. 'On Telepathic Hypnotism, and its Relation to Other Forms of Hypnotic Suggestion'. In *Proceedings of the Society for Psychical Research*. IV (1886–87): 127–88.

Myers, F.W.H. *Human Personality and its Survival of Bodily Death*. 2 Vols. London: Longmans, 1903.

Nabokov, Vladimir. *Vladimir Nabokov: Lectures on Literature*. New York: Harcourt Brace and Company, 1980.

Newbolt, Henry. *My World as in my Time: Memoirs of Sir Henry Newbolt 1862–1932*. London: Faber, 1932.

Newbolt, Henry. *The Later Life and Letters of Sir Henry Newbolt*. Ed. Margaret Newbolt. London: Faber, 1942.

Norton, Robert E. *The Beautiful Soul: Aesthetic Morality in the Eighteenth Century*. Ithaca: Cornell University Press, 1995.

Nussbaum, Martha C. *Love's Knowledge: Essays on Philosophy and Literature*. New York: Oxford University Press, 1990.

Nussbaum, Martha C. *The Fragility of Goodness: Luck and Ethics in Greek Tragedy and Philosophy*. Cambridge: Cambridge University Press, 1986.

O'Toole, F. *A Traitor's Kiss: The Life of Richard Brinsley Sheridan*. London: Granta, 1997.

Parry, Benita. *Delusions and Discoveries*. London: Allen Lane, 1972.

Parssinen, Terry. 'Professional Deviants and the History of Medicine: Medical Mesmerists in Victorian Britain'. In Brian Wallis, ed. *On the Margins of Science: the Social Construction of Rejected Knowledge. Sociological Review Monograph* 27. Keele: Keele University Press, 1979. 103–20.

Pater, Walter. *The Renaissance: Studies in Art and Poetry, the 1893 text*. Ed. Donald L. Hill. Berkeley: University of California Press, 1980.

Paulin, Tom. *Thomas Hardy: the Poetry of Perception*. Basingstoke: Macmillan, 1975.

Pearsall, Ronald. *The Worm in the Bud: the World of Victorian Sexuality*. Harmondsworth: Penguin, 1971.

Perkis, C.L. 'The Ghost in Fountain Lane'. *The Experiences of Loveday Brooke, Lady Detective*. New York: Dover, 1986.

Peterson, William S. *The Kelmscott Press: a History of William Morris' Typographical Adventure*. Berkeley: University of California Press, 1991.

Pick, Daniel. 'Powers of Suggestion: Svengali and the *Fin–de–Siècle'*. In Brian Cheyette and Laura Marcus, eds. *Culture, Modernity and "the Jew"*. Cambridge: Polity, 1998. 105–25.

Pick, Daniel. *Faces of Degeneration: a European Disorder c.1848–c.1914*. Cambridge: Cambridge University Press, 1989.

Pippin, Tina. *Death and Desire: the Rhetoric of Gender in the Apocalypse*. Louisville: John Knox Press, 1992.

Pocock, Tom. *Rider Haggard and the Lost Empire: a Biography*. London: Wiedenfeld and Nicholson, 1993.

Procter, Adelaide. *The Poetical Works*. London: A.L. Burt, n.d.

Punter, David. *The Literature of Terror: a History of Gothic Fictions from 1795 to the Present Day*. London: Longman, 1980, 1996.

Reed, John R. *Victorian Will*. Athens: Ohio University Press, 1989.

Roberts, Pam. 'Julia Margaret Cameron: A Triumph over Criticism'. In Graham Clarke, ed. *The Portrait in Photography*. London: Reaktion Books, 1992. 47–70.

Robertson, Fiona. *Legitimate Histories: Scott, Gothic, and the Authorities of Fiction*. Oxford: Clarendon Press, 1994.

Roe, Andrea, ed. *The Germ: the Literary Magazine of the Pre–Raphaelites*. Oxford: Ashmolean Museum, 1992.

Romer, John. *Valley of the Kings*. London: Michael O'Mara, 1981.

Rossetti, Dante Gabriel. *Dante and His Circle, with the Italian Poets Preceding Him (1100–1200–1300)*. Ed. William Michael Rossetti. London: Ellis and Elvery, 1892.

Rossetti, Dante Gabriel. *Rossetti: Poems and Translations 1850–1870. Together with the Prose Story "Hand and Soul"*. Oxford: Oxford University Press, 1968.

Ruskin, John. *Modern Painters*. Vol. 3. Rpt in Eric Warner and Graham Hough, eds. *Strangeness and Beauty: an Anthology of Aesthetic Criticism, 1840–1910. Volume 1 Ruskin to Swinburne*. Cambridge: Cambridge University Press, 1983.

Ruskin, John. *The Works of John Ruskin*. Volume 5. Eds E.T. Cook and Alexander Wedderburn. London: George Allen, 1904.

Russett, Margaret. *De Quincey's Romanticism: Canonical Minority and the Forms of Transmission*. Cambridge: Cambridge University Press, 1997.

Russo, Mary. *The Female Grotesque: Risk, Excess, and Modernity*. London: Routledge, 1994.

Scott, Walter. 'Introduction to *The Castle of Otranto'*. In Horace Walpole, *The Castle of Otranto*. Int. Marvin Mudrick. New York: Collier Books, 1974. 115–28.

Scott, Walter. *Selected Poems*. ed. James Reed. Manchester: Fyfield Books, 1992.

Sedgwick, Eve Kosofsky. *Between Men: English Literature and Male Homosocial Desire*. New York: Columbia University Press, 1985.

Sedgwick, Eve Kosofsky. *The Coherence of Gothic Conventions*. New York: Methuen, 1986.

Shakespeare, William. *Hamlet*, ed. G.R. Hibbard. Oxford: Clarendon Press, 1987.

Shaw, David. *The Lucid Veil: Poetic Truth in the Victorian Age*. London: Athlone Press, 1987.

Shelley, Percy Bysshe. *Shelley. Poetical Works*. Ed. Thomas Hutchinson. London: Oxford University Press, 1970.

Showalter, Elaine. *Hystories: Hysterical Epidemics and Modern Media*. New York: Columbia University Press, 1997.

Showalter, Elaine. *Sexual Anarchy: Gender and Culture at the Fin de Siècle*. London: Bloomsbury, 1991.

Sichel, Edith, ed. *Gathered Leaves from the Prose of Mary E. Coleridge*. London: Constable and Company, 1910.

Smith, Roberta. 'In Love with the Past and a Vision of Perfect Beauty'. *The New York Times*. June 5, 1998, B32.

Society for Psychical Research. 'First Report of the Committee on Mesmerism'. In *Proceedings of the Society for Psychical Research*. I (1882–83): 220.

Society for Psychical Research. 'Objects of the Society'. In *Proceedings of the Society for Psychical Research*. I (1882–83): 3.

Society for Psychical Research. 'Third Report of the Committee on Thought-Transference'. In *Proceedings of the Society for Psychical Research*. II (1884): 13.

Spacks, Patricia Meyer. *Desire and Truth: Functions of Plot in Eighteenth–Century English Novels*. London: University of Chicago Press, 1968.

Spencer, Kathleen. 'Purity and Danger: *Dracula*, Urban Gothic and the Late Victorian Degeneracy Crisis'. *ELH* 59:1 (1992): 197–225.

Sprinker, Michael. *A Counterpoint of Dissonance: the Aesthetics and Poetry of Gerard Manley Hopkins*. Baltimore: The Johns Hopkins University Press, 1980.

Stead, W.T. 'How We Intend to Study Borderland'. *Borderland* 1:1 (1893): 4–7.

Stead, W.T. 'The Ghost That Dwells in Each of Us'. *Real Ghost Stories*. London: Grant Richard, 1897. 1.

Stephens, Ricardo. *The Cruciform Mark: the Strange Story of Richard Tregenna, Bachelor of Medicine (Univ. Edin.)*. London: Chatto and Windus, 1896.

Stewart, Garrett. 'Count Me In: *Dracula*, Hypnotic Participation and Late Victorian Gothic Reading'. *Literature–Interpretation–Theory* 5:1 (1994): 1–18.

Stoker, Bram. *Dracula*. Harmondsworth: Penguin, 1979.

Stoker, Bram. *Famous Impostors*. London: Sidgwick and Jackson, 1910.

Stokes, John. *Oscar Wilde: Myths, Miracles, and Imitations*. Cambridge: Cambridge University Press, 1996.

Stone, Harry. *The Night Side of Dickens: Cannibalism, Passion, Necessity*. Columbus: Ohio State University Press, 1994.

Stott, Rebecca. *The Fabrication of the Late-Victorian Femme Fatale: the Kiss of Death*. London: Macmillan, 1992.

Sutherland, John. *Victorian Fiction: Writers, Publishers, Readers*. Basingstoke: Macmillan, 1995.

Symons, Arthur. 'The Decadent Movement in Literature'. *Harper's New Monthly Magazine* 87 (November 1893): 858–68.

Tagg, John. *Burden of Representation: Essays on Photographies and Histories*. London: Macmillan, 1988.

Tennyson, Alfred. *The Poems of Tennyson*. Vol. III. Ed. Christopher Ricks. London: Longman, 1987.

Tuckey, C. Lloyd. *Psycho-Therapeutics; or, Treatment by Sleep and Suggestion*. London: Baillière, Tindall and Cox, 1889.

Tuso, Joseph F., ed. *Beowulf: the Donaldson Translation*. London: W.W. Norton and Company, 1975.

Twitchell, James B. *The Living Dead: a Study of the Vampire in Romantic Literature*. Durham: Duke University Press, 1981.

Varma, Devendra P. *The Gothic Flame*. New Jersey: Scarecrow Press, 1987.

Vinaver, Eugène, *et al.*, eds. *Malory: Works*. Oxford: Oxford University Press, 1981.

Vincent, Ralph Harry. *The Elements of Hypnotism*. London: Kegan Paul, 1897.

Warren, Barbara. *The Feminine Image in Literature*. Rochelle Park: Hayden Humanities Series, 1973.

Waters, Chris. *British Socialists and the Politics of Popular Culture 1884–1914*. Manchester: Manchester University Press, 1990.

Weatherby, Harold L. 'Problems of Form and Content in the Poetry of Dante Gabriel Rossetti'. In David G. Reide, ed. *Critical Essays on Dante Gabriel Rossetti*. Oxford: Maxwell Macmillan International, 1992. 67–75.

Weaver, Mike. *Julia Margaret Cameron, 1815–1879*. Southampton: The Herbert Press, 1984.

Weaver, Mike. *Whisper of the Muse*. Malibu: The J. Paul Getty Museum, 1986.

Weintraub, Stanley. *Four Rossettis: a Victorian Biography*. New York: Weybright and Talley, 1977.

Wells, H.G. *Joan and Peter: the Story of an Education*. London: Odhams Press, 1918.

Wheeler, Michael. *Heaven, Hell and the Victorians*. Cambridge: Cambridge University Press, 1994.

White, Norman. *Hopkins: a Literary Biography*. Oxford: Clarendon Press, 1992.

Wilde, Oscar. *Plays, Prose Writings, and Poems*. New York: Everyman's Library, 1991.

Williams, Anne. *Art of Darkness: a Poetics of Gothic*. Chicago: University of Chicago Press, 1995.

Wilson, Edward L. 'Finding Pharaoh'. *The Century Magazine* 34 (May, 1887): 3–10.

Winter, Alison. *Mesmerized: Powers of Mind in Victorian Britain*. Chicago: The University of Chicago Press, 1998.

Witt, Amanda. 'Blushings and Palings: The Body as Text in Wilde's *The Picture of Dorian Gray*'. *Publications of the Arkansas Philological Association* 19 (1993): 85–96.

Wolfreys, Julian. *Writing London: the Trace of the Urban Text from Blake to Dickens*. Basingstoke: Macmillan, 1998.

Wolstenholme, Susan. *Gothic (Re)Visions*. Albany: State University of New York Press, 1993.

Woolf, Virginia. *Collected Essays*. Three Vols. London: Hogarth Press, 1966.

Worth, Katherine. *Sheridan and Goldsmith*. London: Macmillan, 1992.

Index